TENTH EDITION UPDATE

CONNECTICUT
Real Estate
PRACTICE & LAW

Katherine A. Pancak
**Center for Real Estate and
Urban Economic Studies,
University of Connecticut**

Dearborn™
Real Estate Education

President: Roy Lipner
Publisher: Evan Butterfield
Managing Editor, Print Products: Louise Benzer
Development Editor: Tony Peregrin
Production Coordinator: Daniel Frey
Typesetter: Todd Bowman
Creative Art Director: Lucy Jenkins
Cover Design: Gail Chandler

Published by Dearborn™ Real Estate Education
30 South Wacker Drive
Chicago, IL 60606-7481
www.dearbornRE.com

CONTENTS

PREFACE

Connecticut Real Estate: Practice & Law is a key component of Dearborn™ Real Estate Education's complete principles learning system. This system offers students and educators a complete turnkey package for prelicense real estate courses, continuing education, and professional enrichment. As the demographics and structure of the real estate industry change, Dearborn™ Real Estate Education is helping students, instructors, and practitioners adapt to this new environment by providing more accessible and versatile educational tools.

This book can be used with equal effectiveness with *any* of our principles books or software:

- *Modern Real Estate Practice*
- *Mastering Real Estate Principles*
- *Real Estate Fundamentals*
- *National Real Estate Principles*

Connecticut Real Estate: Practice & Law also offers current real estate professionals a practical handbook of Connecticut's real estate law and rules, along with the most current developments. Every effort has been made to ensure that the information contained in this book is both relevant and current. There are also numerous references to Connecticut statutes and the Real Estate Commission's Rules and Regulations, so readers can look up the law themselves in most public and university libraries.

Readers using *Connecticut Real Estate: Practice & Law* to prepare for the state real estate licensing examination should note that this book does not address the national topics that constitute 80 percent of the real estate examination. Students are advised to first read the relevant material in one of the main principles books or software, then turn to *Connecticut Real Estate: Practice & Law* for a focus on Connecticut's particular laws and practices as they relate to that subject. *This book is designed to discuss the statutes, rules, and practical real estate issues that arise in the state of Connecticut.*

■ HOW TO USE THIS BOOK

The conversion table on the next page provides a quick and easy reference for using *Connecticut Real Estate: Practice & Law* in conjunction with various principles books. For instance, *Connecticut Real Estate: Practice & Law's* Chapter 16, "Closing the Real Estate Transaction," may be read in conjunction with Chapter 22 in *Modern Real Estate Practice*, 16th Edition; Chapter 17 in *Real Estate Fundamentals*, 6th Edition; Chapter 12 in *Mastering Real Estate Principles*, 3rd Edition; and Unit 22 in *National Real Estate Principles* software. The chart also provides students with a useful reference to the *Guide to Passing the PSI Real Estate Exam*, 4th Edition, by Lawrence Sager.

Chapter Conversion Table

Connecticut Real Estate: Practice & Law, 10th Edition	Modern Real Estate Practice, 16th Edition	Real Estate Fundamentals, 6th Edition	Mastering Real Estate Principles, 3rd Edition	National Real Estate Principles	Guide to Passing the PSI Real Estate Exam, 5th Edition
1. Real Estate Brokerage and Agency	4, 5	9	13	4, 5	7, 14
2. Listing Agreements and Buyer Agency Contracts	6	7, 9	15	6	9
3. Interests in Real Estate	7	3	7	7	3
4. Forms of Real Estate Ownership	8	5	9	8	3
5. Legal Descriptions	9	2	6	9	3
6. Real Estate Taxes and Other Liens	10	10	5, 25	10	3, 10
7. Real Estate Contracts	11	7	14	11	9
8. Transfer of Title	12	4	10	12	10
9. Title Records	13	6	11	13	10
10. Real Estate License Laws	—	—	16	—	—
11. Real Estate Financing: Principles/Practice	14, 15	12, 13	Unit VII	14, 15	6
12. Leases	16	8	8	16	3
13. Real Estate Appraisal	18	11	Unit VI	18	5
14. Land Use Controls and Property Development	19	14	3	19	4
15. Fair Housing and Ethical Practices	20	15	17	20	11
16. Closing the Real Estate Transaction	22	17	12	22	6 (Math Review)
17. Environmental Issues and the Real Estate Transaction	21	16	3	21	8

ACKNOWLEDGMENTS

The publisher would like to thank Christopher Ashe and Judith I. Johannsen. These individuals provided vital professional guidance and expertise from which everyone benefits.

Thanks also go to the following for permission to reprint forms and documents in this edition: Connecticut Association of REALTORS®, Inc., and Bridgeport Board of REALTORS®, Inc.

Recognition is given to Barbara L. Drisko, DREI, editor of the fifth edition; Judith B. Paesani, Center for Real Estate and Urban Economic Studies at the University of Connecticut for developing the first three editions of this text; Michael L. Galonska, editor of the first edition; and the many students and instructors (users of the text) who have benefited from the materials as a text source and who have made suggestions for its contents.

■ ABOUT THE AUTHOR

Katherine A. Pancak is Associate Professor of Finance and Real Estate at the University of Connecticut School of Business. She is also a member of the faculty in the University's Center for Real Estate and Urban Economic Studies, an internationally recognized academic institute for real estate teaching, research, and service. Prior to joining the University, she was a practicing attorney specializing in the area of real estate.

The author has again dedicated this edition to her parents, Ellen and John Stadtmueller, for all their love and support and for instilling in her a passion for both real estate and education.

1

REAL ESTATE BROKERAGE AND AGENCY

■ OVERVIEW

Connecticut agency law has recently been significantly revised by statute. Formerly, it was the practice in Connecticut for a seller to hire a broker to market the seller's property, and cobrokers (selling brokers) were considered subagents of the seller. Now, subagency in purchase and sale transactions has been significantly limited and is not typically used. The new law does not limit subagency in leasing transactions.

Connecticut real estate license law allows for a broker to be a seller's agent, a buyer's agent, or a dual agent. The law allows brokers to work with a buyer as either a client or a customer. If the broker is going to work with the buyer as a client, a buyer agency agreement must be entered into. If the broker is going to work with the buyer as a customer, the broker must have an agency relationship with the seller. (This means that for in-house sales, the broker represents the seller through a listing agreement, and for cooperating sales, the broker must become the subagent of the seller by obtaining the seller's written consent.)

Salespersons working for a brokerage firm owe the same agency duties to clients as the firm's broker of record. However, real estate brokers are allowed to appoint a separate seller agent and separate buyer agent for the same transaction within the same office. Designated agents are not dual agents.

An agent working with an unrepresented person must clearly disclose the agent's agency affiliation to the unrepresented person using the "Real Estate Agency Disclosure Notice Given to Unrepresented Persons." If a firm represents both the buyer and seller in a transaction (dual agency) and designated agents *are not* assigned, the firm must both disclose this to the parties and obtain the parties' informed consent using the "Dual Agency Consent Agreement." If a firm represents both the buyer and seller in a transaction (dual agency) and designated agents *are* assigned, the firm must both disclose this to the parties and obtain the parties' informed consent using the "Dual Agency/Designated Agency Disclosure Notice and Consent Agreement."

WWWeb.Link   Detailed information on Connecticut real estate brokerage and agency, as well as extensive sample forms, contracts, agreements, and disclosures, can be found at the Connecticut Association of REALTORS®, Inc., Web site at *www.ctrealtor.com*.

■ LICENSING LAW

No individual may conduct business as a real estate broker or salesperson in the state of Connecticut without first obtaining a license from the Connecticut Real Estate Commission (under the Department of Consumer Protection). Partnerships, associations, limited liability companies, or corporations will be granted a license only if every member and officer actively engaging in the real estate business has a broker's license. All agents must be licensed. Although the license law does not require that each licensed broker or salesperson carry an individual bond to protect persons injured by his or her actions, it does require payment of a one-time fee to a real estate guaranty fund. This fund is maintained by the commission to satisfy the substantiated complaints of aggrieved parties.

The complete text of the real estate license law may be found in Title 20 of the Connecticut General Statutes, Chapter 392—"Real Estate Brokers and Salespersons." The law is discussed in detail in Chapter 10.

WWWeb.Link   The Connecticut General Statutes, updated through January 1, 2003, can be found online at the State Legislative Web site at *www.cga.state.ct.us*.

Title 20, Section 20-328 of the Connecticut General Statutes empowers the Commissioner of Consumer Protection, with the assistance of the Connecticut Real Estate Commission, to develop reasonable regulations relating to the form and manner of filing applications for licenses and the manner in which licensed brokers or salespeople conduct day-to-day brokerage operations. These regulations can be found in Sections 20-328-1a through 20-328-10a and are discussed in Chapter 10.

Brokers and salespeople must also recognize the limitations of their authority and should *not* attempt to offer legal advice or any other assistance that requires additional licensing. Such "additional licensing" is not limited to legal counseling alone but also includes licensing for counseling in insurance matters, as Properties Securities Dealers, or for Interstate Land Sales or real estate appraisal. Although the broker's contractual role typically ends at the moment the principal accepts an offer that develops into a sales contract, brokers can and do provide service after the sale.

The Broker

The Connecticut license law carefully defines the term *real estate broker* as any individual, partnership, association, limited liability company, or corporation that *performs, offers, or attempts to perform* any of the following activities pertaining to an estate or interest in real property *for another person and for compensation:* listing for sale, selling, exchanging, buying, renting or collecting rent for the use of, and reselling a mobile home.

Legal entities run as part of a real estate brokerage company must be licensed as a real estate broker. Active owners, members, partners, and officers of a licensed real estate brokerage company must themselves be licensed as either a broker or salesperson. Fifty-one percent of those persons owning or controlling a licensed real estate brokerage company must be licensed real estate brokers.

Although the definition is fairly precise, the Connecticut General Statutes left enough latitude to provide for judicial interpretation. The statutes point out a variety of additional activities that would bring persons under the jurisdiction of the real estate license law. Thus, one must not assume automatically that only the customary agency operations fall within the jurisdiction of licensing requirements. Almost any activity or engagement in the real estate business conducted for a fee and involving the sale, exchange, rental, or purchase of real property falls within the scope of the license law. A separate license for appraisers is required and is discussed in detail in Chapter 13.

The Salesperson

Real estate salespeople are defined as those affiliated with real estate brokers as independent contractors or employed by real estate brokers to carry out the legally authorized functions of real estate brokers on their behalf. The working arrangement between a broker and a salesperson is often a topic of considerable debate. Under one set of circumstances, a salesperson may be considered the broker's employee; under another, he or she may be labeled an independent contractor. In any event, real estate salespeople operate only on behalf of the brokers under whom they are licensed. They are not empowered to engage in the real estate business independently of their brokers.

Unlicensed Personnel

Persons working in real estate offices in primarily custodial (as on-site residential superintendents) or clerical capacities are not considered to be engaging in the real estate business and are not required to be licensed. Such employees are not authorized to render any real estate information to the public. Also exempt from the license law are publishers and advertising salespeople for any medium designed to advertise real estate because these individuals are primarily engaged in the sale of advertising space, not real estate. Other exemptions from the licensing requirements are discussed in Chapter 10.

Personal Assistants

Brokers and salespersons often use unlicensed persons, such as personal assistants, clerical support staff, closing secretaries, and so on to assist them in performing various tasks related to their real estate business. Unlicensed persons are prohibited from negotiating, listing, selling, or buying real estate for a client or customer. The Connecticut Real Estate Commission has adopted a policy on the *Use of Unlicensed Persons by Licensees*. Table 1.1 outlines permitted and prohibited activities. Designated brokers are responsible for ensuring that unlicensed assistants, either directly employed or contracted by the broker or a salesperson under the broker's supervision, are not acting improperly.

TABLE 1.1

Personal Assistant Activities

Permitted Activities	Prohibited Activities
■ Answer phone and forward calls to licensee. ■ Transmit listings and changes to multiple listing services (MLSs). ■ Follow up on loan commitments after a contract has been negotiated. ■ Assemble documents for closing. ■ Secure public documents from city hall, courthouse, sewer/water districts, tax assessor, etc. ■ Have keys made for company listings. ■ Write and prepare ads, flyers, and promotional materials and place such advertising (which must be reviewed by licensee). ■ Record/deposit earnest money and other trust funds. ■ Type contract forms under direction of licensee. ■ Monitor licenses and personnel files. ■ Compute commission checks. ■ Place signs on property. ■ Order items of routine repair as directed by licensee and/or supervising broker. ■ Act as a courier to transport documents, keys, etc. ■ Schedule appointments for licensees to show property. ■ Measure property.	■ Host open houses, kiosks, home show booths or fairs, or hand out materials at such functions. ■ Show property. ■ Answer any questions from consumers on listings, title, financing, closing, etc. ■ Contact cooperating brokers, in person or otherwise, regarding any negotiations or open transactions. ■ Discuss or explain a contract, purchase offer, agreement, listing, or other real estate document with anyone outside of the firm. ■ Be paid on the basis of commission, or any amount based on listings, sales, etc. ■ Negotiate or agree to any commission, commission split, or referral fee on behalf of a licensee. ■ Place calls requiring a license—cold calling, soliciting listings, contacting "For Sale by Owners" or expired listings, extending invitations to open houses, etc. ■ Attend inspections or preclosing walk-throughs unless accompanied by licensee. ■ The unlicensed assistant must not act as a decision maker; rather, he/she shall take all directions from a supervising licensee.

Nonresident Licensing

Connecticut does not have blanket reciprocal licensing arrangements with other states; therefore, having a real estate broker's license from another state does not entitle a person to deal in real estate in Connecticut.[1] A licensed broker from another state who enters into an agency contract for the sale of real property in Connecticut is considered to be unlicensed and would be unable to recover damages as the result of a breach of agency. Other nonresident licensing issues are discussed in Chapter 10.

The Connecticut Real Estate Commission does maintain a reciprocal agreement with the following states that adhere to substantially equivalent licensing requirements: Alabama, Colorado, Georgia, Illinois, Massachusetts, Mississippi, Nebraska, New York, North Carolina, Ohio, Oklahoma, and Rhode Island. However, Connecticut's reciprocal arrangements do not eliminate the necessity of obtaining a Connecticut license—they merely waive some of the examination and application requirements.

The Broker-Salesperson Relationship

Under Connecticut law a real estate salesperson must be affiliated with a specific licensed broker, and under no circumstances can a salesperson accept a listing or perform any brokerage operations on his or her own. A salesperson can work for another broker only with the express knowledge and consent of the broker the salesperson is affiliated with. The specified licensed broker is responsible for liability incurred by the salesperson while conducting real estate business, whether the salesperson is affiliated with the broker as an independent contractor or as an employee.

The real estate salesperson in Connecticut is usually considered an independent contractor rather than an employee of his or her broker/sponsor. For purposes of worker's compensation, brokers and salespeople are not considered employees if all or most of the remuneration for services performed is directly related to sales rather than to number of hours worked. However, in any action brought by a third party against a real estate salesperson affiliated with a real estate broker as an independent contractor, the broker is liable to the same extent as if the salesperson were an employee. An example of a broker-salesperson contract is shown in Figure 1.1.

Agency runs to brokerage firm, not individuals.   Agency relationships are entered into between a client and the brokerage firm's broker of record. Because salespersons work for the broker of record, all clients of the broker are also clients of all the broker's salespersons. (See Figure 1.2, depicting this "agency umbrella" concept.) This means that if the brokerage firm has entered into a listing agreement with a seller, then all of the brokers and salespersons in that firm are agents of that seller, represent that seller, and owe fiduciary duties to that seller. Likewise, if the brokerage firm enters into a buyer agency agreement with a buyer, then all of the brokers and salespersons in that firm are the agents of the buyer, represent that buyer, and owe fiduciary duties to that buyer. Therefore, one salesperson in a firm cannot say that a buyer-client working with another salesperson in the same firm "is not my client." To the contrary, that buyer is the client of each and every salesperson in the firm, and each and every salesperson in the firm must watch out for that buyer's best interests. (The only exception to this running of agency is in the case of appointment of designated agents, which will be discussed later.)

■ AGENCY LAW

The Connecticut Real Estate Commission has provided policy guidance on (1) the various agency documents required to be entered into with or given to buyers and sellers (see Figure 1.3) and (2) an outline of issues to consider regarding the practical application of agency relationships (see Figure 1.4).

Connecticut's real estate license law requires that *listing agreements and buyer agency contracts must be in writing* (see Chapter 2 for a complete inventory of listing agreement and buyer agency requirements). The broker should keep in mind that the contract is more than a simple agreement; it is an employment contract with the principal.

Special agent.   Under a standard listing agreement, the broker does not have the right to convey the principal's property—he or she has only limited authority to act as a *special agent* to locate a buyer and obtain an offer to purchase a specific property. Thus, the listing agreement or contract is an

F I G U R E 1.1

Independent Contractor Agreement

EXPLANATION OF INDEPENDENT CONTRACTOR AGREEMENT

This Independent Contractor Agreement form is revised as of May, 2000. As revised, this form agreement incorporates the contract provisions required by Connecticut Public Act No. 91-364 in order to define real estate brokers and salespersons as independent contractors instead of employees under the Connecticut Workers' Compensation Act. The revised form Agreement continues to include the safe harbor provisions for defining brokers and salespersons as independent contractors for federal tax purposes.

All parties using the form Independent Contractor Agreement should review it thoroughly before such use. Because this form Agreement is intended to comply with the requirements of federal and state laws noted above, you should consult your own attorney before making any changes to this form Agreement.

INDEPENDENT CONTRACTOR AGREEMENT

This Agreement is by and between ————— ——————————————————————
(hereinafter called the "Broker") and ——————
——————————————————————
(hereinafter called the "Salesperson").

INTRODUCTION

The Broker is licensed and authorized to act as a real estate broker in the State of Connecticut and is a member of the Board of ——————————REALTORS®, Inc., the Connecticut Association of REALTORS®, Inc. and the National Association of REALTORS®, Inc.

The Salesperson is licensed and authorized to act as a real estate salesperson or broker in the State of Connecticut.

The Broker operates a real estate brokerage business, maintains an office open to the public for that purpose, and enjoys the reputation of fair dealing with and the goodwill of the public.

SAMPLE INDEPENDENT CONTRACTOR AGREEMENT

The Salesperson wishes to be affiliated with

the Broker as an independent contractor for the purpose of brokering the leasing, sale and purchase of real estate.

In the consideration of their mutual promises, the parties agree to the terms set forth in this Agreement.

TERMS

1. *Relationship of the Parties*. The relationship of the Salesperson to the Broker is that of an independent contractor. The Broker shall have the right to determine the services which the Salesperson shall perform. except to the extent provided in Section 7 (Affirmative Action) of this Agreement, the Broker shall not have the right to control the manner in which the Salesperson performs such services, including the manner in which the Salesperson: (i) handles leads and prospects (including those assigned to him/her by the Broker); (ii) secures and markets listings; and (iii) conducts negotiations. The Salesperson shall be deemed to be a qualified real estate agent under Section 3508 of the Internal Revenue Code of 1986, as amended from time to time, and shall be treated as an independent contractor and not as an employee, servant or partner of the Broker for federal tax purposes or for any other purposes including, without limitation, for the purpose of determining the Salesperson's eligibility for any benefits under the workers' compensation laws of any state.

2. *Obligations of the Broker*. The Broker:

(a) Shall make available to the Salesperson all current office listings, except those which the Broker may from time to time place with another licensee;

(b) Shall provide a desk, phone and clerical services, to be shared by the Salesperson with other licensees, take phone messages relating to the Salesperson's work under this Agreement, and may provide additional office facilities and supplies for the use of the Salesperson;

(c) Shall provide advice and assistance in connection with the Salesperson's work under this Agreement; and

(d) Shall share any benefits the Broker enjoys as a member of a Local, State or National Association of REALTORS®, if

permitted to do so by the respective association.

3. *Salesperson's Obligations*. The Salesperson shall:

(a) At all times maintain a valid Connecticut real estate salesperson or broker license;

(b) Use his/her best efforts to promote the Broker's business, including efforts to sell or rent all property listed with the Broker, obtain and market new listings, and develop and work with leads and prospects;

(c) Use his/her best efforts to develop and maintain his/her goodwill and reputation for fair dealing within the community, as well as the goodwill and reputation of the Broker; and

(d) Advise the Broker immediately of any threatened or pending action or proceeding related to the Salesperson's work for the Broker before an association of REALTORS®, a state agency or any court.

4. *Compensation*. All remuneration for the services performed by the Salesperson under this Agreement shall be directly related to sales or other output, including the performance of services. The Salesperson shall not receive any remuneration related to the number of hours worked. The Broker shall compensate the Salesperson according to the terms set forth in this Section 4.

(a) *Schedule I*. The Salesperson shall be paid commissions for his/her services performed under this Agreement after the deduction of all expenses pursuant to Section 6 hereof, at the rates set forth in Schedule I, attached to and made a part of this Agreement. *[Note: In order to avoid any misunderstandings, Schedule I should be as specific as possible, outlining exactly what duties the Salesperson is expected to perform and exactly how the Salesperson will be paid for each of the duties.]*

(b) *Special arrangements*. In a transaction in which the Salesperson obtains the listing, any deviations from the rates set forth in Schedule I shall be agreed upon by the Broker and the Salesperson. For any listing of the Broker which the Broker assigns to the Salesperson, the Broker shall notify the Salesperson of any deviations from the rates

Independent Contractor Agreement (continued)

> DO NOT COPY <

set forth in Schedule I.

(c) *Joint Servicing.* If two or more salespersons participate in a service, or claim to have done so, the amount of the commission beyond that accruing to the Broker shall be divided between the salespersons according to an agreement between them, or in the absence of an agreement, as determined by the Broker.

(d) *Payment.* All commissions shall be paid to the Broker. The Salesperson shall immediately turn over to the Broker the full amount of any and all commissions collected by the Salesperson. The Salesperson shall be paid a commission based on the Salesperson's gross sales, if any, without deduction for taxes. The Broker shall distribute the Salesperson's commission as soon as practicable after receipt of payment. In no event shall either party be liable for any commission payment to the other party until such commission is received.

5. *Additional Terms.* In addition to any other terms of this Agreement, the Salesperson shall be permitted to: (i) work any hours the Salesperson chooses; and (ii) work either out of the Salesperson's home or at the Broker's office. Subject to laws applicable to real estate brokers and salesmen, the Salesperson shall also be free to engage in outside employment, subject to the limitations found in Connecticut license law, but bound by the confidentiality provisions set forth in Section 11.

6. *Expenses.* The Broker shall not be liable to the Salesperson for any expense incurred by the Salesperson. Expenses which may, by reason of necessity, be payable from a commission or the attempt to collect a commission (such as attorney's fees, costs, documentary stamps, abstracts and the like) shall be paid by the parties in the same proportion as provided for in the division of the commission, pursuant to Schedule I to this Agreement. The Salesperson shall pay all other expenses necessary or related to the conduct of his/her services under this Agreement including, without limitation, automobile, travel, transportation for prospects, entertainment costs, club dues, state or city occupational taxes applicable to that portion of any commission paid to the Salesperson, license fees and taxes and assessments or dues by a board of REALTORS®.

7. *Affirmative Action.* The Broker and the Salesperson both desire to promote fair housing and equal opportunity in housing. Therefore, the Salesperson shall perform his/her obligations under this Agreement in compliance with: (i) federal and state fair housing laws; (ii) the regulations and rules of federal and state agencies responsible for fair housing; and, (iii) Article 10 of the Code of Ethics of the National Association of REALTORS®, Inc. The Salesperson shall make a diligent effort to remain knowledgeable about current fair housing laws, regulations and guidelines.

8. *Agreements.* The Broker hereby specifically appoints the Salesperson as the agent of the Broker solely for the purpose of executing, on behalf of the Broker, any property listing agreements, buyer representation agreements or such other agreements as may relate to such listing agreements and buyer representation agreements. The Salesperson shall take all listings and buyer representation agreements in the name of the Broker and shall file such listings and buyer representation agreements with the Broker immediately after receipt. All listings and buyer representation agreements shall be and remain the exclusive property of the Broker.

9. *Advertising and Marketing.* The Broker advertises publicly and the Salesperson agrees that the Broker may include the Salesperson's name, photograph and/or sales history or performance in such advertisements when deemed appropriate by the Broker to do so. Any public advertising or marketing placed or performed by Salesperson shall conform to the requirements of any Federal or State law regulating such advertising or marketing.

10. *Non-Interference.* The Salesperson shall not contact or otherwise interfere with any leads or prospects of the office that the Broker assigns to other licensees affiliated with the Broker. The Salesperson understands that the Broker may make these assignments to promote the orderly conduct of the business and that any licensee who obtains such an assignment, together with the Broker, shall have the exclusive right to work with the assigned lead or prospect while the assignment is in effect. The Salesperson may also have knowledge of the leads and prospects developed by other licensees affiliated with the Broker. The Salesperson shall not contact or otherwise actively solicit such leads and prospects without the prior written consent of the licensee who developed them and the Broker.

11. *Confidentiality.* The Salesperson understands that he/she may have access to information of the Broker which is not generally known to the public, including, without limitation, office files, client, customer, prospect leads and investor lists, and commission rates. The Salesperson shall keep such information strictly confidential and shall not disclose such information to any person, firm or corporation not affiliated with the Broker.

The obligations of the Salesperson under this Section 11 shall continue after the termination of this Agreement.

12. *Litigation.* Any litigation to collect a commission shall be brought in the name of the Broker, and the Salesperson agrees that the Broker shall have the right and authority to pursue and settle such litigation upon terms and conditions deemed expedient or desirable by the Broker. The Salesperson shall be a subagent of the Broker for the purpose of any litigation to collect a commission and for no other purpose. In any dispute or litigation involving both the Broker and the Salesperson (including litigation to collect a commission), the Broker shall have the right to determine whether the same counsel can represent both the Broker and the Salesperson and to select counsel to represent both, subject to the Salesperson's written agreement to such representation. In any event, the Salesperson agrees to cooperate fully with the Broker and the Broker's counsel. The Broker reserves the right to determine whether and on what terms any litigation or dispute shall be prosecuted, defended, compromised or settled and whether legal expenses shall be incurred.

Subject to the provisions of Section 13, the Broker and Salesperson shall share all expenses arising out of any litigation or dispute (including, without limitation, costs, attorney's fees and insurance policy deductibles) in the same proportion as provided for the division of any commissions, provided, however, if the Broker shall pay such expenses, the Broker may deduct the Salesperson's share from

> DO NOT COPY <

FIGURE 1.1

Independent Contractor Agreement (continued)

future commissions due the Salesperson, if any, or if none shall be due, the Salesperson shall pay his/her proportionate share of such expenses with thirty (30) days after written demand by the Broker.

13. *Indemnity*. Notwithstanding any other provision of this Agreement, the Salesperson agrees to indemnify and hold the Broker harmless for all costs, fines, fees, expenses, assessments and penalties (including, without limitation, costs and attorney's fees) incurred by the Broker because of the Salesperson's negligent or intentional acts or otherwise, misrepresentation, non-disclosure, or promise or untrue statement made by the Salesperson during the course of any transaction handled by the Salesperson under this Agreement. The Broker may deduct any money due the Broker under this Section 13 from any compensation that may be due the Salesperson under this Agreement. The Salesperson shall pay the Broker all money due the Broker under this Section 13 from any compensation that may be due the Salesperson under this Agreement. The Salesperson shall pay the Broker all money due the Broker under this Section 13 within thirty (30) days after written demand by the Broker.

The obligations of the Salesperson set forth in this Section 13 shall continue after the termination of this Agreement.

14. *Termination*. The Salesperson's failure to maintain his/her Connecticut real estate license in effect shall automatically terminate this Agreement. Otherwise, either party may terminate this Agreement at any time by notifying the other party of such termination. Upon the termination of this Agreement, the Salesperson shall turn over to the Broker any and all materials, information and records obtained during the term of the Salesperson's affiliation with the Broker and pertaining to the business of the Broker, including, without limitation, business cards, stationery, signs, books, forms, computer printouts and files. After the termination of this Agreement, the Salesperson shall not use any such materials, record or information or the name of the Broker for his/her own or another's benefit.

Within 10 days after the date of termination, the Broker will give the Salesperson a written statement of all pending listings, transactions and commissions pertaining to the Salesperson.

15. *Nonassignability*. This Agreement is personal to the Salesperson and may not be assigned by the Salesperson to anyone else.

16. *Miscellaneous*. This Agreement shall be interpreted and governed by the laws of the State of Connecticut. This Agreement may be modified only by a written agreement signed by the parties. Should any one or more of the provisions hereunder be determined to be illegal or unenforceable, no other provision hereunder shall be affected. The terms and provisions of this Agreement shall be binding upon and inure to the benefit of the parties hereto and their heirs and personal representatives, as well as to the successors and assigns of the Broker.

IN WITNESS WHEREOF, the parties hereto have executed this Agreement in Connecticut on this _____ day of _____ 20_____. ___

SALESPERSON
BROKER

_____
Signature
Company Name

_____

By:_____
Printed Name
Signature

_____

Printed Name

INDEPENDENT CONTRACTOR AGREEMENT

SCHEDULE I

Commission Rates:

Division of Commission between the Broker and the Salesperson:

Commission and Division of Commissions

THIS SAMPLE AGREEMENT IS FOR ILLUSTRATIVE PURPOSES ONLY. ANY MATTERS PERTAINING TO IT SHOULD BE PRESENTED TO YOUR OWN LEGAL COUNSEL.

Revised 2001

FIGURE 1.2

Agency Umbrella

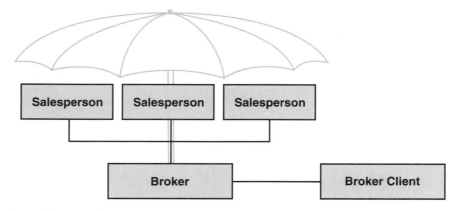

Designated broker in firm enters into agency relationship with client; agency umbrella means that all salespersons that work for broker are then also agents of that client.

FIGURE 1.3

Required Connecticut Agency Documents

	Agency Representation Agreement	Agency Disclosure Notice	Dual Agency/Designated Agency Notice & Consent Agreement
Cooperating Sale			
Broker represents Seller	Listing Agreement	Give to unrepresented potential Buyer at time of first personal meeting concerning Buyer's need (not required if Buyer represented by another agent)	N/A
Broker represents Buyer	Buyer Agency Agreement	Give to unrepresented potential Seller at time of first personal meeting with Seller (not required if Seller represented by another agent)	N/A
Broker working with Buyer, subagent of Seller	Seller Consent to Subagency	Give to unrepresented potential Buyer at time of first personal meeting concerning Buyer's needs	N/A
In-House Sale			
Broker represents both Seller and Buyer, no Designated Agents	Listing Agreement and Buyer Agency Agreement (must contain statement about possibility of dual agency)	N/A	Before Buyer makes a written offer: both Buyer and Seller must sign "Dual Agency Consent Agreement"
Broker represents both Seller and Buyer, Designated Agents have been appointed	Listing Agreement and Buyer Agency Agreement (must contain statement about possibility of dual agency)	N/A	Before Buyer makes a written offer: Buyer, Seller, and Broker must sign "Dual Agency/ Designated Agency Disclosure Notice and Consent Agreement" with names of Designated Agents inserted
Broker represents only Seller, working with Buyer	Listing Agreement	Give to unrepresented potential Buyer at time of first personal meeting concerning Buyer's needs (not required if Buyer represented by another agent)	N/A

From the Connecticut Real Estate Commission Policy on Agency, adopted January 6, 2000.

FIGURE 1.4

Connecticut Real Estate Agency Relationships in Practice

Brokerage Firm Represents Seller	Brokerage Firm Represents Buyer	Brokerage Firm Working with Buyer as Customer
STEP A1. Enter into written Listing Agreement. Go to STEP A2. **STEP A2.** Before Seller's property is shown to each potential Buyer, determine whether Buyer is represented by a brokerage firm. (i) If Buyer is not represented but would like to be represented by your firm, go to STEP B1. (ii) If Buyer is not represented and does not wish to be represented, go to STEP A3. (iii) If Buyer is represented by another firm, go to STEP A4. (iv) If Buyer is represented by your firm, go to STEP A5. **STEP A3.** Give Agency Disclosure Notice to unrepresented Buyer at time of first personal meeting concerning Buyer's needs. Go to STEP A4. **STEP A4.** Proceed as Seller's Agent. **STEP A5.** Have both Buyer and Seller given their informed consent to dual agency? (i) If yes, both Buyer and Seller must sign either Dual Agency Consent Agreement (if not designating agents) or Dual Agency/Designated Agency Disclosure Notice and Consent Agreement (if also designating agent). GO TO STEP A6. (ii) If no, Stop. Cannot represent both parties in the same transaction without obtaining their informed consent. **STEP A6.** Have Brokerage Firm and both Buyer and Seller agreed to the appointment of Designated Agents? (i) If yes, Buyer, Seller, and Broker sign Dual agency/Designated Agency Disclosure Notice and Consent Agreement and Broker must appoint designated agents in that Agreement. Designated agents proceed as such, rest of office proceeds as Dual Agent. (ii) If no, proceed as Dual Agent, with no designated agency.	**STEP B1.** Enter into written Buyer Agency Agreement. Go to STEP B2. **STEP B2.** Before Buyer is shown a property, determine whether the Seller of that property is represented by a brokerage firm. (i) If Seller is not represented, go to STEP B3. (ii) If Seller is represented by another firm, go to STEP B4. (iii) If Seller is represented by your firm, go to STEP A5. **STEP B3.** Give Agency Disclosure Notice to unrepresented Seller at time of first personal meeting with Seller. Go to STEP B4. **STEP B4.** Proceed as Buyer's Agent.	**STEP C1.** Determine whether Buyer seeks representation. (i) If yes, go to STEP B1. (ii) If no, go to STEP C2. **STEP C2.** This is a difficult way to go, although it is allowed by the law. Procedure depends upon whether Buyer is going to be shown an in-house listing or another firm's listing. (i) For in-house listings, go to STEP C3. (ii) For another firm's listings, go to STEP C4. **STEP C3.** Broker may work with Buyer as the Seller's Agent. Go to STEP A3. **STEP C4.** Does Seller agree to Broker being Seller's subagent? (i) If yes, Broker must obtain Seller's written consent to subagency, containing subagent Broker's name and licensee number and containing a statement that the law imposes vicarious liability on the Seller for the acts of the subagent. Go to STEP A3. (ii) If no, Stop. Cannot proceed in this transaction and be legally entitled to compensation.

Note: These are the most common scenarios that a Broker may encounter, although this outline is not all encompassing. Refer to the Connecticut General Statutes for further detail and clarification on Connecticut agency relationships.
From the Connecticut Real Estate Commission Policy on Agency, adopted January 6, 2000.

agency contract of employment in which a broker is provided with limited power and authority to act on behalf of his or her principal. Even though brokers are commonly said to "sell" real estate, "sell" in this sense is not equivalent to "convey." Unless the listing broker has definite authority, such as power of attorney, he or she really does not "sell" at all, but simply brings together buyers and sellers in the marketplace. Hence, the broker is hired to *market* the property for sale, lease, or exchange. The same holds true in the case of buyer agency contracts; a broker is not employed to actually "buy" property, but to conduct research on behalf of the buyer and introduce the buyer to properties.

Dispute over an agency relationship. It is the duty of the party who claims existence of the agency to submit strong evidence to support that allegation.[2] This fact is a key reason why brokers are required to have written listing agreements and buyer agency contracts. Although there may be instances in which brokers are paid commissions without a written listing agreement, the law would not support a broker's right to a commission under these circumstances. Furthermore, brokers should be wary of "for sale" signs including the phrase "brokers protected" and insist upon written contracts before showing such property or divulging any information regarding prospective buyers to the owner.

Fiduciary relationship. A broker must exercise care to avoid violating the trust that is placed in her or him. Furthermore, brokers must avoid making misleading or false statements concerning the properties listed with them or any misrepresentations of actual fact to procure a sale on behalf of the principal. Brokers or salespeople found *guilty of misrepresenting material facts or violating the agency agreement* may be denied the right to collect a commission and are subject to both fines and possible revocation of their licenses.

When a licensed broker/agent submits a written offer to purchase or lease to an owner/principal (or draws up an offer for a buyer), the offer must contain all the essential terms and conditions, including the proposed financing arrangements and any other conditions on which the offer is contingent. In Connecticut, typically a contract, or binder with a stipulation that a contract be drawn up by an attorney at a later date, is presented as the written offer. (Note that the contractual process varies widely across the state. For example, in some areas, negotiation is verbal and nonbinding; in yet other areas, a written offer form is used.) The broker must also diligently and honestly represent his or her principal and present to the principal all legitimate offers received without altering or omitting pertinent details likely to influence any of the parties to the transaction.

Conduct of Brokers and Salespersons

The Connecticut Real Estate Commission has enacted regulations pertaining to the conduct of brokers and salespersons. Among other things, these regulations discuss the duties that brokers and salespersons have to the parties in a real estate transaction; the handling of deposits and escrow monies, compensation, referral fees; and interference with other licensees' agency relationships. See Chapter 10 for a detailed discussion of these regulations.

Disclosure of Agency to Unrepresented Persons

Connecticut real estate licensing law requires *mandatory written disclosure of agency representation* to unrepresented prospective purchasers, sellers, lessors, or lessees. (See Figure 1.5, depicting whom disclosure is given to.) Disclosure is required to be made by the licensed broker or agent representing a seller, purchaser, seller and purchaser (dual agency), lessor, or lessee *only when the agent is also working with another party who is not represented by the agent's firm or another firm.* The required notice form is called the "Real Estate Agency Disclosure Notice Given to Unrepresented Persons," and is set forth in Figure 1.6. Disclosure must be given in residential and commercial purchase and sale transactions as well as in leasing transactions.

FIGURE 1.5

Agency Disclosure

This disclosure must be given at the beginning of the first personal meeting concerning the unrepresented party's needs. It is then required to be attached to any offer, binder, option, or agreement to purchase/lease.

If a person required to sign the disclosure refuses to do so, the agent should note this refusal on the line indicated for the person's signature and attach that disclosure.

The required disclosure need not be given to prospective buyers or lessees at an open house, provided there is a sign or pamphlet disclosing the licensee's agency relationship and the specific real estate needs of the prospective buyer or lessee are not discussed.

Note that the above discussion on agency disclosure details the state law requirements. Members of professional associations, such as the Association of REALTORS®, may be held to stricter requirements.

Subagency

Traditionally, cobrokers were considered subagents of the seller. In Connecticut, subagency is not permitted in a cobrokered transaction without the written consent of the person being represented. Such consent must include the name and license number of all real estate licensees to be appointed as subagents, as well as a statement that the person being represented may be vicariously liable for the acts of the subagent.

This limitation on subagency does not apply to leasing transactions. In a lease transaction (but not a lease-purchase-option transaction), licensees working with a tenant may be a subagent of the landlord without obtaining the landlord's consent. The limitation on subagency does apply to commercial purchase and sale transactions.

Dual Agency

When a brokerage firm represents both the buyer and the seller (or landlord and tenant) in the same transaction, dual agency exists. Dual agency with informed consent is permitted in Connecticut.

Connecticut has provided that a person has given his informed consent to a dual agency agreement if that person signs a statutorily prescribed "Dual Agency Consent Agreement" prior to executing a purchase, sale, or lease contract. Such agreement

FIGURE 1.6

Real Estate Agency Disclosure Notice Given to Unrepresented Persons

REAL ESTATE AGENCY DISCLOSURE NOTICE
GIVEN TO **UNREPRESENTED PERSONS**

This is not a contract. Connecticut law requires that you be given this notice disclosing whom the real estate licensee represents. The purpose of such disclosure is to enable you to make informed choices about your relationship with real estate licensees.

GIVEN TO:_____
(UNREPRESENTED PERSON/PERSONS)

ON _____ (DATE)

OUR FIRM _____ REPRESENTS

❏ SELLER   ❏ LANDLORD   ❏ BUYER   ❏ TENANT

UNREPRESENTED PERSON(S)'S RIGHTS AND RESPONSIBILITIES

1. The broker and salespersons (referred to as agents or licensees) in this transaction owes the other party to this transaction undivided fiduciary obligations, such as: loyalty, reasonable care, disclosure, and obedience to lawful instruction, confidentiality and accountability. The agent(s) must put the other party's interest first and negotiate for the best terms and conditions for them, <u>not for you</u>.

2. All real estate agents, whether representing you or not, are obligated by law to treat all parties to a real estate transaction honestly and fairly.

3. You have the responsibility to protect your own interests. Carefully read all agreements to make sure they accurately reflect your understanding. If you need additional advice for legal, tax, insurance or other such matters, it is your responsibility to consult a professional in those areas.

4. Whether you are a buyer, seller, tenant, or landlord, you can choose to have the advice, assistance and representation of your own real estate brokerage firm and its agents. Do not assume that a real estate brokerage firm or its agents are representing you or are acting on your behalf <u>unless you have contracted in writing</u> with that real estate brokerage firm.

ACKNOWLEDGMENT
OF UNREPRESENTED PERSON(S)*

_____
Signature(s)

_____
Print Name(s)

_____
Date

ACKNOWLEDGEMENT OF AGENT

_____
Signature

_____
Print Name

_____
Date

*To be signed by the buyer/tenant when the agent represents the seller/landlord, or
To be signed by the seller/landlord when the agent represents the buyer/tenant

Connecticut Department of Consumer Protection form issued June, 2002 is shown in Figure 1.7. The Consent Agreement form specifies what disclosures can and cannot be made to the dual parties.

Timing of dual agency documentation. In a dual agency situation, the Dual Agency Consent Form must be signed by both the buyer and seller before the buyer makes an offer on the seller's property.

Many brokers have clients sign the Dual Agency Consent Form at the time an agency agreement is entered into. This is permitted as a way of introducing the client to the concept of dual agency but does not meet the statutory informed consent requirement if a specific buyer has not yet been matched with a specific seller's property.

The Real Estate Commission provides us with the following policy guidance. The Dual Agency Consent Form may be generically signed by the seller at the time a listing agreement is entered into, identifying the buyer as "all buyers that the licensee now represents or may represent in the future." Likewise, the Dual Agency Consent Form may be generically signed by the buyer at the time the buyer agency agreement is entered into, identifying the seller as "all sellers that the licensee now represents or may represent in the future" and the property as "all property currently listed with the licensee or listed with the licensee in the future." Additionally, however, before a specific buyer-client makes an offer on a specific seller-client's property, both the buyer and seller must execute a specific Dual Agency Consent Form, listing the proper parties and property.

Possibility of Dual Agency must be stated in agency agreements. If a brokerage firm represents both buyers and sellers (or landlords and tenants), the firm's agency agreements must contain a statement that the potential exists for the firm to be a dual agent.

Designated Agency

When a real estate brokerage firm represents both the buyer and seller (or landlord and tenant) in the same transaction (which amounts to dual agency), the firm may appoint a separate seller agent and separate buyer agent to represent the parties, if the parties agree. This type of agency is referred to as *designated agency*, and the appointed agents would be designated agents. Designated agents are not dual agents, although the brokerage firm and all non-designated licensees would be dual agents.

If a firm is going to designate agents in a dual agency situation, the Dual Agency Consent Form is not used. Instead, to disclose the dual/designated agency situation and to obtain all parties' informed consent to the dual/designated agency, the Dual Agency/Designated Agency Notice and Consent Agreement is to be used (see Figure 1.8). Before a buyer makes a written offer, the buyer, seller, and firm's broker must sign the form with the names of the designated agents inserted. As with the Dual Agency Consent Form, the Dual Agency/Designated Agency Notice and Consent Agreement may be generically signed at the time an agency agreement is entered into, but must be reexecuted at the appropriate time with the appropriate information included.

Dual Agency Consent Agreement

DUAL AGENCY CONSENT AGREEMENT
Pursuant to Public Act 96-159

Property Address: _____

Seller(s) or Landlord(s):   _____

Buyer(s) or Tenant(s):   _____

(1) This Dual Agency Consent Agreement is an addendum to and made part of (check all that apply):

❑ Listing Agreement dated _____ between brokerage firm and seller or landlord.

❑ Buyer or tenant agency agreement dated _____ between brokerage firm and buyer or tenant.

(2) Seller and buyer (or landlord and tenant, as the case may be) hereby acknowledge and agree that _____ _____ (name of brokerage firm) is representing both buyer and seller (or landlord and tenant, as the case may be) in the purchase and sale (or lease) of the above referenced property and that brokerage firm has been and is now the agent of both seller and buyer (or landlord and tenant, as the case may be). Seller and buyer (or landlord and tenant, as the case may be) have both consented to and hereby confirm their consent to this dual representation.

(3) Seller and buyer (or landlord and tenant, as the case may be) agree:

(A) The brokerage firm shall not be required to and shall not disclose to either buyer or seller (or landlord or tenant, as the case may be) any personal, financial or other confidential information to such other party without the express written consent of the party whose information is disclosed, other than information related to material property defects which are known to the brokerage firm and other information the brokerage firm is required to disclose by law.

(B) The brokerage firm may not disclose: (i) To the buyer that the seller (landlord) will accept less than the asking or listed price, unless otherwise instructed to do so in writing by the seller (landlord); (ii) to the seller (landlord) that the buyer (tenant) can or will pay a price greater than the price submitted in a written offer to the seller (landlord), unless otherwise instructed to do so in writing by the buyer (tenant); (iii) the motivation of the seller or buyer (or landlord or tenant, as the case may be) for selling, buying or leasing property, unless otherwise instructed in writing by the respective party; or (iv) that a seller or buyer will agree to financing terms other than those offered, unless instructed in writing by the respective party.

(4) Property information available through the multiple listing service or otherwise, including listed and sold properties, which has been requested by either the seller or the buyer (or landlord or tenant, as the case may be) shall be disclosed to both seller and buyer (or landlord and tenant, as the case may be).

(5) Both parties are advised to seek competent legal and tax advice with regard to this transaction, and with regard to all documents executed in connection with this transaction, including this Dual Agency Consent Agreement.

I have read and understand the above agreement.

Buyer (Tenant)	**Seller (Landlord)**	**Brokerage Firm**
_____	_____	_____
		Company Name
_____	_____	_____
		Authorized Signature
Date:_____	Date:_____	Date:_____

Dual Agency/Designated Agency Notice and Consent Agreement

Dual Agency/Designated Agency
Disclosure Notice and Consent Agreement
Given to <u>Persons Represented by the Same Brokerage Firm</u>

Brokerage Firm: _____

Property Address: _____

Buyer (Tenant): _____

Seller (Landlord): _____

The Brokerage Firm has entered into a written agency relationship with both Buyer and Seller (or Tenant and Landlord). Buyer (Tenant) is now interested in buying (leasing) Seller's (Landlord's) Property. If this transaction proceeds, Brokerage Firm will be a dual agent, since Brokerage Firm represents both parties. Connecticut law allows Brokerage Firm to be a dual agent, but only after both Buyer and Seller (or Tenant and Landlord) understand what dual agency is and consent to it.

Connecticut law also allows Brokerage Firms that are dual agents to appoint individual designated agents within their firm to solely represent Buyer and Seller (or Tenant and Landlord); again, this designation can only be made after both Buyer and Seller (or Tenant and Landlord) understand what designated agency is and consent to it.

Both Buyer and Seller (or Tenant and Landlord) are free to seek legal and tax advice with regard to this <u>transaction, and with regard to all documents signed in connection with this transaction.</u>

Understanding Dual Agency

Dual Agency means that the Brokerage Firm, and all the brokers and salespersons for the firm (unless designated agency *is* chosen) act in a fiduciary capacity for both Buyer and Seller (or Tenant and Landlord). In Dual Agency, the Brokerage Firm does not represent either the Buyer or Seller (or Tenant or Landlord) exclusively, and the parties can not expect the Brokerage Firm's undivided loyalty.

The Brokerage Firm may not disclose to either the Buyer or Seller (or Tenant or Landlord) any personal, financial, or confidential information to the other party except as authorized by either party or required by law. The Brokerage Firm may not disclose, unless otherwise instructed by the respective party:

–   to Buyer (Tenant) that Seller (Landlord) will accept less than the asking or listed price

–   to the Seller (Landlord) that the Buyer (Tenant) can pay a price greater than otherwise instructed to do so in writing by the Buyer (Tenant);

–   the motivation of either Buyer or Seller (or Tenant or Landlord) for selling, buying, leasing the Property; and that

–   that Buyer or Seller will agree to financing terms other than those offered.

Dual Agency/Designated Agency Notice and Consent Agreement (continued)

Dual Agency Consent

Buyer and Seller (or Landlord and Tenant) understand dual agency and
consent to Brokerage Firm acting as a dual agent in this transaction.

Understanding Designated Agency

Designated Agency means the appointment by the Brokerage Firm of one broker or salesperson (referred to as agent) affiliated with or employed by the Brokerage Firm to solely represent Buyer (Tenant) as a Designated Buyer's Agent and appoint another to solely represent Seller (Landlord) as a Designated Seller's Agent in this transaction.

A Designated Buyer's Agent and Designated Seller's Agent owe the party for whom they have been appointed undivided fiduciary obligations, such as loyalty, reasonable care, disclosure, obedience to lawful instruction, confidentiality and accountability. The Designated Agent is not deemed to be a Dual Agent, and thus does not owe fiduciary duties to the other party. A designated agent may use confidential information obtained about the other party while a designated agent for the benefit of the party for whom they have been appointed, however, information obtained before the designation is still confidential. In the case of Designated Agency, Brokerage Firm is still considered a Dual Agent.

Appointment of Designated Agents

Buyer and Seller (or Landlord and Tenant) understand designated agency and have
agreed to the appointment of designated agents.

If designated agency has been agreed to, the following designated agents have been appointed:

_____ has been designated to solely represent Buyer (Tenant) as a Designated Buyer Agent.

_____ has been designated to solely represent Seller (Landlord) as a Designated Seller Agent.

Appointing broker/authorized agent: _____   Date: _____

Acknowledgment of Buyer (Tenant)

_____

_____

Signature(s)   *Date*

_____

Print Name(s)

Acknowledgement of Seller (Landlord)

_____

_____

Signature(s)   *Date*

_____

Print Name(s)

Designated Agency is not available to only one party in a transaction. For example, a brokerage firm cannot designate a designated agent solely to represent a buyer without also designating an agent for the seller.

Confidential Information

The real estate *licensee may not reveal confidential information about a client at any time during or after an agency relationship.* Further, the licensee may not use confidential information about the person that he or she represented to that person's disadvantage or to the advantage of another. Confidential information means facts concerning a person's assets; liabilities; income; expenses; motivations to purchase, rent, or sell; and previous offers received or made that are not a matter of public record.

■ BROKER COMPENSATION

The amount of compensation is an integral part of the contract between principal and broker-agent. Commissions, unlike interest rates, are not subject to usury law (maximum interest rates allowed by statute). A broker may request any compensation he or she feels is commensurate with the duties expected of him or her under the listing or buyer agency contract. Compensation can be paid by either the seller or buyer. The compensation can be a percentage of sales price or a flat fee.

The broker may not accept a commission or listing agreement based on a net price.   This type of arrangement, whereby the broker retains all funds above a certain net-to-the-seller figure as compensation, is illegal in Connecticut (refer to Chapter 6 of *Modern Real Estate Practice*).

Written agreements must state (in boldface type or in another prominent manner) that compensation may be negotiable (see Chapter 10 for more details). Section 20-325b of the Connecticut General Statutes requires that the following language be inserted in listing agreements and buyer agency contracts immediately preceding any provision relating to compensation:

> **NOTICE: THE AMOUNT OR RATE OF REAL ESTATE BROKER COMPENSATION IS NOT FIXED BY LAW. IT IS SET BY EACH BROKER INDIVIDUALLY AND MAY BE NEGOTIABLE BETWEEN YOU AND THE BROKER.**

A broker in Connecticut is not entitled to compensation unless *reasonable cause for payment exists*. In the case of a listing agreement, if an offer meets all the terms and conditions agreed to under the contract, the broker is deemed to have produced a ready, willing, and able buyer, and reasonable cause exists to award him or her a commission. Furthermore, when a broker procures a buyer who is ready, willing, and able to purchase on terms other than those on the listing agreement but that are acceptable to the seller, the broker is entitled to a commission once the seller has formally accepted the offer of the prospective buyer and all the conditions prescribed by the offer have been met. The fact that a sale may not actually take place does not change the right of a licensed broker to recover a commission from the principal. If the seller defaults on the sales contract, the broker is still entitled to a commission. If the buyer procured by the broker defaults, however, the broker has no recourse against the seller for collecting a commission but may sue the buyer to recover damages.

In the case of a buyer agency contract, if the broker meets the requirements of the contract, the broker will be owed the agreed-on compensation.[3] A broker entering into a buyer brokerage agreement with a buyer is required to accurately explain the provisions of the agreement that detail the compensation arrangement. If a buyer brokerage agreement calls for zero (or blank) compensation, the buyer's broker cannot look to the buyer for compensation even if the seller's agent does not agree to compensate the buyer's broker. A broker cannot advertise or state that buyers can be represented with no liability to pay a fee or commission, unless in fact the buyer has no obligation to pay compensation in any circumstances under the agreement. (Note that a buyer brokerage agreement where the buyer has no obligation to the broker may not be legally enforceable for lack of consideration.)

Brokers may be denied the right to collect compensation under a variety of circumstances, ranging from fraud and misrepresentation to criminal intent and operating without a license. Commissions may be denied by virtue of an aggrieved party's substantiated complaint (through the Real Estate Commission) or by court action. Any actions by a broker that violate his or her agency relationship or the laws governing licensing and conduct may be sufficient cause for denial of compensation.

■ BROKER'S LIEN

A broker who has performed services relating to *residential* or *commercial* real estate has the right to place a *lien on the real estate* to secure payment of compensation pursuant to Section 20-325a of the Connecticut General Statutes. The lien does not attach until it is recorded in the land records in the town where the property is located. At the time of recording, the broker must be entitled to compensation, without any contingencies (except the transfer of title), under terms set forth in a written contract.

For services relating to a seller, the claim of lien must be recorded prior to conveyance. Where the broker represents a lessor in a lease transaction, the claim must be recorded within 30 days after the tenant takes possession, unless the broker receives notice of the lease signing date in advance, in which case the lien must be recorded prior to the lease signing. If compensation is due in installments, any claim for lien for amounts owing after a conveyance or lease must be recorded subsequent to the transaction. In the case of a broker representing a buyer or a tenant, the claim of lien must be filed within 30 days of the conveyance or lease signing.

The claim for lien must include

- the name of the property owner,
- the commission amount that is being claimed in the lien,

- the name of the broker,
- the broker's real estate license number,
- a description of the real estate on which the lien is being claimed, and
- a statement sworn to and signed by the broker that states that the information contained in the notice is true and accurate to his/her knowledge (as of October 1, 2004, an authorized agent of the broker can sign).

The broker's lien law goes into detail about what types of notices must be served and procedures followed to claim and enforce the lien, including a notice of intent to lien. Enforcing the lien requires filing an action in superior court and is very much like foreclosing on a mortgage. See Figure 1.9 for examples of a broker's lien notice and filing. *If a broker does not file a suit to enforce the lien within one year of filing it, the lien is extinguished.* The owner of the property can demand that the broker commence an action sooner, in which case the suit must be filed within 45 days of the demand or the lien is extinguished.

A closing or leasing cannot be prevented solely on the basis of a recorded broker's lien. If a recorded lien creates a problem in the transaction, the law requires that an escrow account for the amount of the disputed compensation be established from the proceeds of the transaction. The broker is then required to release the claim for lien. The escrow is released to the appropriate party when the dispute is resolved.

■ NOTICE OF COMMERCIAL LEASE COMMISSION RIGHTS

A broker who is entitled to a future commission for a commercial lease transaction can protect his or her right to receive that commission in the event the landlord sells the property. To do so, the broker must record a Notice of Commission Rights in the municipal land records in the municipality where the leased property is located. This notice must be recorded within 30 days of execution of the lease or when the tenant takes occupancy of the leased property, whichever is later. Section 20-325k of the Connecticut General Statutes dictates the form of notice and provisions for release. If the notice requirements are followed properly, future owners of the leased property will be bound to pay the future commission owed. See Figure 1.10 for the required notice form.

■ MORTGAGE BROKERAGE SERVICES

A real estate broker or salesperson may not receive any type of referral fee for the referral of any buyer to an attorney or mortgage broker/lender.[4] Likewise, no attorney or mortgage lender may receive a referral fee for the referral of a person to a real estate broker or salesperson (unless the attorney or mortgage lender holds a real estate license). It is not unusual, however, for a real estate broker to act as a mortgage broker for the buyer. The broker's fee must be for negotiating or arranging for a mortgage loan for the buyer and not for the referral of the buyer to a mortgage lender. A real estate broker acting as a

Broker's Lien Notice and Filing

BROKER'S LIEN

This is to certify that [*Broker Name and Address*], Connecticut in accordance with a certain listing contract/buyer representation agreement [*specify type of agreement*] with [*Name and address of Property Owner or Person executing agreement*], for the sale/purchase [*specify which*] of real property located at [*Property Address*] in the Town of _____, County of _____, and State of Connecticut has a lien under P. A. 95-186 on the following described premises owned by [*Name of Property Owner (or Buyer, if buyer representation agreement)*] in the amount of [*Amount of Commission Claimed*] which amount is justly due.

The subject premises are bounded and described as follows: {Attach legal description of property}

SEE SCHEDULE A ATTACHED HERETO AND MADE A PART HEREOF

IN WITNESS WHEREOF, I have hereunto set my hand and seal this _____ day of_____, 20____.

By: _____ License Number: _____

STATE OF CONNECTICUT   )

)   SS:

COUNTY OF   )

Personally appeared _____, signer and sealer of the foregoing instrument, who acknowledged the same to be his free act and deed, before me.

_____

Notary Public
Commissioner of Superior Court

NOTICE OF INTENT TO CLAIM BROKER'S LIEN

THIS NOTICE IS GIVEN TO

Seller Name and Address   Buyer Name and Address

[*Name and Address of Real Estate Broker*], Connecticut, real estate broker, hereby gives you notice pursuant to P. A. 95-186 that said real estate broker claims a lien on certain real property located at [*Property Address*], Connecticut, owned by [*Name and address of Property Owner or Person executing agreement*] on account of services performed under a certain listing contract/buyer agency agreement [*Specify type of agreement*] and that said real estate broker intends to claim a lien therefore on said premises to the amount of [*Amount of Commission Claimed*].

The said premises are situated in the Town of _____, County of _____ and State of Connecticut, recorded in the name of _____ in volume _____ at page _____ of the Town of _____ land records and bounded and described as more fully appears on schedule A attached hereto.

Dated at _____, Connecticut, this _____ day of_____, 20____.

By: _____ License Number: _____

Notice of Commission Rights

NOTICE OF COMMISSION RIGHTS

The undersigned licensed Connecticut real estate broker does hereby publish this NOTICE OF COMMISSION RIGHTS to establish that the lease referenced below was procured by a real estate broker pursuant to a written brokerage commission agreement providing for the payment or promise of payment of compensation for brokerage services.

Owner: _____

Landlord: _____

Tenant: _____

Lease date: _____

Lease term: _____

Project or building name (if any): _____

Real estate broker name _____

Address _____

Telephone number _____

Real estate license number _____

---

mortgage broker for a buyer should be familiar with the law governing the licensure of first and second mortgage brokerage, which is described in Chapter 11.

When a real estate broker or salesperson receives a commission for the sale of the property, a fee for placing the mortgage loan can be received *only with full disclosure* of the following statement, printed in at least 10-point boldface capital letters:

> **I UNDERSTAND THAT THE REAL ESTATE BROKER OR SALESPERSON IN THIS TRANSACTION HAS OFFERED TO ASSIST ME IN FINDING A MORTGAGE LOAN. ADDITIONALLY, I UNDERSTAND THAT THIS REAL ESTATE BROKER OR SALESPERSON DOES NOT REPRESENT ANY PARTICULAR MORTGAGE LENDER AND WILL ATTEMPT TO OBTAIN THE BEST TERMS AVAILABLE WITHIN THE MORTGAGE LOAN MARKET FOR MY SPECIFIC HOME FINANCING NEEDS. IF THE REAL ESTATE BROKER OR SALESPERSON DOES NOT FULFILL HIS OR HER FIDUCIARY OBLIGATION I MAY FILE A COMPLAINT WITH THE DEPARTMENT OF BANKING. I ALSO UNDERSTAND THAT I MAY ATTEMPT TO FIND A MORTGAGE LOAN TO FINANCE THE PURCHASE OF MY HOME WITHOUT THE ASSISTANCE OF THE REAL ESTATE BROKER OR SALESPERSON IN WHICH CASE I WILL NOT BE OBLIGATED TO PAY A FEE TO THE REAL ESTATE BROKER OR SALESPERSON.**[5]

■ ENDNOTES

1. *Harris v. Kent House Corp.* (DC 1954) 127 F. Sup. 44.
2. *Baskin v. Dam* (1968) 239 A. 2d 549, 4 Conn. Cir. 702.
3. *Ditchkus Real Estate Company v. Storm*, 25 Conn. App. 51, 592 A. 2d 959 (1991).
4. Section 20-325c of the Connecticut General Statutes.
5. Section 20-325c of the Connecticut General Statutes.

QUESTIONS

1. Under Connecticut licensing law, a partnership, association, or corporation will be granted a license only if
   a. the broker retains a current license.
   b. every member and officer actively participating in the brokerage business has a broker license.
   c. all papers are filed with the Secretary of State.
   d. the brokerage business has paid a one-time fee to the guaranty fund.

2. A licensed broker procures a ready, willing, and able buyer for his or her seller-principal. The seller first accepts the buyer's offer in writing, then experiences a change of heart and withdraws the original acceptance. The broker in this instance
   a. is entitled to collect a commission.
   b. is out of luck because the transaction was never completed.
   c. may sue the buyer.
   d. may retain the deposit as commission.

3. Brenda Broker of Hart Realty has entered into a listing agreement with Seller. Through the MLS, Beau Broker of Fair Realty has been working with Buyer, who is interested in making an offer on Seller's property. In this transaction, typically Beau Broker would enter into a written representation contract with
   a. Seller as a subagent.
   b. Buyer as an agent.
   c. Buyer as a subagent.
   d. neither Buyer nor Seller.

4. In Question 3, if Beau Broker wishes to represent Buyer, Connecticut licensing law requires that he enter into a(n)
   a. oral agency agreement.
   b. written agency agreement.
   c. dual agency agreement.
   d. cobrokerage agreement.

5. When a broker represents the seller of real estate, an agency disclosure must be given to
   a. the seller, at the time the listing agreement is signed.
   b. the purchaser, before the purchase and sale contract is signed.
   c. all potential purchasers, at the beginning of the first personal meeting with the purchaser.
   d. any potential unrepresented purchaser, at the beginning of the first personal meeting with the purchaser.

6. Shoreline Realty has entered into agency agreement with both Seller and Buyer. Buyer is interested in making an offer on Seller's property. Can this occur?
   a. No, Shoreline Realty would then be a dual agent.
   b. Yes, as long as written agency agreements have been entered into with both parties.
   c. Yes, only if Shoreline Realty designated separate agents to represent each party.
   d. Yes, if both Buyer and Seller give their consent to dual agency.

7. Shoreline Realty has entered into agency agreements with both Seller and Buyer. Seller and Buyer agreed to dual agency, but not designated agency. Cal, a salesperson with Shoreline Realty, has been working with Buyer. Legally, Cal is not allowed to do any of the following *except*
   a. provide comparable market data to Seller, after Buyer requests and receives such data from Cal.
   b. disclose Buyer's financial qualifications to Seller.
   c. disclose to Buyer that Seller will accept less than the listing price.
   d. disclose to Seller that Buyer will pay more than the offering price.

8. Sal's listing agreement with Seller has terminated. Seller now enters into a listing agreement with another brokerage firm. Sal has a buyer interested in Seller's property. Sal
   a. is a dual agent.
   b. cannot disclose to the buyer offers received on Seller's property while it was listed with him.
   c. cannot disclose to the buyer information about the physical condition of the property.
   d. cannot represent the buyer.

9. Buona Vista Realty has entered into agency agreements with both Seller and Buyer. Angela, a salesperson with Buona Vista, has been designated to represent Seller, and Bao, another salesperson, has been designated to represent Buyer. In this situation
   a. Angela and Bao are dual agents.
   b. all the other salespersons that work for Buona Vista are dual agents, but not Angela and Bao.
   c. Buona Vista Realty has violated the licensing laws.
   d. Angela and Bao may reveal confidential information about their clients to each other.

10. Elaine, a real estate broker, has been working with the Seinfields. After helping them negotiate for their dream home in Greenwich, the Seinfields ask Elaine if she can help them secure a mortgage. Big Bank will pay Elaine a fee for referring purchasers to them. This is
    a. not allowed.
    b. allowed if Elaine and the Seinfields have entered into a written buyer agency agreement.
    c. allowed if Elaine discloses the referral fee to the Seinfields.
    d. allowed if Big Bank offers the best interest rates and terms available in the market.

11. To secure payment of compensation for her services, a broker may place a lien on a(n)
    a. condominium unit.
    b. four-family apartment building.
    c. office building.
    d. All of the above

2

LISTING AGREEMENTS AND BUYER AGENCY CONTRACTS

■ OVERVIEW

The Connecticut licensing laws and regulations allow a broker to enter into buyer-agency contracts with potential purchasers/lessees as well as listing contracts with potential sellers/lessors.

WWWeb.Link

Sample Connecticut agency agreements, as well as agency-related legal alerts and guidelines, can be found at *www.ctrealtor.com*.

Electronic agency contracts (including e-mails and faxes) must meet federal and state guidelines for electronic documents and signatures. See Appendix E for a discussion of the requirements.

■ AGENCY AGREEMENTS

Listing agreements. To represent a seller or landlord, a written listing agreement must be entered into. The agreement must be entered into before a broker or salesperson attempts to negotiate on behalf of the seller or landlord. Three basic types of listing agreements are recognized in Connecticut: exclusive right to sell, exclusive agency, and open listing. (Examples of these types of listing contracts can be found in Figures 2.1, 2.2, and 2.3, respectively.)

Buyer agency contracts. To represent a buyer, a written buyer agency agreement must be entered into. Three basic types of buyer agency agreements are recognized in Connecticut: exclusive right to represent buyer, exclusive agency right to represent buyer, and open right to represent buyer. (Examples of these types of buyer agency contracts can be found in Figures

2.4, 2.5, and 2.6, respectively.) As a practical matter, the exclusive-agency-right-to-represent-buyer agreement is rarely used.

The agreement must be entered into before a broker or salesperson attempts to *negotiate* on behalf of a prospective buyer or tenant. "Negotiate" has been defined to include showing the buyer any property, discussing an offer with the buyer, engaging in negotiation on behalf of the buyer, *or* giving advice to the buyer about particular real estate.

Preliminary activities for buyer.[1]   A licensee may conduct preliminary activities for a buyer before a written buyer representation agreement is entered into, given that the following Real Estate Commission policy guidelines are met.

Before a licensee works with a buyer, the licensee should

(i)   ask whether the buyer is currently being represented by another firm;
(ii) explain the real estate firm's office policy on the various agency and customer relationships that the licensee could potentially have with the buyer; and
(iii) specifically tell the buyer not to provide confidential information unless and until the buyer and licensee have entered into an agency relationship.

A licensee can do the following for a buyer without entering into a written buyer agency agreement:

(i)   Give the buyer property information;
(ii) Give the buyer information on the licensee's firm; and
(iii) Give the buyer information on mortgage rates and lending institutions.

A licensee *cannot* do the following for a buyer unless either (1) a written buyer agency agreement is entered into, or (2) the licensee is going to represent the seller and has presented the buyer with an Agency Disclosure Notice stating that the licensee represents the seller (and for cooperating sales, obtains the seller's consent to subagency):

(i)   Ask the buyer to disclose confidential information (including information about the buyer's financial status, reasons for purchasing, etc.);
(ii) Express an opinion or give advice about particular real estate (note that a licensee representing the seller should be cautious expressing an opinion or giving advice);
(iii) Physically show the buyer in-house listings;
(iv) Physically show the buyer property listed with another firm;
(v)   Discuss an offer with the buyer; or
(vi) Engage in any verbal or written negotiations concerning purchase price, terms, or conditions.

F I G U R E   2.1

Exclusive-Right-to-Sell Listing Contract

Exclusive Right to Sell Agreement

Date of this Agreement: _____ / _____ / _____

Address of Property: _____

Owner(s): _____

_____

List Price: _____

Present Encumbrances: _____

_____

Terms of Sale: _____

_____

_____

Term of Listing Beginning Date: _____ / _____ / _____

Term of Listing Ending Date: _____ / _____ / _____

Service Fee: _____

Procuring Cause Protection Period: _____

Special Showing Instructions including Internet display: _____

_____

ENVIRONMENTALLY HAZARDOUS CONDITIONS AND MATERIALS

	Is Present	Is Not Present	Was Removed	No Knowledge of its presence
Lead Paint	☐	☐	☐	☐
Asbestos	☐	☐	☐	☐
Mold	☐	☐	☐	☐
Underground Storage Tank	☐	☐	☐	☐
Hazardous Waste	☐	☐	☐	☐
Radon	☐	☐	☐	☐

A G R E E M E N T

1. **Fees:** The Owner(s) agrees to pay the Broker the service fee specified above (1) if the Broker or its agent(s) produces a purchaser who is ready, willing and able to purchase the Property at the List Price and on the Terms stated, or at such other price or such other terms as may be acceptable to Owner(s), or (2) if a sale or exchange of said Property is made by the Owner(s) or any other person during the term of this Exclusive Right to Sell or any Procuring Cause Protection period set forth above.

2. **Procuring Cause Protection Period:** The Owner(s) agrees to pay the service fee to the Broker should a sale be made directly or indirectly within the Procuring Cause Protection Period to parties the Broker or its agent(s) has submitted the Property to during the term of this Exclusive Right To Sell Agreement and Broker notifies Owner(s) in writing of the submissions during the Term of this Exclusive Right To Sell Agreement. This paragraph shall not apply if the Owner(s) subsequently executes a valid exclusive listing with any other real estate broker.

3. **Marketing:** The Broker agrees to market the Property for sale and to make a diligent effort to sell at the List Price and on the Terms stated herein until there is an enforceable contract for the sale of the Property or this Exclusive Right To Sell Agreement expires, whichever occurs first.

4. **Signs and Keys:** The Owner(s) gives the Broker the right to place a "For Sale" sign on the Property and to remove all other "For Sale" signs during continuance of this Exclusive Right To Sell Agreement. The Owner(s) agrees to furnish the Broker with a key to the Property and to permit the Broker to place a keybox on the door.

©2002 Connecticut Association of REALTORS®, Inc.   1
May 23, 2002
Revised July 16, 2002

EQUAL HOUSING OPPORTUNITY   REALTOR®

Exclusive-Right-to-Sell Listing Contract (continued)

5. **Entry and Control:** The Broker or any of its agent(s) may enter the Property at reasonable times for the purpose of showing it to prospective purchasers in accordance with any Special Showing Instructions as noted above. Owner(s) acknowledges that the Broker has a duty under state regulations and the Code of Ethics to cooperate with other brokers to show the Property. Owner(s) and Broker agree that Owner(s) shall at all times have control over the Property, its maintenance and preparation for showing to prospective purchasers.

6. **Owner(s)' Agreements:**
   (a) Owner(s) agrees to complete and keep updated a Connecticut Residential Property Condition Disclosure Report and Title X Lead-based paint disclosure (if applicable) and authorizes the Broker to disclose the information contained therein.
   (b) Owner(s) is either the Owner(s) of the Listed Property or has full authority to enter into this Agreement.
   (c) Owner(s) has received a copy of this Agreement.
   (d) Owner(s) represents that there are no other listings or agreements in effect concerning this Property, including open listings.
   (e) Owner(s) understands that names of attorneys, contractors, and other professionals are furnished as an accommodation to Owner(s) and do not constitute an endorsement or guaranty of such professional or the professional's work product.
   (f) Owner(s) agrees to pay reasonable attorney's fees that Broker may incur to collect monies due under this Agreement.
   (g) Broker reserves the right to terminate this Contract by written notice to the Owner(s) if the Broker has reasonable cause to believe the Owner(s) may be unable to consummate a sale of the Listed Property for the List Price set forth above by reason of liens, encumbrances, title disputes or other matters affecting title to the Property.
   (h) Owner(s) agrees to refer to Broker all requests for information about showings or offers for the Property, and to advise said Broker of any contacts made by any prospective buyer, tenant, or other broker.

7. **Property Information:** Owner(s) has reviewed the information contained on this Exclusive Right To Sell Agreement or the property data sheet and any other disclosure of information forms where Owner(s) supplies information. To the best of Owner's knowledge and belief, Owner(s) represents that any material defects regarding the Listed Property have been disclosed to Broker and the information contained in such information forms are complete and accurate. Owner(s) agrees to indemnify and hold the Broker or its agent(s) harmless from any claim, action, damage or cost including attorney fees that Broker or its agent(s) may incur resulting from an incorrect or inaccurate representation, a misrepresentation or lack of representation of any of the information contained in such forms. Any representations made by Owner(s) are not warranties of any kind and may not be a substitute for an inspection or warranties that a prospective buyer may obtain. Owner(s) authorizes Broker as Owner's agent to disclose any information that Owner(s) provides to Broker concerning the Property.

8. **Multiple Listing Service and Internet Display:** Broker is authorized to submit the Property to the Multiple Listing Service noted above for publication to and by its participants. Unless otherwise indicated under "special showing instructions" above, Owner(s) agree to permit other Brokers to display Property on their web site(s) as part of the Internet Data Exchange program or otherwise. Broker may display the Property on its web sites. Owner(s) agrees that neither the provider of the MLS nor Broker are responsible for errors or omissions appearing in the MLS. The Owner(s) authorizes Broker to provide timely notice of status changes of this Exclusive Right To Sell Agreement and to provide sales information including selling price upon sale of the Property to any agreed upon Multiple Listing Service(s).

9. **Statements Required By Law or the REALTOR® Code of Ethics:**
   (a) This Agreement is subject to the Connecticut General Statutes prohibiting discrimination in commercial and residential real estate transactions (Connecticut General Statute Title 46a, Chapter 814c).
   (b) The real estate broker may be entitled to certain lien rights pursuant to subsection (d) of Section 20-325a of the Connecticut General Statutes.
   (c) **NOTICE: THE AMOUNT OR RATE OF REAL ESTATE BROKER COMPENSATION IS NOT FIXED BY LAW. IT IS SET BY EACH BROKER INDIVIDUALLY AND MAY BE NEGOTIABLE BETWEEN YOU AND THE BROKER.**
   (d) Federal law requires the Owner(s) of "target property," which is generally property built prior to 1978, to disclose the presence of lead-based paint or lead-based paint hazards and to furnish any records, reports, inspections, or other documents in the Owner's possession concerning these items.
   (e) Agency Relationships: While Broker shall generally act as the agent for Owner(s), it may be necessary or appropriate for Broker to act as agent of both Owner(s) and buyer(s), exchange party, or one or more additional

May 23, 2002
Revised July 16, 2002

F I G U R E 2.1

Exclusive-Right-to-Sell Listing Contract (continued)

parties. Broker shall provide agency disclosure as required by law. Owner(s) understands that Broker may have or obtain listings on other properties and that potential buyers may consider, make offers on, or purchase other property through use of Broker's services.

10. **Electronic Signatures:** Broker and Owner(s) agree that they may use an electronic record, including fax or e-mail, to make and keep this Agreement. Either Broker or Owner(s) has the right to withdraw consent to have a record of this Agreement provided or made available to them in electronic form, but that does not permit that party to withdraw consent to the Agreement itself once it has been signed. Broker's and Owner's agreement to use electronic records applies only to this particular real estate transaction and not to all real estate transactions.

For access to and retention of faxed records, there are no special hardware or software requirements beyond access to a fax machine or fax modem and accompanying software connected to a personal or laptop computer. For access to and retention of e-mail records, Owner(s) will need a personal or laptop computer, Internet account and e-mail software.

Owner(s) wishes to use (check one) ❏ Fax machine. Fax number is : _____
❏ E-mail. E-mail address is : _____

Each party will promptly inform the other of any change in e-mail address or fax number in writing or electronically.

11. The Owner(s) and Broker acknowledge, agree and understand that although this form has been furnished by the Connecticut Association of REALTORS®, Inc., the Association assumes no responsibility for its content and is not a party to this Agreement. **This Contract is binding and legal.**

_____   _____   _____
OWNER   DATE   BROKER/AGENCY NAME

_____   _____
STREET   STREET

_____   _____
CITY/STATE/ZIP   CITY/STATE/ZIP

_____   _____   _____
OWNER   DATE   AUTHORIZED AGENT

_____   _____
STREET   E-MAIL ADDRESS

_____
CITY/STATE/ZIP

F I G U R E   2.2

Exclusive-Agency Listing Contract

Exclusive Agency Right to Sell Agreement

Date of this Agreement: _____/_____/_____

Address of Property: _____

Owner(s): _____
_____

List Price: _____

Present Encumbrances: _____
_____

Terms of Sale: _____
_____
_____

Term of Listing Beginning Date: _____ / ____ / ____

Term of Listing Ending Date: _____ / ____ / ____

Service Fee: _____

Procuring Cause Protection Period: _____

Special Showing Instructions including Internet display: _____
_____

ENVIRONMENTALLY HAZARDOUS CONDITIONS AND MATERIALS

	Is Present	Is Not Present	Was Removed	No Knowledge of its presence
Lead Paint	☐	☐	☐	☐
Asbestos	☐	☐	☐	☐
Mold	☐	☐	☐	☐
Underground Storage Tank	☐	☐	☐	☐
Hazardous Waste	☐	☐	☐	☐
Radon	☐	☐	☐	☐

A G R E E M E N T

1. **Fees:** The Owner(s) agrees to pay the Broker the service fee specified above if the Broker or its agent(s) produces a purchaser who is ready, willing and able to purchase the Property at the List Price and on the Terms stated, or at such other price or such other terms as may be acceptable to Owner(s).

2. **Procuring Cause Protection Period:** The Owner(s) agrees to pay the service fee to the Broker should a sale be made directly or indirectly within the Procuring Cause Protection Period to parties the Broker has submitted the Property to during the term of this Exclusive Agency To Sell Agreement and Broker notifies Owner(s) in writing of the submissions during the Term of this Exclusive Agency To Sell Agreement. This paragraph shall not apply if the Owner(s) subsequently executes a valid exclusive listing with any other real estate broker.

3. **Marketing:** The Broker agrees to market the Property for sale and to make a diligent effort to sell at the List Price and on the Terms stated herein until there is an enforceable contract for the sale of the Property or this Exclusive Agency To Sell Agreement expires, whichever occurs first.

4. **Signs and Keys:** The Owner(s) gives the Broker the right to place a "For Sale" sign on the Property and to remove all other "For Sale" signs during continuance of this Exclusive Agency To Sell Agreement. The Owner(s) agrees to furnish the Broker a key to the Property and permit the Broker to place a keybox on the door.

5. **Entry and Control:** The Broker or its agent(s) may enter the Property at reasonable times for the purpose of showing it to prospective purchasers in accordance with any Special Showing Instructions as noted above. Owner(s) acknowledges that the Broker has a duty under state regulations and the Code of Ethics to cooperate with other brokers to show the Property. Owner(s) and Broker agree that Owner(s) shall at all times have control over the Property and its maintenance.

©2002 Connecticut Association of REALTORS®, Inc.   1
Revised May 23, 2002

Exclusive-Agency Listing Contract (continued)

6. **Owner(s)'s Agreements:**
   (a) Owner(s) agrees to complete and keep updated a Connecticut Residential Property Condition Disclosure Report and authorizes the Broker to disclose the information contained therein.
   (b) Owner(s) is either the Owner(s) of the listed property or has full authority to enter into this Agreement.
   (c) Owner(s) has received a copy of this Agreement.
   (d) Owner(s) represents that there are no other listings or agreements in effect concerning this Property, including open listings.
   (e) Owner(s) understands that names of attorneys, contractors, and other professionals are furnished as an accommodation to Owner(s) and do not constitute an endorsement or guaranty of such professional or the professional's work product.
   (f) Owner(s) agrees to pay reasonable attorney's fees that Broker may incur to collect monies due under this Agreement.
   (g) Broker reserves the right to terminate this Contract by written notice to the Owner(s) if the Broker has reasonable cause to believe the Owner(s) may be unable to consummate a sale of the listed property for the List Price set forth above by reason of liens, encumbrances, title disputes or other matters affecting title to the Property.

7. **Property Information:** Owner(s) has reviewed the information contained on this Exclusive Agency To Sell Agreement or the property data sheet and any other disclosure of information forms where Owner(s) supplies information. To the best of Owner's knowledge and belief, Owner(s) represents that any material defects regarding the Listed Property have been disclosed to Broker and the information contained in such information forms are complete and accurate. Owner(s) agrees to indemnify and hold the Broker and its agent(s) harmless from any claim, action, damage or cost, including attorney fees, that the Broker or its agent(s) may incur resulting from an incorrect or inaccurate representation, a misrepresentation or lack of representation of any of the information contained in such forms. Any representations made by Owner(s) are not warranties of any kind and may not be a substitute for an inspection or warranties that a prospective buyer may obtain. Owner(s) authorizes Broker as Owner's agent to disclose any information that Owner(s) provides to Broker concerning the Property.

8. **Multiple Listing Service:** Broker is authorized to submit the Property to the Multiple Listing Service noted above for publication to and by its participants. Unless otherwise indicated under "special showing instructions" above, Owner(s) agree to permit other Brokers to display Property on their web site(s) as part of the Internet Data Exchange program or otherwise. Broker may display the Property on its web sites. Owner(s) agrees that neither the provider of the MLS nor Broker are responsible for errors or omissions appearing in the MLS. The Owner(s) authorizes Broker to provide timely notice of status changes of this Exclusive Agency Right To Sell Agreement and to provide sales information including selling price upon sale of the Property to any agreed upon Multiple Listing Service(s).

9. **Statements Required By Law or the REALTOR® Code of Ethics:**
   (a) This Agreement is subject to the Connecticut General Statutes prohibiting discrimination in commercial and residential real estate transactions (Connecticut General Statute Title 46a, Chapter 814c).
   (b) The real estate broker may be entitled to certain lien rights pursuant to subsection (d) of Section 20-325a of the Connecticut General Statutes.
   (c) **NOTICE: THE AMOUNT OR RATE OF REAL ESTATE BROKER COMPENSATION IS NOT FIXED BY LAW. IT IS SET BY EACH BROKER INDIVIDUALLY AND MAY BE NEGOTIABLE BETWEEN YOU AND THE BROKER.**
   (d) Federal law requires the Owner(s) of "target property," which is generally property built prior to 1978, to disclose the presence of lead-based paint or lead-based paint hazards and to furnish any records, reports, inspections, or other documents in the Owner's possession concerning these items.
   (d) **Agency Relationships:** While Broker shall generally act as the agent for Owner(s), it may be necessary or appropriate for Broker to act as agent of both Owner(s) and buyer(s), exchange party, or one or more additional parties. Broker shall provide agency disclosure as required by law. Owner(s) understands that Broker may have or obtain listings on other properties and that potential buyers may consider, make offers on, or purchase other property through use of Broker's services.

10. **Electronic Signatures:** Broker and Owner(s) agree that they may use an electronic record, including fax or e-mail, to make and keep this Agreement. Either Broker or Owner(s) has the right to withdraw consent to have a record of this Agreement provided or made available to them in electronic form, but that does not permit that party to withdraw consent to the Agreement itself once it has been signed. Broker's and Owner's agreement to use an electronic record applies only to this particular real estate transaction and not to all real estate transactions.

FIGURE 2.2

Exclusive-Agency Listing Contract (continued)

For access to and retention of faxed records, there are no special hardware or software requirements beyond access to a fax machine or fax modem and accompanying software connected to a personal or laptop computer. For access to and retention of e-mail records, Owner(s) will need a personal or laptop computer, Internet account and e-mail software.

Owner(s) wishes to use (check one) ❑ Fax machine. Fax number is:_____
                                      ❑ E-mail. E-mail address is:_____

Each party will promptly inform the other of any change in e-mail address or fax number in writing or electronically.

11. The Owner(s) and Broker acknowledge, agree and understand that although this form has been furnished by the Connecticut Association of REALTORS®, Inc., the Association assumes no responsibility for its content and is not a party to this Agreement. **This Contract is binding and legal.**

_____	_____	_____
OWNER	DATE	BROKER/AGENCY NAME
_____		_____
STREET		STREET
_____		_____
CITY/STATE/ZIP		CITY/STATE/ZIP
_____	_____	_____
OWNER	DATE	AUTHORIZED AGENT
_____		_____
STREET		E-MAIL ADDRESS
_____		
CITY/STATE/ZIP		

©2002 Connecticut Association of REALTORS®, Inc.   3
Revised May 23, 2002

Open Listing Contract

Open Listing Agreement

PARTIES AND PROPERTY:

I/We _____ , Owner(s), give you, _____
_____ REALTOR® the right to list for sale my/our real property on a
non-exclusive basis at _____ , in _____ , CT

SELLING TERMS:

The Listed Price shall be $_____ .

TERM OF THIS LISTING:

This Listing Agreement will take effect on _____ , 20____ , and will remain in effect through
and including _____ , 20____ , provided however that this Listing Agreement shall terminate
sooner if I/We notify you that I/We have entered into an Exclusive Agency or an Exclusive Right to Sell Listing Agreement
for the Listed Property and you have not yet earned a commission as provided in this Agreement. Upon full execution of
an agreement for the sale of the Listed Property, all rights and obligations under this Listing Agreement will automatically
extend through the date of the actual closing of the Listed Property and may not be revoked or canceled once you have
executed a purchase contract for the sale of the property to a buyer we found.

PAYMENT OF SERVICE OR FEE:

**NOTICE: THE AMOUNT OR RATE OF REAL ESTATE BROKER COMPENSATION IS NOT FIXED BY
LAW. IT IS SET BY EACH BROKER INDIVIDUALLY AND MAY BE NEGOTIABLE BETWEEN YOU AND
THE BROKER.**

If during the term of this Listing Agreement you find a buyer ready, willing and able to buy the Listed Property, either on
the terms specified in this Listing Agreement or on any other terms acceptable to me/us, I/We will pay you a service fee of:
(check one)

❏ _____ % (percent) of the agreed upon sale price.
❏ a retainer of $_____ .
❏ a flat fee of $_____ .
❏ an hourly rate of $_____ per hour.

OFFERS OF PURCHASE:

You will continue to submit all offers to me/us until (select one):
❏ a written Agreement has been signed by me/us and a buyer.
❏ a written Agreement has been signed by me/us and a buyer and all contingencies have been met.
❏ title passes.

OWNER'S AND REALTOR'S® AGREEMENTS:

1. This is NOT an Exclusive Agency or Exclusive Right to Sell Listing Agreement. I/We understand that the Listed Property
    will not be placed in any multiple listing service. I/We may sell the Listed Property myself/ourselves or through another
    broker or agent.
2. If this is a 1-4 family residential property, I/We represent that I/We have good title to the Listed Property and that I/We
    have the right to sell the Listed Property.

Copyright© 1997-2002 Connecticut Association of REALTORS®, Inc.
Revised April 4, 1997
Revised January 29, 1998
Revised July 31, 2002

Page 1 of 2

Open Listing Contract (continued)

3.   I/We have received a copy of this Listing Agreement.
I/We agree to pay any costs and attorney's fees which you may incur to collect any monies due to you under this Listing Agreement.

4.   I/We authorize you, as my/our agent, to disclose any information that I/We provide you concerning the Listed Property. You may market this Property on the Internet or World Wide Web. You are not responsible for the accuracy of the information supplied to you by me/us.

5.   You are not responsible for the management, maintenance or upkeep of, or for any physical damage to, the Listed Property or its contents.

6.   This Listing Agreement is binding upon me/us, or against my/our heirs, administrators, executors, successors and assigns, and your successors and assigns.

7.   The real estate broker may be entitled to certain lien rights pursuant to sub-section(d) of Section 20-325a of the Connecticut General Statutes.

8.   **Notice to Seller:** Federal law requires the seller of a dwelling which is considered to be "target housing" (meaning with some exceptions, housing built before 1978) to disclose the presence of lead-based paint and lead-based paint hazards, and to furnish any records or reports concerning lead-based paint or lead-based paint hazards to a buyer. A seller must permit a buyer a 10-day period (unless the parties mutually agree in writing to a different time period) to conduct a risk assessment or inspection of the property for the presence of lead-based paint and lead-based paint hazards before a buyer is obligated to proceed with any Agreement.

9.   Other terms

STATEMENT REQUIRED BY LAW:

THIS AGREEMENT IS SUBJECT TO CHAPTER 814c OF TITLE 64a OF THE GENERAL STATUTES AS AMENDED (HUMAN RIGHTS AND OPPORTUNITIES). IT IS UNLAWFUL UNDER FEDERAL AND STATE LAW TO DISCRIMINATE ON THE BASIS OF RACE, COLOR, RELIGION, NATIONAL ORIGIN, SEX, MARITAL STATUS, FAMILIES WITH CHILDREN AND/OR PHYSICAL HANDICAP IN THE ACQUISITION OR DISPOSITION OF REAL PROPERTY.

REALTOR® Firm Name	Owner Date
Authorized Representative Date	Owner Date
Street	Street
City State Zip	City State Zip
Telephone	Telephone

Copyright© 1997-2002 Connecticut Association of REALTORS®, INC.
Revised April 4, 1997
Revised January 29, 1998
Revised July 31, 2002

Page 2 of 2

Exclusive Right to Represent Buyer Authorization

EXCLUSIVE RIGHT TO REPRESENT BUYER OR TENANT AUTHORIZATION

I.   Exclusive Right Appointment.

You (Buyer(s) or Tenant(s)) _____ appoint us (Firm) _____ (broker/agent) as your exclusive representative to assist you to locate and purchase, exchange or lease real property acceptable to you and generally described as: _____ (the "Property").

II.   Geographical Area.

This Authorization is limited to the following areas of the State of Connecticut: _____ _____

III.   Term of Authorization.

This Authorization is in effect from _____ to _____, inclusive.

IV.   Broker's Duties.

   A.   We will attempt to locate the property.
   B.   We will negotiate on your behalf for terms and conditions agreeable to you.
   C.   We will assist you in the purchase, exchange or lease, as the case may be, of the Property.
   D.   We will act in your interest regarding the location and purchase, exchange or lease of the Property.

V.   Buyer's/Tenant's Duties.

   A.   You will tell us about all past and current contacts with any real property or any other real estate agents and refer all leads or information about property to us.
   B.   You will cooperate with us and be reasonably available to examine real property.
   C.   Upon request, you will give us financial and personal information regarding your purchase abilities and needs.
   D.   You are notified that the Department of Environmental Protection is required pursuant to Section 22a-134f of the Connecticut General Statutes to furnish lists of hazardous waste facilities located within the town to the Town Clerk's office. You should refer to these lists and the Department of Environmental Protection for information on environmental questions concerning any property in which You are interested and the lands surrounding that Property.
   E.   **Questions concerning the legal title to property, the residence of convicted persons, tax considerations, wood destroying pests, environmental conditions, property inspection, engineering, or the uses or planned uses of neighboring properties should be referred to your attorney, tax advisor, building inspector or appropriate governmental agency.**

VI.   Other Terms and Conditions.

   A.   You understand and agree that we may also become a seller's or landlord's agent for the Property. In that event we would become dual agents, representing both you and the seller or landlord. If this situation should arise, we will promptly disclose all relevant information to you and discuss the appropriate course of action to take under the circumstances. We will also discuss a dual agency consent agreement with you and present a statutory form of such an agreement for your review and signature.

   B.   You agree that we may represent other buyers or tenants.

Connecticut Association of REALTORS®, Inc.
111 Founders Plaza, Suite 1101
East Hartford, Connecticut 06108
Copyright© 1996-2002 Connecticut Association of REALTORS®, Inc.
Revised February 27, 1997
Revised July 22, 2002

Page 1 of 3

Exclusive Right to Represent Buyer Authorization (continued)

C. We may share and disclose financial and personal information regarding your purchase abilities and needs with other agents who offer real property to us.

D. This Authorization is binding upon and shall inure to the benefit of you and us, and each of our heirs, administrators, executors, successors and assigns. You may not assign this Authorization.

E. You agree to pay any costs and attorneys' fees which we may incur to collect any monies due us under this Authorization.

F. This Authorization may be modified, waived or discharged only by a written agreement signed by the parties.

G. You will advise us immediately if you execute an exclusive buyer representation agreement or Authorization with any other firm. You represent that you have not signed any exclusive representation Authorizations or agreements with any other broker or brokerage firm covering the same geographical area stated in this Authorization.

H. You acknowledge receipt of a copy of this Authorization.

NOTICE: THE AMOUNT OR RATE OF REAL ESTATE BROKER COMPENSATION IS NOT FIXED BY LAW. IT IS SET BY EACH BROKER INDIVIDUALLY AND MAY BE NEGOTIABLE BETWEEN YOU AND THE BROKER.

VII. Fees.

A. In consideration of the services provided hereunder, you agree to pay us the fee(s) checked below: **(ANY SECTION NOT FILLED IN IS INAPPLICABLE)**

1. **PROFESSIONAL SERVICE FEE.** You are obligated to pay our professional service fee. However, you hereby authorize and instruct us to request payment of all or any part of this fee from ❏ the seller of the Property and/or the seller's listing agent, if any; ❏ the landlord of the Property and/or the landlord's listing agent, if any; or ❏ other. If the seller, landlord or listing broker offers us a professional service fee in excess of the amount stated in this Section VII, you agree that we may accept that amount as our fee.

a. If you are purchasing real estate, you will pay us a professional service fee of $_____ or _____ % of the purchase price of the Property purchased by you, or of the value of Property obtained by you in an exchange.

b. If you are leasing real estate, you will pay us a professional service fee of $_____ or _____ % of the yearly rental of the Property leased by you. You also agree to pay a commission in the amount noted above on any renewals, enlargements, exercise of lease options, or new leases between yourself and the landlord. Such commission shall be due and payable at the commencement of the new lease, enlargement, renewal, or option term.

c. We earn the professional service fee if you (i) enter into a contract for the purchase or exchange of real property during the term of this Authorization and all material conditions have been met or are subsequently met; (ii) enter into a lease, whether oral or written, for the rental of real property during the term of this Authorization and all material conditions have been met or are subsequently met or a lease entered into during the term of this Authorization is renewed or enlarged, you or a landlord exercise a lease

Connecticut Association of REALTORS®, Inc.
111 Founders Plaza, Suite 1101
East Hartford, Connecticut 06108
Copyright© 1996-2002 Connecticut Association of REALTORS®, Inc.
Revised February 27, 1997
Revised July 22, 2002

Page 2 of 3

Exclusive Right to Represent Buyer Authorization (continued)

option or you enter into a new lease with the landlord even if such renewal, enlargement, new lease or exercise of option takes place after the expiration of this Authorization; or (iii) you are introduced or take occupancy to real property during the term of this Authorization and obtain title to such property within _____ (_____) months after the expiration of this Authorization, provided, however, that no fee will be due and payable under this Section VII.A.1.c(iii) if you sign an exclusive agreement or Authorization with another real estate broker after the expiration of this Authorization.

    d. _____ (other)

2. **RETAINER FEE.**

    a. You will pay us a non-refundable retainer fee of $_____, due and payable when you sign this Authorization.

    b. We __ will __ will not apply this retainer fee toward the payment of any professional service fee that we earn under this Authorization.

3. You will pay us our professional service fee no later than the date on which title to the real property transfers to you or the date on which you occupy, renew, enlarge a lease or an option is exercised whichever date is applicable to the type of transaction.

B. The real estate broker may be entitled to certain lien rights pursuant to Subsection (d) of Section 20-325a of the Connecticut General Statutes.

VIII. **Fair Housing**

This Authorization is subject to the Connecticut General Statutes prohibiting discrimination in commercial and residential real estate transactions (C.G.S. Title 46a, Chapter 814c).

IT IS UNLAWFUL UNDER FEDERAL AND/OR STATE LAW TO DISCRIMINATE ON THE BASIS OF RACE, CREED, COLOR, NATIONAL ORIGIN, ANCESTRY, SEX, SEXUAL ORIENTATION, MARITAL STATUS, AGE, LAWFUL SOURCE OF INCOME, LEARNING DISABILITY, MENTAL RETARDATION, FAMILIAL STATUS AND MENTAL OR PHYSICAL DISABILITY.

REALTOR® FIRM NAME: _____

By:_____

_____
Street

_____
City, State, Zip

_____
Telephone number and/or e-mail address

_____
Date

BUYER/TENANT: _____

BUYER/TENANT: _____

_____
Street

_____
City, State, Zip

_____
Telephone number

_____
Date

F I G U R E 2.5

Exclusive Agency Right to Represent Buyer Authorization

EXCLUSIVE AGENCY RIGHT TO REPRESENT BUYER OR TENANT AUTHORIZATION

I.   **Exclusive Right Appointment.**

You (Buyer(s) or Tenant(s)) _____ appoint us (Firm) _____ (broker/agent) as your exclusive real estate brokerage to assist you to locate and purchase, exchange or lease real property acceptable to you and generally described as: _____ (the "Property").

II. **Geographical Area.**

This Authorization is limited to the following areas of the State of Connecticut: _____

III. **Term of Authorization.**

This Authorization is in effect from _____ to _____, inclusive.

IV. **Broker's Duties.**

A.   We will attempt to locate the property.
B.   We will negotiate on your behalf for terms and conditions agreeable to you.
C.   We will assist you in the purchase, exchange or lease, as the case may be, of the Property.
D.   We will act in your interest regarding the location and purchase, exchange or lease of the Property.

V.   **Buyer's/Tenant's Duties.**

A.   You will tell us about all past and current contacts with any real property or any other real estate agents and refer all leads or information from other real estate brokerages about property to us.
B.   You will cooperate with us and be reasonably available to examine real property.
C.   Upon request, you will give us financial and personal information regarding your purchase abilities and needs.
D.   You are notified that the Department of Environmental Protection is required pursuant to Section 22a-134f of the Connecticut General Statutes to furnish lists of hazardous waste facilities located within the town to the Town Clerk's office. You should refer to these lists and the Department of Environmental Protection for information on environmental questions concerning the any property in which You are interested and the lands surrounding that Property.
E.   **Questions concerning the legal title to property, the residence of convicted persons, tax considerations, wood destroying pests, environmental conditions, property inspection, engineering, or the uses or planned uses of neighboring properties should be referred to your attorney, tax advisor, building inspector or appropriate governmental agency.**

VI. **Other Terms and Conditions.**

A.   You understand and agree that we may also become a seller's or landlord's agent for the Property. In that event we would become dual agents, representing both you and the seller or landlord. If this situation should arise, we will promptly disclose all relevant information to you and discuss the appropriate course of action to take under the circumstances. We will also discuss a dual agency consent agreement with you and present a statutory form of such an agreement for your review and signature.

B.   You agree that we may represent other buyers or tenants.

C.   We may share and disclose financial and personal information regarding your purchase abilities and needs with other agents who offer real property to us.

Copyright© 1996-2002 Connecticut Association of REALTORS®, Inc.
Revised February 27, 1997
Revised July 22, 2002

Page 1 of 3

FIGURE 2.5

Exclusive Agency Right to Represent Buyer Authorization (continued)

D. This Authorization is binding upon and shall inure to the benefit of you and us, and each of our heirs, administrators, executors, successors and assigns. You may not assign this Authorization.

E. You agree to pay any costs and attorneys' fees which we may incur to collect any monies due us under this Authorization.

F. This Authorization may be modified, waived or discharged only by a written agreement signed by the parties.

G. You will advise us immediately if you execute an exclusive buyer representation agreement or Authorization with any other firm. You represent that you have not signed any exclusive representation Authorizations or agreements with any other broker or brokerage firm covering the same geographical area stated in this Authorization.

H. You acknowledge receipt of a copy of this Authorization.

NOTICE: THE AMOUNT OR RATE OF REAL ESTATE BROKER COMPENSATION IS NOT FIXED BY LAW. IT IS SET BY EACH BROKER INDIVIDUALLY AND MAY BE NEGOTIABLE BETWEEN YOU AND THE BROKER.

VII. **Fees.**

A. In consideration of the services provided hereunder, you agree to pay us the fee(s) checked below: **(ANY SECTION NOT FILLED IN IS INAPPLICABLE)**

1. **PROFESSIONAL SERVICE FEE.** You are obligated to pay our professional service fee. However, you hereby authorize and instruct us to request payment of all or any part of this fee from ❑ the seller of the Property and/or the seller's listing agent, if any; ❑ the landlord of the Property and/or the landlord's listing agent, if any; or ❑ other. If the seller, landlord or listing broker offers us a professional service fee in excess of the amount stated in this Section VII, you agree that we may accept that amount as our fee.

    a. If you are purchasing real estate, you will pay us a professional service fee of $_____ or _____ % of the purchase price of the Property purchased by you, or of the value of Property obtained by you in an exchange.

    b. If you are leasing real estate, you will pay us a professional service fee of $_____ or _____ % of the yearly rental of the Property leased by you. You also agree to pay a commission in the amount noted above on any renewals, enlargements, exercise of lease options, or new leases between yourself and the landlord. Such commission shall be due and payable at the commencement of the new lease, enlargement, renewal, or option term.

    c. We earn the professional service fee if you (i) enter into a contract for the purchase or exchange of real property during the term of this Authorization and all material conditions have been met or are subsequently met; (ii) enter into a lease, whether oral or written, for the rental of real property during the term of this Authorization and all material conditions have been met or are subsequently met or a lease entered into during the term of this Authorization is renewed or enlarged, you or a landlord exercise a lease option or you enter into a new lease with the landlord even if such renewal, enlargement, new lease or exercise of option takes place after the expiration of this Authorization; or (iii) you are introduced or take occupancy to real property during the term of this

Copyright© 1996-2002 Connecticut Association of REALTORS®, Inc.
Revised February 27, 1997
Revised July 22, 2002

Page 2 of 3

Exclusive Agency Right to Represent Buyer Authorization (continued)

Authorization and obtain title to such property within _____ (____) months after the expiration of this Authorization, provided, however, that no fee will be due and payable under this Section VII.A.1.c(iii) if you sign an exclusive agreement or Authorization with another real estate broker after the expiration of this Authorization.

d. _____ (other)

2. **RETAINER FEE.**

    a. You will pay us a non-refundable retainer fee of $_____, due and payable when you sign this Authorization.

    b. We __ will __ will not apply this retainer fee toward the payment of any professional service fee that we earn under this Authorization.

3. You will pay us our professional service fee no later than the date on which title to the real property transfers to you or the date on which you occupy, renew, enlarge a lease or an option is exercised whichever date is applicable to the type of transaction.

B. The real estate broker may be entitled to certain lien rights pursuant to Subsection (d) of Section 20-325a of the Connecticut General Statutes.

VIII. **Fair Housing**

A. This Authorization is subject to the Connecticut General Statutes prohibiting discrimination in commercial and residential real estate transactions (C.G.S. Title 46a, Chapter 814c).

IT IS UNLAWFUL UNDER FEDERAL AND/OR STATE LAW TO DISCRIMINATE ON THE BASIS OF RACE, CREED, COLOR, NATIONAL ORIGIN, ANCESTRY, SEX, SEXUAL ORIENTATION, MARITAL STATUS, AGE, LAWFUL SOURCE OF INCOME, LEARNING DISABILITY, MENTAL RETARDATION, FAMILIAL STATUS AND MENTAL OR PHYSICAL DISABILITY.

REALTOR® Firm Name

_____

By:_____

_____
Street

_____
City, State, Zip

_____
Telephone number and/or e-mail address

_____
Date

BUYER/TENANT:

_____

BUYER/TENANT:

_____

_____
Street

_____
City, State, Zip

_____
Telephone number

_____
Date

Copyright© 1996-2002 Connecticut Association of REALTORS®, Inc.
Revised February 27, 1997
Revised July 22, 2002

Page 3 of 3

Open Right to Represent Buyer Authorization

OPEN RIGHT TO REPRESENT BUYER OR TENANT AUTHORIZATION

[R] REALTOR®

I.   Appointment.

You (Buyer(s) or Tenant(s))_____ appoint us
(Firm) _____ (broker/agent) as your real
estate agent to assist you in locating, purchasing or exchanging real property acceptable to you and generally
described as:_____
_____(the "Property").

II.   Geographical Area.

This Authorization is limited to the following areas of the State of Connecticut: _____
_____

III.   Term of Authorization.

This Authorization is in effect from _____ to _____, inclusive.

IV.   Broker's Duties.

A.   We will attempt to locate the property.
B.   We will negotiate on your behalf for terms and conditions agreeable to you.
C.   We will assist you in the purchase, exchange or lease, as the case may be, of the Property.
D.   We will act in your interest regarding the location and purchase, exchange or lease of the Property.

V.   Buyer's/ Tenant's Duties.

A.   You will tell us about all past and current contacts with any real property or any other real estate agents.
B.   You will cooperate with us and be reasonably available to examine real property.
C.   Upon request, you will give us financial and personal information regarding your purchase abilities and needs.
D.   **Questions concerning the legal title to property, tax considerations, property inspection, engineering, or the uses or planned uses of neighboring properties should be referred to your attorney, tax advisor, building inspector or appropriate governmental agency.**
E.   You are notified that the Department of Environmental Protection is required pursuant to Section 22a-134f of the Connecticut General Statutes to furnish lists of hazardous waste facilities located within the town to the Town Clerk's office. You should refer to these lists and the Department of Environmental Protection for information on environmental questions concerning the any property in which You are interested and the lands surrounding that Property.

VI.   Other Terms and Conditions.

A.   You understand and agree that we may also become a seller's or landlord's agent for the Property. In that event we would become dual agents, representing both you and the seller or landlord. If this situation should arise, we will promptly disclose all relevant information to you and discuss the appropriate course of action to take under the circumstances. We will also discuss a dual agency consent agreement with you and present a statutory form of such an agreement for your review and signature.
B.   You agree that we may represent other buyers or tenants.
C.   We may share and disclose financial and personal information regarding your purchase abilities and needs with other agents who offer real property to us.
D.   This Authorization is binding upon and shall inure to the benefit of you and us, and each of our heirs, administrators, executors, successors and assigns. You may not assign this Authorization.

Copyright© 1996-2002 Connecticut Association of REALTORS®, Inc.
Revised February 27, 1997
Revised June 5, 1997
Revised July 22, 2002

Page 1 of 3

F I G U R E   2.6

Open Right to Represent Buyer Authorization (continued)

E. You agree to pay any costs and attorneys' fees which we may incur to collect any monies due us under this Authorization.

F. This Authorization may be modified, waived or discharged only by a written agreement signed by the parties. This Authorization will lapse upon notice to us that you have executed an exclusive representation agreement with another broker, provided, however, that execution of an exclusive representation agreement with another broker shall not act to deprive Us of compensation already earned under this Authorization.

G. You will advise us immediately if you execute an exclusive buyer representation agreement or authorization with any other firm. You represent that you have not signed any exclusive representation authorizations or agreements with any other broker or brokerage firm covering the same geographical area stated in this Authorization.

H. You acknowledge receipt of a copy of this Authorization.

NOTICE: **THE AMOUNT OR RATE OF REAL ESTATE BROKER COMPENSATION IS NOT FIXED BY LAW. IT IS SET BY EACH BROKER INDIVIDUALLY AND MAY BE NEGOTIABLE BETWEEN YOU AND THE BROKER.**

VII.   Fees.

A. In consideration of the services provided hereunder, you agree to pay us the fee(s) checked below: **(ANY SECTION NOT FILLED IN DOES NOT APPLY).**

1. ☐ **PROFESSIONAL SERVICE FEE.** You are obligated to pay our professional service fee. However, you hereby authorize and instruct us to request payment of all or any part of this fee from ☐ the seller of the Property and/or the seller's listing agent, if any; ☐ the landlord of the Property and/or the landlord's listing agent, if any; or ☐ other _____. If the seller, landlord or listing broker offers us a professional service fee in excess of the amount stated in this Section VII, you agree that we may accept that amount as our fee.

(a) If you are purchasing real estate, you will pay us a professional service fee of ☐ $ _____ o ☐ _____ % of the purchase price of the Property purchased by you or of the value of Property obtained by you in an exchange.

(b) If you are leasing real estate, you will pay us a professional service fee of ☐ $ _____ or ☐ _____% of the yearly rental of the Property leased by you. You also agree to pay a commission in the amount noted above on any renewals, enlargements, exercise of lease options, or new leases between yourself and the landlord. Such commission shall be due and payable at the commencement of the new lease, enlargement, renewal, or option term.

(c) We earn the professional service fee if (i) during the term of this Authorization you enter into a contract for the purchase or exchange of real property we have introduced to you and all material conditions have been met or are subsequently met; (ii) during the term of this Authorization you enter into a lease, whether oral or written, for the rental of real property we have introduced to you and all material conditions have been met or are subsequently met or a lease entered into during the term of this Authorization is renewed or enlarged, you or a landlord exercise a lease option or you enter into a new lease with the landlord even if such renewal, enlargement, new lease or exercise of option takes place after the expiration of this Authorization; or (iii) you are introduced or take occupancy to real property during the term of this Authorization and obtain title to such property within _____ (_____) months after the expiration of this Authorization, provided however, that no fee will be due and payable under this Section VII.A.1.c.(iii). if you sign an exclusive agreement or authorization with another real estate broker after the expiration of this Authorization.

(d) _____
             (other)

Copyright© 1996-2002 Connecticut Association of REALTORS®, Inc.
Revised February 27, 1997
Revised June 5, 1997
Revised July 22, 2002

Page 2 of 3

FIGURE 2.6

Open Right to Represent Buyer Authorization (continued)

2. ☐ RETAINER FEE.

    (a)   You will pay us a non-refundable retainer fee of $_____ , due and payable when you sign this Authorization.

    (b)   We ☐ will ☐ will not apply this retainer fee toward the payment of any professional service fee that we earn under this Authorization.

3.   You will pay us our professional service fee no later than the date on which title to the real property transfers to you or the date on which you occupy, renew, enlarge a lease or an option is exercised, whichever date is applicable to the type of transaction.

B.   The real estate broker may be entitled to certain lien rights pursuant to Subsection (d) of Section 20-325a of the Connecticut General Statutes.

VIII. Fair Housing

A.   This Authorization is subject to the Connecticut General Statutes prohibiting discrimination in commercial and residential real estate transactions (C.G.S. Title 46a, Chapter 814c).

IT IS UNLAWFUL UNDER FEDERAL AND/OR STATE LAW TO DISCRIMINATE ON THE BASIS OF RACE, CREED, COLOR, NATIONAL ORIGIN, ANCESTRY, SEX, SEXUAL ORIENTATION, MARITAL STATUS, AGE, LAWFUL SOURCE OF INCOME, LEARNING DISABILITY, MENTAL RETARDATION, FAMILIAL STATUS AND MENTAL OR PHYSICAL DISABILITY.

REALTOR® FIRM NAME: BUYER/TENANT:

_____   _____

                                      BUYER/TENANT:

By:_____   _____

_____   _____
Street Address   Street Address

_____   _____
City, State, Zip   City, State, Zip

_____   _____
Telephone   Telephone

_____   _____
Date   Date

■ CONTENT OF LISTING AND BUYER AGENCY CONTRACTS

The license laws require that agency contracts must be *in writing* and contain the following information[2]:

- The name and address of broker performing the services and the name of the person or persons for whom the acts were done or services rendered
- All the terms and conditions to the contract
- An identification of the compensation to be paid and, in boldface type immediately preceding the provision relating to compensation, the following statement:

NOTICE: THE AMOUNT OR RATE OF REAL ESTATE BROKER COMPENSATION IS NOT FIXED BY LAW. IT IS SET BY EACH BROKER INDIVIDUALLY AND MAY BE NEGOTIABLE BETWEEN YOU AND THE BROKER.

- The date on which the agreement is entered into
- The expiration date of the agreement
- The type of listing agreement
- A statement acknowledging adherence to the Connecticut statutes pertaining to fair housing:

THIS AGREEMENT IS SUBJECT TO THE CONNECTICUT GENERAL STATUTES PROHIBITING DISCRIMINATION IN COMMERCIAL AND RESIDENTIAL REAL ESTATE TRANSACTIONS (CGS Title 46A, Chapter 814C).

- The signature of the real estate broker or the broker's authorized agent
- The signature(s) of the person(s) for whom the services will be rendered or an agent authorized to act on behalf of such person(s) (except that listing contracts for one- to four-family residences must be signed by the owner(s) of the property or an agent authorized to act pursuant to a written agreement)
- The following statement regarding broker's lien rights:

THE REAL ESTATE BROKER MAY BE ENTITLED TO CERTAIN LIEN RIGHTS PURSUANT TO SUBSECTION (d) OF SECTION 20-325a OF THE CONNECTICUT GENERAL STATUTES.

- If a brokerage firm represents both buyers and sellers (or landlords and tenants), a statement that the potential exists for a broker to be a dual agent

Additional Requirements for Listing Contracts

The licensing regulations additionally require that listing agreements contain the following[3]:

- A proper identification of the property.
- If the broker or agent has a present or contemplated interest in the property, the listing agreement must contain a disclosure of the interest.
- If the broker is going to allow unaffiliated brokers to advertise the listing, the listing agreement must contain a disclosure as to who will be allowed

to advertise the property, exceptions to the advertising, and an authorization by the seller/landlord for such advertising.

While local practice or individual preference may dictate the additional provisions, the law requires only what is listed above. Licensees are required to immediately deliver a copy of an executed listing or buyer agency agreement to any party or parties who have executed it.

Agreements Other Than Listing Agreements or Buyer Agency Contracts

For all contractual commitments other than listing or buyer agency agreements, licensees are required to use their best efforts to ensure that the agreements are in writing, dated, and express the agreement of the parties involved.[4] The licensee is responsible for immediately delivering a copy of such agreement to the party or parties executing it.

■ NET LISTINGS

Connecticut law imposes relatively few limitations on listing arrangements; the only strict prohibition concerns *net listings*.[5] A net listing is defined as a listing contract in which the broker receives as a commission all excess monies above a minimum sales price agreed on by the broker and seller. Regulations of the Connecticut license law provide that a licensed broker may not accept a listing that is based on a "net" price.

■ OBLIGATIONS ASSOCIATED WITH EXCLUSIVE AGREEMENTS

When an *exclusive-right-to-sell* or *exclusive-agency* agreement is drawn up between an owner and a broker (or brokerage agency), this fact must be *clearly indicated in the wording of the agency contract*. A broker who enters into an exclusive listing with a seller or lessor must make a diligent effort to sell or lease the property involved because an exclusive-agency contract severely limits the number of persons who may market the property.[6]

A broker that enters into an exclusive agency agreement with a prospective buyer or lessee must make a diligent effort to find a property within the prospective buyer's or lessee's specifications.

■ FAIR HOUSING

Connecticut statutes pertaining to Fair Housing have important regulations on the broker's conduct in the marketplace. They prohibit discrimination (on the basis of Connecticut's protected classes) with respect to rental housing, commercial property, the sale of building lots, and other real property interests. All listing agreements and buyer agency agreements *must* clearly state their adherence to the Connecticut Statutes pertaining to fair housing with language to the following effect[7]:

"This agreement is subject to the Connecticut General Statutes prohibiting discrimination in commercial and residential real estate transactions (CGS Title 46a, Chapter 814c)."

Regulations of the license law prohibit licensees from participating in activities that constitute blockbusting or steering. They cannot obtain or seek to obtain listings for the sale or lease of residential property by suggesting or contending that the property may be subject to a loss in value as the result of the entry or prospective entry of any minority group(s) into the neighborhood. This practice, as well as other discrimination practices, is discussed at some length in the principles books (see the conversion table in the Preface of this book for chapter references).

■ DISCLOSURE OF PROPERTY INFORMATION

Real estate brokers and salespersons **cannot misrepresent or conceal any** *material fact* **about a property.**

Connecticut law does not deem certain psychological facts about a property to be material: that a person who was HIV-positive or had AIDS lived at the property or that a suicide, murder, or other felony occurred on the property. Note, however, that information about suicide, murder, or other felony (but not HIV-status) does become material and must be disclosed if a buyer states in writing that such information is important for his or her decision.[8] Information about HIV-status never becomes material, and in fact disclosure of such information by a real estate licensee may be in violation of state and federal fair housing laws.

Effective October 1, 2004, this law changes. Sellers, landlords, and licensees will not be liable for failure to disclose a "nonmaterial fact," which is a fact related to whether a property occupant has or had a disease listed by the Public Health Commissioner, or the fact that there was a death or felony on the property.

Sellers are required to provide prospective purchasers with a *Property Condition Disclosure Report* in all residential real estate transactions (with few exceptions). (See Chapter 7 for further information on this disclosure requirement and form report.)

It is also common practice in Connecticut (although not required by state law) for brokers to prepare a separate information or fact sheet containing data about the physical and economic characteristics of a property. This sheet may include the lot size, age of the residence, type of construction, square footage, tax assessments, special features, and other miscellaneous facts that might be of value or particular interest to a prospective buyer or the agent handling the property.

Brokers, salespersons, and owners *should disclose* to prospective purchasers and tenants information about UFFI (urea-formaldehyde foam insulation) and other hazardous waste including, but not limited to, lead-based paint, radon, and asbestos. This disclosure information should be compiled at the time of taking the listing.

The Hazardous Waste Law (Super Lien) affects certain nonresidential properties in Connecticut that are deemed an "establishment." It is required that such properties be inspected, analyzed, and treated, if necessary, to clean up the land where hazardous waste exists. To avoid liability potential and to protect the public, the real estate agent must disclose this law to the owner and encourage the owner to comply with the law at the time of listing. The Connecticut Department of Environmental Protection administers the Hazardous Waste Law.

Many purchasers are concerned about hazardous waste facilities located near listed properties. A seller and the seller's broker have met their duty to a potential buyer to disclose the presence of off-site hazardous waste facilities if the seller provides the buyer with a written notice of the availability of hazardous waste facility inventory lists.

More detail about the above three environmental disclosures, as well as other environmental concerns, is provided in Chapter 17.

■ ADVERTISING

For purposes of the licensing law, advertising is defined as "all forms of identification, representation, promotion, and solicitation disseminated in any manner and by any means of communication to the public for any purposes related to real estate activity."

The license law and regulations prohibit brokers and salespersons from advertising in a manner that misrepresents material facts or makes false promises. In addition, the following rules apply to ads.

- Salespersons cannot advertise listed property in their own name. All advertisements placed by a salesperson must be made in the name of the broker (or brokerage agency) under whom the salesperson is licensed.
- A broker must identify himself or herself or the brokerage agency in ads. A broker cannot imply in an ad that a non–real estate person is offering property. Ads containing only a post office box number, telephone number, or street address and no other identifying information are known as *blind ads*, and are illegal.
- A broker must get permission to advertise real estate listed with another broker (in turn, that listing broker was required to get seller authorization to allow others to advertise the property) and also permission to modify any of the other broker's listing information. Advertising of real estate listed with another broker must specifically state that the real estate is not listed with the advertising broker and must be updated at least once every 72 hours.

Electronic Advertising

All requirements outlined in the above section apply to advertising on the Internet. In addition, all Internet advertising by a broker or salesperson must include the following **on every page** of the Internet site.

- Licensee's name and office address.
- Name of real estate broker that the licensee is affiliated with.
- All states where the licensee is licensed.
- Last date when the site property information was updated.

Any electronic communication of advertising or marketing material must contain the first three items above on the first or last page of the communication. Electronic communication includes e-mail, e-mail discussion group postings, and bulletin board postings.

Signs

Brokers are not permitted to place "for sale" or "for rent" signs on the property of another without the consent of the owner or without a valid listing contract that authorizes use of the sign.[9]

Although local municipalities in Connecticut have shied away from placing limitations on real estate advertisements, several of the larger cities have taken a strong interest in this area. It is believed that the placement of "for sale" signs on properties located in deteriorating sections of cities has some detrimental effects on neighboring property values and hastens the further decline of these areas. To avoid this negative impact on attempts to rehabilitate and preserve such neighborhoods, a number of local ordinances have been initiated to prohibit the use of signs. A licensee, however, must make a diligent effort to market the property listed until the owner accepts an offer. Historically, under normal circumstances, signs sell more property than any other form of marketing nationwide.

TELEPHONE SOLICITATION

Connecticut law prohibits unsolicited telephone calls between 9:00 P.M. and 9:00 A.M. to any Connecticut resident, and further prohibits all unsolicited phone calls to any Connecticut resident who wishes to be included in a to-be-established "no sales solicitation calls" listing.[10] This law prohibits real estate cold calling.

WWWeb.Link   For information on the Connecticut No-Call list see *http://www.state.ct.us/dcp/nocall.htm.*

ENDNOTES

1. Connecticut Real Estate Commission Policy on Agency, adopted January 6, 2000 (CRECPA).
2. Sections 20-325a (b) and 20-325b of the Connecticut General Statutes; Sections 20-328-4a and 20-328-6a of the Connecticut Regulations Concerning the Conduct of Real Estate Brokers and Salespersons; Number 8 of the CRECPA.
3. Section 20-328-6a (a) of the Connecticut Regulations Concerning the Conduct of Real Estate Brokers and Salespersons.
4. Section 20-328-6a.
5. Section 20-328-6a.
6. Section 20-328-2a (c) of the Connecticut Regulations Concerning the Conduct of Real Estate Brokers and Salespersons.
7. Section 20-328-4a (c) of the Connecticut Regulations Concerning the Conduct of Real Estate Brokers and Salespersons.
8. Sections 20-329cc through 20-329ff of the Connecticut General Statutes.
9. Section 20-328-2a (g) of the Connecticut Regulations Concerning the Conduct of Real Estate Brokers and Salespersons.
10. Section 42-288a of the Connecticut General Statutes.

QUESTIONS

1. Betty Buyer contacts Hartfield Realty and is interested in potentially purchasing a home in the Hartfield area. Without entering into a buyer agency relationship with Betty, a salesperson from Hartfield Realty can do all of the following for her *except*
   a. give Betty information on properties for sale in Hartfield.
   b. give Betty information on mortgage interest rates and terms.
   c. prequalify Betty for a mortgage.
   d. explain to Betty about buyer agency, seller agency, and dual agency.

2. Betty is interested in seeing a house listed with Hartfield Realty but does not wish to enter into a buyer agency agreement with Hartfield Realty. A salesperson from Hartfield Realty can show Betty an in-house listing if
   a. the salesperson obtains the seller's permission.
   b. Betty verbally agrees to buyer agency.
   c. the salesperson provides Betty with an Agency Disclosure Notice, stating that Hartfield Realty represents the seller.
   d. the salesperson provides Betty with a Dual Agency Consent Form.

3. Betty is interested in seeing a house listed with Fairford Realty but does not wish to enter into an agency relationship. A salesperson from Hartfield Realty can show Betty the house if
   a. Hartfield Realty obtains the seller's written consent to subagency, and Betty is given an Agency Disclosure Notice stating that Hartfield Realty represents the seller.
   b. Hartfield Realty obtains Fairford Realty's consent to subagency, and Betty is given an Agency Disclosure Notice stating that Hartfield Realty represents the seller.
   c. Betty verbally agrees to buyer agency.
   d. This cannot occur

4. In Connecticut, an exclusive-right-to-buy contract
   a. is illegal.
   b. is equivalent to a listing agreement.
   c. must be indicated as such in the buyer agency agreement.
   d. requires the signature of the principal only.

5. A broker who enters into an exclusive-agency listing contract
   a. is guaranteed a commission.
   b. must split his/her commission.
   c. must make a diligent attempt to sell or lease the property.
   d. has violated the law.

6. In Connecticut a net listing is
   a. based on a set rate of commission.
   b. similar to an open listing.
   c. illegal.
   d. common.

7. A broker who wishes to place a "for sale" sign on a listed property must first
   a. obtain the consent of the owner of the property.
   b. sell the property.
   c. list the property.
   d. Cannot do so

8. A broker cannot
   a. advertise listed property for sale or lease in a newspaper.
   b. advertise property listed with another broker in the newspaper without the other broker's knowledge.
   c. include the broker's name and telephone number in any advertisement.
   d. advertise property listed for sale without the express written consent of the owner.

9. In Connecticut, real estate commissions are
   a. set by law.
   b. set by the Real Estate Commission.
   c. determined by local groups of brokers.
   d. negotiable between the seller/buyer and broker.

10. Buyer-brokerage contracts in Connecticut
    a. must be in writing to be enforceable.
    b. must be on specific forms.
    c. are not regulated under the license laws.
    d. are illegal.

11. Bob Broker has obtained permission from Sonjay Broker and Ken Broker to advertise Sonjay and Ken's listings on his office Web site. Bob Broker now has an obligation to
    a. obtain the seller's permission for such advertising.
    b. advertise Sonjay and Ken's listings on the first page of the Internet site.
    c. include Sonjay and Ken's names and e-mail addresses under the listing information.
    d. update the listing information at least every 72 hours.

12. Susie Salesperson sends out an e-mail to all the parents in her daughter's first-grade class, informing them that she is a real estate agent and providing them with pictures of houses that she has currently listed. In this e-mail Susie is legally required to also include
    a. the name of the real estate broker she is affiliated with.
    b. the listing prices of the property.
    c. the last date when the property information was updated.
    d. none of the above, as a simple e-mail such as this is not considered advertising.

3

INTERESTS
IN REAL ESTATE

■ OVERVIEW

Although never officially recognized, many of the statutory and common-law concepts relating to real property ownership and land title in Connecticut were developed from English common-law principles. In general, Connecticut laws recognize the various types and categories of estates discussed in the principles books (see the conversion table in the Preface for chapter references); however, there are several exceptions. Connecticut does not recognize curtesy and dower rights or the homestead exemption. Further, easements in Connecticut generally "run with the land."

■ DOWER AND CURTESY

Since 1877 neither dower nor curtesy has been recognized in Connecticut. The interest of a person in the property of his or her spouse is provided for via statutory survivorship rights under laws pertaining to the property rights of husband or wife or to a joint tenancy with survivorship rights (see Chapter 4).

Under the statutes relating to the property rights of a surviving spouse, the husband or wife would be entitled to a life estate equal in value to one-third of the deceased partner's property (real and personal).[1] This interest attaches to the survivor on the death of his or her spouse, so it is not necessary for a nonowning spouse to sign any conveyances of an owning spouse's real estate to release these statutory survivorship rights while the owning spouse is alive. The statutory survivorship interest flows to the surviving spouse regardless of the terms of a will that might dispose of the estate to other parties. Such survivorship interest must be declared in writing, signed by the surviving spouse, and lodged with the court of probate within 150 days of the appointment of the administrator of the estate. An estranged spouse has no right to such a declaration. Should the deceased partner die without a will, or should a portion of the estate remain undisposed of after all dispositions have been made, the surviving spouse would inherit as prescribed by the intestate law of descent (see Chapter 8).

■ HOMESTEAD PROPERTY

Connecticut does not recognize a homestead exemption. It does provide, however, for a temporary application of homestead in its probate court procedures and for a homestead exemption in debt collection procedures.

Probate court procedure has stipulated that the family of a deceased property owner may occupy the property designated as the homestead during the period of estate settlement. Once the estate has been settled, however, the executor or administrator of the estate may require that the property be vacated. For the purposes of this statute, the word *family* refers to the collective group of blood relatives and relatives by marriage. To enforce homestead occupancy, the family members in question must have been members of the household at the time of the decedent's death.[2] The probate judge's decision is final in all cases.

A homeowner subject to a debt collection procedure due to an involuntary lien or money judgment may exempt his or her homestead from the collection up to a value of $75,000 (value is defined as fair market value of the property less any consensual lien, so this value figure is more akin to equity in the home). This exemption is not allowed for collection of debt due to loans secured by a mortgage on the property, mechanics' liens, tax liens, and other liens consented to by the homeowner.[3]

■ DEED RESTRICTIONS

Conservation and preservation restrictions may be acquired by any governmental body, charitable corporation, or trust and are not unenforceable on account of lack of privity of estate or contract.[4] Such restrictions can take the form of a deed restriction, easement, covenant, or condition in any deed. The purpose of a *conservation* restriction is to retain land or water areas in agricultural, farming, forest, or open space use. The purpose of a *preservation* restriction is to preserve historically significant structures or sites.

■ EASEMENTS BY PRESCRIPTION

Easements created in Connecticut generally "run with the land," which means they pass with the property ownership rights on conveyance. The manner in which easements may be created is essentially equivalent to the methods discussed in the principles books. With respect to the acquisition of prescriptive easements, Section 47-37, Chapter 822 of the Connecticut General Statutes states: "No person shall acquire a right-of-way or any other easement from, in, upon, or over the land of another, by adverse use and enjoyment thereof, unless such use has been continued uninterrupted for *fifteen years*."

Extent of right. When an easement in Connecticut is created by prescription,[5] the very use that establishes the right also limits and qualifies the right. In other words, the user who acquires the easement may not expand his or her use to exceed the original use. For example, if a right-of-way is acquired across another's property for the purpose of hauling logs, the easement cannot be enlarged to encompass any other use, such as hauling cut lumber or finished wood products back across the land.

Location of boundaries. The boundaries within which a right-of-way acquired through prescription will be exercised must be defined with reasonable explicitness to be valid.[6] Once these boundaries have been established, the user cannot expand them to enlarge the right-of-way or to extend the uses possible under such right-of-way.

Burden of proof. In nearly all instances, the burden of proof in matters concerning rights-of-way and other easements lies with the defendant (user). The owner of the servient tenement (the land over which the right-of-way passes) does not have to disprove the user's right to an easement; the user must establish his or her rights with adequate proof.[7]

Question of fact. In determining whether an easement has been acquired through prescription, the court must decide whether in fact all the requirements for this have been met.[8] Although the burden of proof still lies on the person claiming the right to the easement, it is trier (the court) who makes the final decision.

Light and air. Easement of light and air cannot be acquired by prescription if the creation of such an easement would make it unlawful for an adjoining landowner to erect a structure, even though all the requirements for the creation of an easement by prescription have been met.[9] A person who has owned a building adjacent to a vacant lot for the prescribed 15 years cannot claim an easement for light and air that would deny the vacant lot owner the right to build a structure—even though that structure would intercept cool breezes and sunlight.

Abandonment. An easement by prescription may be extinguished if the owner of the property on which the easement has been made takes, obtains, or regains open and continuous control and possession of the property for the prescriptive period of 15 years.[10]

Preventing acquisition by prescription. When the owner of a property seeks to prevent another's acquisition of a right-of-way or easement, he or she must abide by the statutory procedures. Mere letters to, or verbal contact with, the persons claiming the right will not qualify as an interruption of use in most cases.

The owner must issue a written notice to the person claiming the right or privilege in the same manner as one would serve an original summons in a civil action (usually by a sheriff or other court-appointed process server). The notice must be signed and returned to the owner and recorded within three months of the date when the notice was served. If the claimant is not available, the notice may be served on his or her agent or guardian. If the claimant resides out of state, it may be served on the occupant of the claimant's estate. When neither the claimant nor an estate occupant can be located, the property owner can prevent the acquisition of an easement by posting a conspicuous notice on the property and serving notice on the person to whom the premises were last assessed for tax purposes and by recording this service within three months. Once notice is served, the owner has effectively disturbed the claimant's right and interrupted the claimant's use.[11]

■ LICENSE

License in Connecticut is defined essentially as it is in the principles books. For a licensor to revoke or cancel a license under Connecticut law, there must be a valid reason—it cannot be merely at the whim of the licensor.

■ WATER RIGHTS

Connecticut laws relating to riparian rights are generally the same as those described in the principles books. Under law, a riparian landowner may use the water while it runs over his or her land but cannot unreasonably contain, divert, or destroy it.[12]

The most critical factor in establishing boundary of an upland owner is the determination of whether the body of water adjoining the owner's property is navigable. If it is navigable, upland owners own to the water's edge; if it is not navigable, they own to the center of the stream or water body. In Connecticut the decision as to navigability is generally accorded to the state, through its court procedures. There is no single state agency charged with the responsibility of defining navigable waters. Such decisions are typically made on the basis of widely accepted court interpretations and the advisement of the U.S. Army Corps of Engineers in cases involving bodies of water located in more than one state.

■ ENDNOTES

1. Section 45 of the Connecticut General Statutes.
2. *Hall v. Meriden Trust and Safe Deposit Co.* (1925) 130 A. 157, 103 Conn. 226.
3. Sections 52-352a and 52-352b of the Connecticut General Statutes.
4. Sections 47-42a, 47-42b and 47-42c of the Connecticut General Statutes.
5. *New Canaan County School v. Rayward* (1957) 136 A. 2d 742, 144 Conn. 637.
6. *City of Derby v. Di Yanno* (1955) 111 A. 2d 23, 19 Conn. Supp. 218, affirmed 118 A. 2d 308, 142 Conn. 708; and *Taylor v. Dennehy* (1950) 71 A. 2d 596, 136 Conn. 398.
7. *Bradley's Fish Co. v. Dudley* (1870) 37 Conn. 136.
8. *Klein v. DeRosa* (1951) 79 A. 2d 773, 137 Conn. 586.
9. *Puroto v. Chieppa* (1905) 62 A. 664, 78 Conn. 401.
10. *Miller v. State* (1936) 183 A. 17, 121 Conn. 43.
11. Sections 47-38 through 47-41 of the Connecticut General Statutes.
12. *Parker v. Griswold*, 17 Conn. 388 (1845).

QUESTIONS

1. In Connecticut dower and curtesy are
   a. currently recognized.
   b. recognized voluntarily.
   c. recognized but not enforced.
   d. not recognized.

2. If a husband dies in Connecticut, his wife is entitled to
   a. a life estate in all property owned by the husband during his life.
   b. a life estate in all property owned by the husband at the time of his death.
   c. an election to take a life estate equal to one-third of the property owned by the husband at the time of his death.
   d. nothing.

3. A homeowner may exempt the following amount from debt owed a foreclosing mortgagee:
   a. $75,000
   b. $150,000
   c. The value of the home
   d. Nothing

4. The burden of proof in acquiring an easement by prescription lies with the
   a. party claiming the easement.
   b. court in equity.
   c. party protesting the claim of right.
   d. owner of the land on which the easement is to be laid.

5. In Connecticut, the prescriptive period to acquire an easement is
   a. 100 months.   c. 15 years.
   b. 12 years.   d. 30 years.

6. To be extinguished by law, a right-of-way must have been abandoned for at least
   a. 100 months.   c. 15 years.
   b. 12 years.   d. 30 years.

7. The decision as to whether a claimant has met all the requirements for acquiring an easement by prescription is made by the
   a. attorney of the person claiming the right.
   b. court.
   c. owner's attorney.
   d. user of the right or privilege.

8. Seth and Beth are neighboring property owners. Beth has been crossing Seth's property to get to a state beach. Seth wishes to prevent Beth from acquiring an easement to cross his land. To do so effectively, he can
   a. follow Connecticut's statutory procedures.
   b. write her a letter granting her permission to cross the property.
   c. write her a letter forbidding her to cross the property.
   d. put up a "no trespassing" sign.

9. A UConn student has been given a ticket (license) to enter Gampel Pavilion to watch the Huskies basketball team. UConn can revoke or cancel this license for all of the following reasons *except*
   a. the student was throwing popcorn.
   b. the student attempted to jump onto the court.
   c. UConn decided to revoke all student tickets.
   d. the Pavilion had a power outage.

10. What is the most critical factor in establishing riparian rights?
    a. Determining whether the body of water adjoining the owner's property is navigable
    b. Determining the size of the body of water adjoining the owner's property
    c. Determining the number of states the body of water passes through
    d. Determining the depth of the waterway adjoining the owner's property

4

FORMS OF REAL ESTATE OWNERSHIP

■ OVERVIEW

In Connecticut, ownership rights or interests in land may be held in severalty, in co-ownership, or in trust. Connecticut recognizes two forms of co-ownership: tenancy in common and joint tenancy. For joint tenancy in Connecticut, property can be held in equal or unequal shares. Real estate may also be owned by trusts and by business entities such as partnerships and corporations. Connecticut allows for condominium and cooperative ownership under the Common Interest Ownership Act.

■ CO-OWNERSHIP

A conveyance by deed to two or more people is presumed to be as tenants in common, unless the conveyance includes specific language creating a right of survivorship. If there is language stating that the grant includes a right of survivorship, then a joint tenancy with right of survivorship is created.[1]

Unlike other states that require that all tenants hold equal shares in a joint tenancy, in Connecticut property can be held in equal or unequal shares in a joint tenancy. That means, for example, that if two people own property together as joint tenants, one can own ⅔ of the property and the other ⅓, and still have rights of survivorship.

Connecticut allows conveyance of a deed directly from a grantor to himself or herself and others as joint tenants without the use of a third party. Joint tenants may convey or encumber their interests, but a conveyance from fewer than all the joint tenants to a person other than another joint tenant would sever the joint tenancy as to that portion conveyed. A lien on a joint tenant's interest is still valid against that interest after death.

Ownership by Married Couples

Connecticut law does not recognize a tenancy by the entirety.[2] Any conveyance to a husband and wife, without specific language indicating otherwise, would be treated in the same manner as a conveyance to two or more unrelated parties—as a tenancy in common.[3] If the deed contains specific language indicating a joint tenancy, the law will recognize it as such. The joint tenancy with the right of survivorship is the most common form of property ownership between a husband and wife in Connecticut.

Under Connecticut statutes, property rights acquired by either husband or wife prior to marriage remain as separate interests.[4] However, either spouse may acquire and hold property acquired after marriage as an individual in severalty or with persons other than his or her spouse. The interests of the surviving spouse in such property are discussed in Chapter 3.

When a husband and wife hold real estate as joint tenants (by themselves or with others) and subsequently file for and obtain a divorce, the divorce decree usually serves to extinguish the joint tenancy and convert it to a tenancy in common.[5] Because property owned jointly by a husband and wife almost always falls under the provisions of a joint tenancy with survivorship rights, the concept of community property (as discussed in the principles texts) is of no particular importance and is not recognized as a form of ownership in Connecticut.

■ PARTITIONS

Partition is the physical division of co-owned property. An estate in land may be partitioned in several different ways under Connecticut law.[6] Sometimes the administrator or executor of an estate left undivided at the time of the owner's death will request that the probate court order an estate to be partitioned. Under all forms of concurrent ownership, the parties may voluntarily partition an estate at any time. When the owners do not all agree to a partition, they must petition the courts for equitable relief. The court appoints a committee to accomplish the partition. This is the most common partition in cases involving the dissolution of joint tenancies or other forms of co-ownership.

Occasionally, it is physically impossible to fairly and equitably partition an estate. In the event of such a situation, the court may order the property sold and the proceeds distributed in proportion to each owner's undivided interest (if interest is not stated in the owner's deed, the property will be divided equally). Alternatively, if one or more of the owners has only a minimal interest, the court may decide to distribute the property to the majority owners and order just compensation to be paid to those owners with a minimal interest. All partitions (whether voluntary or involuntary) must be recorded in the land records.

■ TRUSTS

The types of trusts outlined in the principles books are equivalent to those recognized in Connecticut. The Fiduciary Powers Act specifically outlines a trustee's duties and the relationship between trustee and beneficiaries.[7]

■ OWNERSHIP OF REAL ESTATE BY BUSINESS ORGANIZATIONS

Connecticut law permits business organizations to own real estate. Types of organizations include general partnerships, limited partnerships, corporations, S corporations, and limited liability companies.

Partnerships

General and limited partnerships may own real property. The partners' responsibilities and liabilities are spelled out in both the partnership agreement and the statutes pertaining to partnerships.

In Connecticut the use of limited partnerships as a form of real property ownership is particularly important. Under a limited partnership, a property is divided (monetarily) into units, each of which can be purchased by a limited partner. The financial liability of each limited partner extends no further than his or her initial capital outlay unless the partnership agreement specifically provides for additional contributions of liability. Under a typical arrangement, one or more general partners will be selected to manage the partnership property and are responsible for reporting to the limited partners as required by the agreement. The general partner is empowered to carry out management and financing duties and retains unlimited liabilities unless specified otherwise. The principal attractions of limited partnerships (much like those of real estate investment trusts or syndicates) lie with their financial accessibility to the smaller investor and their freedom from management burdens.

The specific statutory provisions covering the setup and operation of both general and limited partnerships can be found under Title 34 of the Connecticut General Statutes: Chapter 611—Uniform Partnership Act and Chapter 610—Uniform Limited Partnership Act.

Corporations

Corporations and S corporations in Connecticut are equivalent to the descriptions discussed in the principles books. They are formed by making appropriate filings with the secretary of state.

Connecticut allows a relatively new form of corporation, known as a *limited liability company*.[8] The LLC, which is neither a corporation nor partnership, combines the tax status of partnerships with the limited liability of corporations. Unlike a limited partnership, there is no requirement that a general partner be generally liable. An LLC is less restrictive than an S corporation because it does not limit the number of owners to 35 or restrict business entities or foreign investors from becoming partners. This form of entity has become popular for ownership of investment real estate.

■ COMMON INTEREST OWNERSHIP ACT

The Connecticut Common Interest Ownership Act regulates the development of common interest ownership properties.[9] This law covers condominiums, cooperatives, and all other forms of real property unit ownership including planned unit developments (PUDs). The Common Interest Ownership Act identifies these types of ownership as "common interest communities," where ownership of a unit requires financial contribution for the maintenance of common areas.

Since 1976, Connecticut has had a law that regulates the development of condominiums and protects the rights of condominium buyers. However, there was no law to control the development of cooperatives and planned communities and to protect the rights of these ownership buyers. The old law (Unit Ownership—Condominium Acts of 1976) is still in effect for condominiums developed before January 1, 1984.

Types of Communities

Common interest communities are one of three types: a condominium, cooperative, or planned community. A *condominium* is a community where the units are owned separately and the common areas are owned by all of the unit owners together as tenants in common. In a *cooperative*, all the real property is owned by an association (even the units). The unit owners are members of the association and have the right to exclusive possession of a particular unit. A *planned community* is a catchall category, including any type of common interest community that is not a condominium or cooperative. Typically, planned unit developments, or PUDs, where the unit owners own their lots and an association owns the common areas, would be a planned community. (Note that if the common areas were owned by the unit owners as tenants in common, this PUD would be a condominium, not a planned community.)

Leasing

Common interest units may be leased under certain conditions specified in the bylaws. When a unit is leased, written notice must be given to a tenant informing him or her that the unit is in a common interest community. An explanation of the rights, privileges, and obligations of the tenant is most important.

Management Services

Those who offer or provide association management services to condominium or other common interest communities are required to obtain a certificate of registration ($60 first year, $100 annually thereafter) from the Department of Consumer Protection.[10] Certificates of registration expire on January 31. Anyone who manages and handles or has access to association funds is to furnish a fidelity bond sufficient to cover the maximum association funds in the manager's custody; in no case may the bond be for less than three months' assessments plus reserve funds. A separate bond is required for each association. All contracts to provide association management services must meet certain minimum standards, and specific practices are prohibited.

Condominium developers are required to register as community association managers if they receive compensation for any management function performed in developing communities. The law applies to developers of developments greater than four units, and where the developer controls more than two-thirds, but fewer than all, the votes within an association. If the law applies, in addition to registering, a developer also has to be bonded for the maximum amount of funds under the association's control.

Lien for Assessments

The association has a statutory lien on a unit for any unpaid common charges, assessments, and fines. This lien is known as a *"super" lien* because it takes priority over many other liens or encumbrances that may attach to the real estate, including mortgages recorded after the date of delinquency of the unpaid charges. The association is not required to record a separate notice of lien because recording of the declaration constitutes record notice and perfection of the lien. The lien may be foreclosed on in the same manner as a mortgage foreclosure.

Creation-Declaration

The Common Interest Ownership Act requires that a *declaration be filed and recorded in the land records of the town(s)* where the common interest ownership property is located; this declaration is for all aspects of common interest ownership, including condominiums, cooperatives, and planned communities. In general, the declaration must contain the following information:

- The name of the common interest community and the community association; a statement that the common interest community is a condominium, cooperative, or planned community
- The name of every town in which any part of the common interest community is located
- A legally sufficient description of the real property included in the community
- A statement of the maximum number of units that the owner/developer reserves the right to create
- For a condominium or planned community, a description of the boundaries of each unit, including an identifying number
- A description of any limited common element
- A description of any development rights
- Any restrictions on use, occupancy, and alienation of the units
- The recording date for any easements and/or appurtenances

In addition to these general requirements, the declaration has particular requirements for development rights and for cooperatives. At the time the declaration is recorded, the owner/developer must also record a set of floor plans, a land survey, and a copy of the association's bylaws.

Initial Sale—Public Offering Statement

Before an owner/developer of a common interest ownership property can offer units for sale, she or he must prepare a public offering statement. The public offering statement provides purchasers with full disclosures regarding the common interest community. This statement must be provided to all prospective purchasers not later than the date of the contract of sale. A *purchaser, before conveyance, may cancel a contract of sale within 15 days after executing it and receiving the public offering statement.* The requirements for the public offering statement are very detailed and designed to protect the purchasing public. Brokers who are involved in developing common interest ownership units should be well versed in the requirements of the public offering statement.

Exception: Common interest communities that contain no more than 12 units (and that may not be further developed) do not need to provide a public offering statement or resale documents as discussed below.

The Common Interest Ownership Act has great impact on anyone who deals with common interest ownership, including developers, bankers, real estate agents, and homeowners' associations, because more and more people are choosing common interest ownership as a mode of housing. More information about the very complicated procedures and regulations governing common interest ownership may be obtained from the Connecticut Department of Housing and/or an attorney.

Resale of Units

After the initial sale by the developer and prior to subsequent conveyances, common interest ownership unit sellers are required to give buyers a copy of the declaration, bylaws, rules, and regulations, and a resale certificate is prepared by the association. There is an exception for communities that contain no more than 12 units (and that may not be further developed). The resale certificate provides information on the following:

- The effect of the sale on any right of first refusal
- The amount of the monthly common expense assessment and any unpaid common expense or special assessment currently due from the owner
- Any other fees payable by the owner
- Any capital expenditures in excess of $1,000 approved by the executive board for the current and next succeeding fiscal year
- The amount of any reserves for capital expenditures
- The current operating budget of the association
- Any unsatisfied judgments against the association and any pending suits in which the association is a defendant
- The insurance coverage provided for the benefit of unit owners
- Any restrictions in the declaration affecting the amount that may be received by a unit owner on the sale, condemnation, casualty loss to the unit or the common interest community, or termination of the common interest community
- In a cooperative, an accountant's statement, if any was prepared, as to the deductibility for federal income tax purposes by the unit owner of real property taxes and interest paid by the association
- If the association is unincorporated, the name of the statutory agent for service of process filed with the Connecticut secretary of state
- A statement of any pending sale or encumbrances of common elements
- A statement disclosing the effect on the unit to be conveyed of any restrictions on the owner's right to use or occupy the unit or to lease the unit to another person

These resale documents must be furnished to the purchaser or his or her attorney before the closing or transfer of possession. Before conveyance, *purchasers have a right to cancel the contract until five business days after the certificate and documents have been delivered* to the purchaser or purchaser's attorney (or seven days after they are sent by registered or certified mail). When a unit owner (seller) requests a resale certificate from the association in writing, the association must provide it within ten business days of the request. The maximum fee the association can charge for preparation of the resale certificate is $125. The fee charged must reflect actual cost to prepare; an additional $10 is allowed if documents are delivered in three days.

Recording Updates

In January of each year, a condominium association must file with the town clerk a certificate with the name and address of the officer of the association or managing agent from whom the resale documents may be requested. Any change in this data must be filed within 30 days.

Condominium Conversion

The Common Interest Ownership Act prohibits municipalities from banning the conversion of buildings to condominiums and other types of common interest housing.

The Common Interest Ownership Act also protects the tenants living in units undergoing conversion and requires that owners and/or developers give tenants at least 180 days' notice of the conversion, a public offering statement, and a conversion notice. The conversion notice must include information on the rights of tenants during this transition period. Certain tenants may qualify for relocation assistance, based on their age and gross adjusted income of the tenants. During the transition period of the conversion, tenants' rents may not be increased for any reason.

■ ENDNOTES

1. Section 47-14a through 47-14k of the Connecticut General Statutes.
2. *Whittlesy v. Fuller* (1836) 11 Conn. 337.
3. *New Haven Trolley and Bus. Emp. Credit Union v. Hill* 142 A. 2d 730, 145 Conn. 332.
4. Section 46b-3b of the Connecticut General Statutes.
5. Section 47-14g of the Connecticut General Statutes.
6. Chapter 919 of the Connecticut General Statutes.
7. Chapter 708b, Connecticut General Statutes, Title 45, Sections 100d-g.
8. Public Act 93-267.
9. Title 47, Chapter 828 of the Connecticut General Statutes.
10. Sections 20-450 through 20-462 of the Connecticut General Statutes.

QUESTIONS

1. Which of the following forms of ownership is
   not recognized under Connecticut law?
   a. Tenancy in common
   b. Joint tenancy with survivorship rights
   c. Condominium
   d. Tenancy by the entireties

2. The maximum fee that can be charged for the
   condominium resale documents is
   a. $75. c. $180.
   b. $100. d. $225.

3. Annually, a condominium association must file
   the name and address of the officer or managing
   agent of the association from whom a resale
   certificate can be requested with the
   a. secretary of state.
   b. town clerk's office.
   c. Real Estate Commission.
   d. Department of Housing.

4. Connecticut law will allow the partition of
   concurrent ownership in real estate
   a. when it is voluntary.
   b. when it is involuntary.
   c. voluntarily and involuntarily.
   d. only on the death of a tenant in common.

5. Alex and Adam own property as tenants in
   common. Alex requests a court to partition the
   property, but the court finds that it is physically
   impossible to do so. Therefore, the court may
   a. refuse the request to partition.
   b. require the sale of the property and a distribution of the proceeds of sale.
   c. instruct Alex to purchase Adam's interest at
   market value.
   d. escheat the property to the state until a satisfactory settlement can be made between
   Adam and Alex.

6. Husband and Wife, who own their home as joint
   tenants, obtain a divorce. At that time, the joint
   tenancy
   a. extinguishes and becomes a tenancy in
   common.
   b. continues until one of them dies.
   c. extinguishes and becomes a tenancy at
   sufferance.
   d. reverts to common interest ownership.

7. What types of properties are governed by the
   Common Interest Ownership Act?
   a. Condominiums
   b. Condominiums and cooperatives
   c. PUDs
   d. Condominiums, cooperatives, and planned
   communities

8. A condominium is created by filing a _____
   in the land records.
   a. public offering statement
   b. unit deed
   c. declaration
   d. resale certificate

9. On the initial sale of a cooperative unit, the
   developer must give the purchaser a
   a. resale certificate.
   b. proprietary lease.
   c. public offering statement.
   d. conversion notice.

10. Bob has just entered into a contract to buy a
    condominium unit from Cal (who originally
    bought the unit from the developer and has
    lived there for the past ten years). Cal has
    delivered the resale documents to Bob. Bob has
    a right to cancel the contract within
    a. 5 days of receipt of resale documents.
    b. 15 days of receipt of resale documents.
    c. 5 days from the date Bob executed the
    contract.
    d. Bob does not have the right to cancel a
    signed contract in this situation.

CHAPTER FIVE

LEGAL DESCRIPTIONS

■ OVERVIEW

For legal descriptions of property, Connecticut predominantly follows the metes-and-bounds method. The government survey system is not used in Connecticut. When a parcel of land is a lot within an approved subdivision or has been subdivided out of a larger tract, the legal description will often identify and refer to the original subdivision map.

Although a metes-and-bounds description is legally preferred in Connecticut, other less exact descriptions are generally considered valid to make the contracts or documents on which they appear enforceable. Thus, not all documents or instruments pertaining to a particular parcel of real property will contain a full legal description. A sale contract may contain as simple a description as the street address and still be a binding contract. A property description in a mortgage deed may indicate the boundaries as public roads and thoroughfares or even lands "now or formerly of" rather than using precise distances and courses.

■ METES AND BOUNDS

A typical full legal description is given below. Monuments are used to establish boundaries. Commonly, these monuments are iron pins. (It is unlawful to disturb boundary markers set by a surveyor.[1])

■ **EXAMPLE** A certain piece or parcel of land with the buildings and improvements thereon situated on the southerly side of Woodmont Drive in the Town of East Hartford, County of Hartford and State of Connecticut, known and designated as Lot No. 57 on a map entitled "Section A Subdivision Plan 'Eastonbury Estates' Town of East Hartford, Conn. Owner—Arbeiter Liedertafel, Inc., Subdivider—Harry James and Edwin Hoberman, 303 Burnside Ave., E. Hartford, Conn. Everett O. Gardner and Assoc., 576 Old Post Road, Tolland, Connecticut, Professional Engineers Land Surveyors. Scale 1" = 40". Date 1/20/76" which map is on file in the Town Clerk's Office in said Town of East Hartford.

Said premises are more particularly bounded and described as follows:

Northerly: by Woodmont Drive a distance of One Hundred Seventy-Eight and Thirty-Nine One-Hundredths (178.39) feet;

Easterly: by land now or formerly of Hand J. Builders and Developers, Inc., being Lot No. 56 on a map for "Section B Subdivision Plan Eastonbury Estates" a distance of Two Hundred Twenty-Seven and Fifty-Eight One-Hundredths (227.58) feet;

Southerly: by land now or formerly of Anna S. Holm and Ellis O. Sahlberg situated in the Town of Glastonbury as shown on said map One Hundred Eighty-Five (185) feet; and

Westerly: by Lot No. 58 as shown on said map a distance of Two Hundred Fifty-One and Sixty One-Hundredths (251.60) feet.

Said premises are also known as 61 Woodmont Drive in said Town of East Hartford.

In some instances, the distances between monuments or benchmarks may not be mentioned in the description unless it becomes absolutely necessary to establish the boundaries. Thus, a description as follows would be acceptable in most instances even though it makes no specific reference to every linear dimension of the parcel.

■ **EXAMPLE**   All that certain piece or parcel of land with the buildings and all other improvements thereon and the appurtenances thereto, located and situated in the Town of South Windsor, County of Hartford and State of Connecticut, containing approximately One Hundred (100) acres, and being more particularly bounded and described as follows, to wit:

Easterly: by Sullivan Avenue and Pierce Road, so-called;

Southerly: by land now or formerly of Harold J. A. Collins, Stanley H. Lorenson, Asher A. Collins, and Strong Road, in part by each;

Westerly: by West Road, so-called; and

Northerly: by land now or formerly of Herbert Tomlinson, et ux., and land now or formerly of Annette Frink partly by each.

Said premises are the same as were conveyed by Ella A. West, to the grantor herein by Warranty Deed dated August 8, 1958, and recorded in Volume 66 at Page 330 of the South Windsor Land Records.

■ GOVERNMENT SURVEY SYSTEM

While the government survey system is not used in Connecticut, the legislature has created a coordinated system for the purpose of defining geographic locations of points.[2] Referring to the system of plane coordinates established pursuant to the system is considered a sufficient legal description describing a land boundary corner.

■ LOST BOUNDARY

In the event of a lost or uncertain boundary, Connecticut law provides for the establishment or reestablishment of the boundary on the complaint of one of the adjoining landowners.[3] The superior court will appoint a committee of not more than three persons to investigate the situation and erect and establish the lost or uncertain boundary. The committee may engage a surveyor to assist and will record a certified copy of the findings to establish the boundary between the adjoining landowners. Unless it can be proven that the committee made an error of law in reaching its conclusion, the findings of the committee are held to be conclusive.

■ COMMON INTEREST OWNERSHIP

The conveyance of any legal interest in a condominium unit is treated in a manner similar to any other real property conveyance. The essential difference lies in the description of the unit's undivided interest in the common areas and facilities.[4] A legally sufficient description of a common interest ownership unit must contain: (1) the name of the common interest community, (2) the recording data for the original declaration, (3) the town in which the common interest community is located, and (4) the identifying number of the unit. A typical condominium unit is described below.

■ **EXAMPLE**   Unit No. 62 of South Mountain Townhouses, Bristol, Connecticut, together with an interest in the common areas and facilities, appurtenant said unit and common areas and facilities being more specifically designated and described in the Declaration of Condominium establishing the plan for Unit Ownership under the "Unit Ownership Act" of the State of Connecticut made by the Grantors entitled "South Mountain Townhouses Declaration of Condominium" dated May 31, 1973, and recorded in Volume 614 at Pages 310 through 340 inclusive of the Land Records of said City of Bristol, the floor plans of which are set forth on drawings entitled "South Mountain Townhouses, Bristol, Connecticut, David Butts Associates, architect, 1019 Farmington Avenue, Bristol, Conn."[5]

Said premises are conveyed together with and subject to all of the covenants, restrictions, reservations, limitations, conditions, uses, agreements, easements, appurtenances, and other provisions set forth in the aforesaid Declaration of Condominium.

Said premises are further subject to any and all provisions of any ordinance, municipal regulation, or public or private laws; and to easements as of record appears.

■ ENDNOTES

1. Section 47-34a of the Connecticut General Statutes.
2. Section 13a-255 of the Connecticut General Statutes.
3. Section 47-34 of the Connecticut General Statutes.
4. Section 47-223 of the Connecticut General Statutes.
5. *Post v. Perkins* (1913) 86 A. 762, 87 Conn. 70.

QUESTIONS

1. The principal method of delineating property boundaries or legal descriptions in Connecticut is known as the
   a. colonial block grant system.
   b. system of principal meridians and baselines.
   c. system of metes and bounds.
   d. rectangular survey system.

2. An iron pin, used as a point on a property boundary, would be the same thing as a
   a. monument.   c. base point.
   b. meridian.   d. plat.

3. When an adjoining property owner files suit to establish or reestablish a lost boundary, a committee to carry out the task is usually appointed by the
   a. real estate commission.
   b. superior court.
   c. court of appeals.
   d. town clerk.

4. The findings of a committee appointed to establish a lost boundary are considered conclusive unless it can be proven that the
   a. adjoining landowners are related.
   b. committee made an error of law.
   c. committee did not employ a surveyor.
   d. boundary was between three or more properties.

5. A legally sufficient description of a condominium unit must contain the
   a. name of the condominium unit.
   b. dimensions of the unit.
   c. boundaries of the common interest community property.
   d. recording data for the original declaration.

6. Ken has agreed to buy Mary's house, and they draw up their own purchase contract. The contract describes the property as "90 Fairweather Lawn, Bridgeport." Based on the property description, is this contract binding?
   a. No, Connecticut requires a metes-and-bounds description.
   b. No, at the minimum, a reference to a subdivision map must be made.
   c. Yes, such a simple description may be used for purposes of a purchase and sale contract.
   d. Yes, Ken was fully aware of the boundaries of the property.

6

REAL ESTATE TAXES AND OTHER LIENS

■ OVERVIEW

Real estate is taxed at the municipal level in Connecticut. The amount of tax is based on the value of the property. Unpaid municipal property taxes become a lien on the property and take precedence over all other liens. In addition to tax liens, Connecticut recognizes the other types of liens that are described in the principles texts.

■ PROPERTY TAXES—THE LOCAL DOMAIN

Title 12 of the Connecticut General Statutes provides local municipalities with broad powers to assess and evaluate real property and to levy local property taxes. The real property tax in Connecticut is the exclusive domain of the local municipality and is considered to be an *ad valorem* tax (based on value). The local tax rate is set by each individual town according to its estimated expenses for the forthcoming year and the property list provided by the local assessor's office. The state itself does not levy a real property tax.

Assessment

Local tax assessors are required to maintain a list of taxable properties in their municipalities, including real estate and such tangible personal property as automobiles. This list, often called the *Grand List*, also contains an estimate of the value of these properties. Properties owned by nonresidents are assessed and taxed in the same manner as those owned by residents.

The state requires that the values placed on all properties reflect their market value. However, there are three important considerations that must be addressed in light of this statutory requirement.

Periodic reassessment. Few towns have either the manpower or financial resources to annually reassess each parcel of real property in the town to establish current market values (although municipal assessors may hire a revaluation company to assess property within a town). Connecticut law requires that towns revalue properties every five years, by either physical observation or statistical analysis. Reassessment based on a physical inspection is required every ten years.

Farm, forest, and open-space lands.   Specific categories of land have been established by the state of Connecticut. For tax purposes, farm, forest, and open-space land are not assessed at market value. If the owners of such land follow the proper registration procedures, their assessments are lowered to provide considerable tax relief.[1]

Assessment appeals.   A property owner who feels that his or her property has been assessed incorrectly may appeal to the local *board of tax review* for a revaluation of the property. Such appeals must be made during the appropriate month (usually February or March) for the upcoming tax year unless, by a special act, the town provides additional time periods. Assessment appeals can be made during the intervening years between revaluations.[2] Appeals from the municipal board of tax review are made to the Connecticut Appeals Board for Property Valuation.

Exempted Properties

The law provides for the exemption of certain kinds of property from local property taxes. Most of these exempted properties correspond to those mentioned in the principles texts. In addition, there are statutory provisions that allow for possible reduction or elimination of taxes for certain kinds of property or properties owned by certain classes of owners. The following is a representative (though not a complete) list of these "special" properties and owners:

Tax Abatement

- Structures of architectural or historical merit
- Environmentally impacted or contaminated sites—if remediated and redeveloped
- Various types of low-income and moderate-income housing
- Corporations (under specified circumstances)
- Others (by authority of the taxing body)

Tax Relief

- Persons over 65 years old
- Disabled or handicapped persons
- Veterans (usually limited to a $1,000 exemption)
- Farm, forest, and open-space land (as discussed earlier)
- Others (by authority of the taxing body)

The Calculation of Taxes

While the exact procedure used to calculate an individual property owner's tax bill might vary somewhat from town to town, there are some generally accepted principles.

In most Connecticut towns each parcel of real property is assessed for tax purposes at a certain percentage of its market value. This percentage is called an *assessment ratio*. Connecticut law requires an assessment ratio of 70 percent. The property is first appraised to obtain an estimate of market value. The market value is then trended (adjusted) back to the market value that would have been in effect at the date of the last town assessment. Then the assessment ratio is applied to the trended market value to obtain the assessed value. The tax rate (expressed in *mills* and equivalent to dollars of tax per thousand dollars of assessed value) is then calculated on the basis of the revenues required by the municipality and the total list of taxable property. Each town sets its own mill rate. Some municipalities also have different mill rates for different districts within that town. Last, the assessed value of the property is divided by 1,000, and this figure is multiplied by the tax rate to obtain the tax bill. To illustrate:

■ **EXAMPLE**
- Property: single-family home and lot
- Appraised market value: $100,000
- Trended market value: $80,000
- Assessment ratio: 70 percent
- Assessed value: $80,000 × .70 = $56,000
- Tax rate: 42 mills (or $42.00 per $1,000 of assessed value)
- Indicated property tax: $\frac{\$56,000}{\$1,000} = \$56 \times \$42 = \$2,352$

Special Taxes or Assessments

Every parcel of real property in a Connecticut town does not necessarily carry an equal tax burden. Frequently, a special service—a fire district or a sewer facility—that benefits only properties within a given area will require that a special tax or assessment be levied on the properties in that area. Special taxes or assessments are levied on these benefiting properties as described in the principles texts. Owners of properties within these special service areas, then, must pay not only the standard property tax rate but also an additional rate for the special facility.

Timing of Property Tax Payments

The tax year in Connecticut is generally the same as the state's fiscal year and runs from July 1 to June 30. In the majority of Connecticut towns, real property taxes are payable for the current tax year on July 1 and January 1 (six-month taxes on each date). Typically, there is a 30-day grace period after these dates before any penalties (interest) begin to accrue. In several towns, however, payments are made quarterly. In any real estate sales transaction, one should be particularly careful to determine the timing and manner of local tax payments well ahead of any closing to avoid unanticipated problems with pro rata adjustments. (Calculations of prorations are discussed in Chapter 16 of the text.)

Assessment dates.   Property on the Grand List for the next tax year must be assessed by October 1 of the preceding year. Thus, taxes payable on July 1, 2004, and January 1, 2005, are determined from assessments computed by the town assessor prior to October 1, 2003.

Tax bills issued.   Although the exact timing may vary somewhat from town to town, tax bills are issued at least 30 days prior to the date on which the first installment is due and payable (and often earlier).

Property Tax Liens

In the event that real property taxes or assessments are not paid in accordance with the legally prescribed schedule, such taxes become a lien on the property until they are paid or the property is sold at public auction to satisfy the delinquent sums owed. From a strictly legal standpoint, *the taxes are actually a lien on the property from the date of assessment* (generally October 1), but this lien is never enforced by law unless the taxpayer violates the prescribed payment schedule. As stated previously, municipal tax liens take precedence over all other liens. The possible exception would be a federal tax lien recorded against the property that became attached to the property and was completed prior to the municipal lien.[3]

The statutes generally hold tax liens to a 15-year maximum, although this period may be extended by court order. To be valid, tax liens must be recorded by the agency levying the tax within two years from the due date of the taxes in question.

A municipality may, through superior court action, foreclose a tax lien, take possession of the delinquent taxpayer's property, and order it sold at a tax or sheriff's sale. However, the taxpayer has a period of six months from the date of the sale to exercise his or her *right of redemption* as described in the principles texts. (The redemption period may be as short as 60 days if the property was abandoned or meets other conditions established by local ordinance.) If the sale produces a sum in excess of that needed to satisfy the lien and any other costs of the sale, the excess will be turned over to the taxpayer.

■ CAPITAL GAINS TAX

The full amount of capital gains is taxed as income by the state of Connecticut. The tax is calculated in the same manner as that of the federal government. Hence a separate state tax is imposed. The law also requires that a husband and wife who file a single return jointly for IRS tax purposes file a single return jointly for the tax imposed under Connecticut General State Statutes.

The state capital gains tax applies to nonresidents on gain realized from the sale or exchange of real property located in Connecticut. If a nonresident is a party in a partnership that sells or exchanges realty in Connecticut and realizes a gain, that individual shall be taxed for each gain in the same manner as occurs with the federal tax. Similar taxes are also levied for individuals as shareholders in S corporations or beneficiaries of trusts or estates that sell or exchange real estate located in Connecticut.

WWWeb.Link   Specific details about income taxes in Connecticut are available through the Department of Revenue Services Web site at *www.drs.state.ct.us.*

■ CONVEYANCE TAX

Connecticut levies two types of taxes on the seller at the time of transfer of title: a state conveyance tax and a municipal conveyance, both based on a percentage of the selling price. These are paid at the time of closing (transfer of title). A more detailed explanation of these taxes is presented in Chapter 8.

■ OTHER LIENS AND TRANSFER TAXES

Mechanics', judgment, and other liens generally operate as described in the text. Additionally, in Connecticut, a broker who has performed services relating to real estate has the right to place a lien on the real estate to secure payment of compensation. (See Chapter 1 for a complete discussion of Broker's Lien.)

The usual test applied to establish the priority of liens other than tax or municipal liens is the date of *recording*. However, with respect to mechanics' liens, the primary test for priority lies with the establishment of the date on which the mechanic in question delivered materials or commenced work.[4] To be valid, a mechanic's lien must be recorded within 90 days from the time the mechanic's work ceases and will extinguish in one year from that date unless action to foreclose is begun.

In Connecticut, mechanic's liens can attach to leasehold interests as well as the underlying interest of leased property, if certain conditions are met. Additionally, a property owner who has a lien placed on his property can seek a court order substituting a bond for the lien.

Connecticut also allows for a purchaser's lien to secure a purchaser's deposit paid in connection with a purchase and sale contract. The actual contract can be recorded as evidence of the lien, or a notice of contract can be recorded. In order to be valid, the recorded document must be signed by the owner of the property. This lien takes priority over any liens or encumbrances placed on the property after its recording. It can be foreclosed in the same way a mortgage lien is foreclosed.

■ ENDNOTES

1. Section 12-107a, Chapter 203—Assessment of Property Taxes, Connecticut General Statutes. *Jupiter Realty Company v. Board of Tax Review of the Town of Vernon*, 242 Conn. 363, 698 A.2d 312 (1997).
2. *Pitt v. City of Stamford* (1933) 167 A. 919, 117 Conn. 388.
3. *U.S. v. City of New Britain, Conn.* (1954) 74 S. Conn. 367, 347 U.S. 81, 98 L. Ed. 520.
4. *Waterbury Lumber and Coal Company v. Asterchinsky* (1913) 87 A. 739, 87 Conn. 316, Ann. Cas. 1916 B, 613.

QUESTIONS

1. In Connecticut the real property tax is essentially a(n)
   a. ad hoc tax.
   b. ad valorem tax.
   c. state tax.
   d. title lien.

2. With respect to real property taxation, Connecticut statutes require that assessments reflect
   a. reproduction value.
   b. insurable value.
   c. intrinsic value.
   d. market value.

3. The Connecticut statutes require a complete physical revaluation of real properties in any given town once every
   a. ten years.
   b. year.
   c. four years.
   d. time the Grand List increases by 10 percent.

4. Certain types of land are eligible for tax relief through special assessment allowances under the general statutes. Which of the following does not fall into this category?
   a. Farm land
   b. Open-space land
   c. Forest land
   d. Wetlands

5. The basic unit of real property tax rate in Connecticut is called
   a. a quota.
   b. a mill.
   c. a percentum.
   d. the assessment ratio.

6. Bill has just bought a home in Glastonbury for $150,000. The town has calculated its market value at $100,000. Glastonbury's mill rate this year is 20 mills. Bill has asked you to compute his yearly property taxes. You tell him
   a. you need to know the assessment ratio in Glastonbury before you can do so.
   b. $1,400.
   c. $2,000.
   d. $2,100.

7. From a strictly legal standpoint, real property taxes become a lien on the property as of the
   a. due date.
   b. 30th day from the due date.
   c. date of assessment.
   d. date a foreclosure suit is filed *and* recorded.

8. Jen contracted with ABC Construction Company to put a new deck on her house. They began work on May 1 and finished on June 1, but Jen never paid them. On July 1, Jen sold her house to Tom, who received a mortgage loan from Country Bank and a mortgage loan from City Bank. City Bank recorded its mortgage on July 1. Country Bank recorded its mortgage on July 2. ABC Construction Company records a mechanic's lien on July 3. What is the priority of the liens?
   a. ABC Construction, City Bank, Country Bank
   b. City Bank, Country Bank, ABC Construction
   c. ABC Construction, then City Bank and Country Bank equal
   d. City Bank and Country Bank equal, then ABC Construction

9. The conveyance tax levied by the state on the seller of the property is based on
   a. the selling price.
   b. earnest money.
   c. the amount of the mortgage.
   d. the time of the purchase.

10. The town of Goshen has recently revalued a piece of property at a market value of $200,000. Goshen's mill rate is 25 mills. How much property tax will be owed on the property this year?
    a. $5,000
    b. $500
    c. $3,500
    d. $350

CHAPTER SEVEN

REAL ESTATE CONTRACTS

■ OVERVIEW

Connecticut requires that all contracts affecting title to real estate must be in writing to be enforceable (Statute of Frauds).

Connecticut also requires that sellers provide prospective purchasers with a property condition report in all residential real estate transactions (with few exceptions).

Electronic contracts (including e-mails and faxes) must meet federal and state guidelines for electronic documents and signatures. See Appendix E for a discussion of the requirements.

■ BROKER'S AUTHORITY TO PREPARE DOCUMENTS

Connecticut laws are somewhat vague regarding the extent to which a broker is authorized to prepare documents and contracts associated with the sale of real property. *The law,* however, *clearly prohibits brokers from engaging in activities that require a license to practice law.* This would seem to deny the broker's authority to prepare all but the most elementary of contracts, such as sales or listing contracts. The use of standardized contract forms drawn up and approved by attorneys and Boards of REALTORS® is so widespread among real estate brokers that there are few instances that would require a broker to prepare his or her own documents. The law would not, however, keep a broker from preparing sales or listing contracts, subject to approval of legal counsel, if desired.

It is customary practice, then, for brokers to use preapproved forms for almost all their day-to-day operations. Frequently, local real estate boards retain attorneys to draw up an appropriate array of standard contracts and encourage their membership to use them. In the event that a broker is faced with an unusual situation for which no standard form is appropriate, it would be wisest to consult legal counsel rather than struggle with the preparation of an appropriate and acceptable contract document.

■ STANDARD CONTRACTUAL REQUIREMENTS

Written contracts.   Like other contracts, real estate contracts must contain the basic legal elements to be valid and enforceable. These include legally competent parties, offer and acceptance, valid consideration, and legality of object. The necessity that they be *in writing,* describe the property, and be signed by all the parties to the contract are elements particular to real estate contracts. But in Connecticut the statute of frauds requires that all contracts involving consideration in excess of $500 be in writing. It is presumed, however, that the mutual agreement of the parties to a contract is not marred by mistakes, misrepresentation, fraud, duress, or undue influence. In any of these situations, the statute of frauds will void the contract regardless of whether all other elements are present.

Regulations of the Connecticut Real Estate Commission require that all listing and buyer brokerage agreements also be in writing. Because these contracts do represent the broker's contract of employment, it would be important to a broker to have the contract in writing. Oral (parol) contracts are not enforceable by law, and the broker is urged to avoid them.

Capacity of parties.   In Connecticut the attainment of the age of majority (currently 18) gives a person the capacity to enter into legally enforceable contracts. While minors may enter into contracts prior to attaining majority (the law sets no absolute minimum), other parties to the contract should understand that minors generally are permitted to void their contracts at their own discretion.[1] Because of this, it is important to ascertain the capacity of an individual to sign a legally enforceable contract, particularly with reference to his or her age. Also, any person signing a contract on behalf of a corporation must have authority to act.

Offer and acceptance.   The Connecticut laws requiring written contracts for realty transactions make it easier to determine whether an offer and acceptance have occurred. When the seller signs the buyer's offer, that constitutes the seller's acceptance, and the offer to purchase *ripens* into a sales contract. The same would apply to a *bond for deed,* although a simpler format of sales contract might be drawn. The bond for deed is discussed later in this chapter. It is customary practice for the selling broker to sign the sales contract, even though his or her signature is not required to create an enforceable contract.

■ REAL ESTATE CONTRACTS

Listing and Buyer Brokerage Contracts

Because it forms the foundation of the real estate broker's legal relationship with his or her principal, listing contracts and buyer brokerage contracts are of utmost importance. As discussed in Chapter 2, these contracts must contain a number of elements besides those found in an ordinary contract. The additional items are principally the terms and conditions essential to the purchase or sale, the compensation to be paid, the expiration date of the contract, and a statement of the broker's adherence to the General Statutes pertaining to

Fair Housing (see Chapter 2 for a complete inventory of listing requirements). While other items might be added to the contract at the specific request of either party, as long as the minimal elements are present, the contract will be enforceable. See the sample listing and buyer brokerage forms provided in Chapter 2 for a representative sample of these contracts used in Connecticut.

Listing contracts are bilateral contracts in which the principal promises to pay a commission to the broker and the broker promises to attempt to procure a ready, willing, and able buyer (with the exception of an open listing contract, which is a unilateral contract). Similarly, buyer agency agreements are bilateral contracts. Because agency contracts are primarily contracts of employment and do not have direct application to the actual conveyance of title to real property, they are not usually considered to fall within the jurisdiction of the statute of frauds.[2] The regulations of the Connecticut Real Estate Commission do require, however, that to be enforceable, agency agreements must be in writing and contain a minimum of information. Listings are discussed in Chapters 1 and 2.

Sales Agreements

One of the broker's primary responsibilities is to negotiate a valid sales contract between the buyer and the seller. In performing this task, it is often the broker who will draw up the actual contract. It is, therefore, quite important that brokers be fully aware of the implications of such agreements. The sales contract is the instrument that establishes the rights and obligations of both buyer and seller and thus should be prepared with great care.

It is common practice in Connecticut for agents to use forms that have been prepared by an attorney and have been endorsed by their local real estate boards. As an alternative, the buyer or seller may use the services of a broker and have a *bond for deed* (see discussion below) drawn up by an attorney to act as substitute for the sale agreement. It is generally advisable to use this format when there are many specific provisions included in the contract that deviate from standard agreements. If a buyer seeks advice on whether a bond for deed or a standard sales contract should be used, refer the buyer to a legal adviser. *An agent must not give legal advice on whether the buyer should use a binder, sales contract, or bond for deed as the document for purchase.*

The sales agreement is considered to be a bilateral contract in Connecticut because it involves a promise for a promise. The buyer promises to pay an amount of money for the seller's property as of a certain date, and the seller promises to convey his or her property to the buyer in exchange for the stipulated amount.

The sales contract frequently contains much the same information as a listing or buyer brokerage contract. However, those contracts contain additional elements, such as the expiration date of the listing, computation of the broker's compensation, and other data of no particular significance in the sales contract. The sales contract, on the other hand, usually stipulates the terms and conditions on which the buyer is making his or her offer to purchase contingent. These might include the buyer's successful procurement of a mortgage loan in a specific amount; the loan's terms and interest rate; a satisfactory report on any inspections made for such things as termites, structural soundness, and so on; a stipulation that the conveyance should take place no later than some specific date; or any other items the buyer may deem important to the contract. In the event of any inspections, it is typical practice for the buyer to bear any costs associated with them. Although results may be communicated either orally or in writing, it is generally best to insist on a written statement to avoid subsequent problems regarding the outcome of any inspection. A standard Sales Contract form currently in use in Connecticut (Figure 7.1), Contingency Addendum to Purchase and Sale contract (Figure 7.2), contract contingency waiver (Figure 7.3), Hubbard Clause contract addendum (Figure 7.4), and a Binder of Sale (contract) (Figure 7.5) appear in this chapter, along with a Residential Property Condition Disclosure Report (Figure 7.6).

Bonds for deed.   A bond for deed is essentially the same thing as a sales contract with several subtle but important differences. Bonds for deed are witnessed, acknowledged, and drawn up in proper form for recording. Recording legally establishes the date of the contract and prevents any earlier contracts from resurfacing to the disadvantage of the buyer. Even if the date on a newly discovered contract predates the bond for deed, the date of recording would establish priority. A bond for deed also provides the maximum *flexibility* in the content of the sales agreement. It is typical practice to use a bond for deed in lieu of a standard form sales contract if there are a large number of terms or very specific and detailed terms and conditions. In such cases, a simpler form of sales contract is used first that includes a provision for the subsequent preparation of a bond for deed on the seller's acceptance. The standard sales contract is designed to accommodate only relatively uncomplicated sales. A bond for deed provides the *maximum degree of safety* to the buyer and seller. Because it is recorded, it typically provides a full legal description of the property, recites the terms and conditions of the sale in detail, and leaves the least room for error, fraud, collusion, or conspiracy to defraud. Bonds for deed are always drawn up by an attorney (typically the buyer's but sometimes the seller's). The bond for deed and the sales contract are equally enforceable.

Personal property and items of real estate.   In general, the law presumes that if the sales contract is silent on the point, any items of real estate attached to the property being sold will be conveyed with the property, and any items of personal property will be removed before the buyers take possession. If the sale is to include any items of personal property (such as drapes, lawn furnishings or equipment, aboveground pools, movable appliances, and so on), these items must be specifically identified in the sales contract. No separate bill of sale is drawn up for these items, and the sales agreement for the real property doubles as a bill of sale for the personal property. The opposite is true for items of real property, such as television antennas, sconces, or chandeliers. Any such items that will *not* be conveyed must be so specified in the sales contract.

F I G U R E   7.1

Purchase and Sale Agreement

This is a legally binding contract. If either party has any questions about any aspect of this transaction, he/she should either consult with an attorney before signing this Agreement or request an attorney-approval contingency. Not intended for use with commercial property or new construction.

PURCHASE AND SALE AGREEMENT

1.   **Parties.**
     Buyer(s):_____
            Name(s)

            _____
            Address   Phone

     Seller(s):_____
            Name(s)

            _____
            Address   Phone

2.   **Property.** Buyer agrees to purchase from Seller and Seller agrees to sell to Buyer certain real property known as:_____, Connecticut ("Property") along with the following personal property_____
_____

3.   **Purchase Price.** The Purchase Price for the Property is $_____.

     $_____   Initial Deposit receipt of which is hereby acknowledged.
     $_____   Additional Deposit to be paid on or before _____.
     $_____   Balance of Purchase Price to be paid at closing.

4.   **Mortgage Contingency.** Buyer will make diligent, good faith efforts to obtain a written commitment for a mortgage loan ("Mortgage") from a bank or other institutional lender on or before _____ ("Mortgage Contingency Date"). Buyer will provide Seller and Broker, no later than the Mortgage Contingency Date, with a copy of any written commitment for a Mortgage obtained by Buyer. Buyer will pay all application fees, points (not to exceed ___), and other charges in accordance with the policies established by the applicable lender.

The Mortgage must be on the following terms:

     (a) Loan Amount $_____   (b) Maximum initial interest rate _____ % per annum
     (c) Minimum term _____ years.

Types of mortgage: (CHECK THE FOLLOWING AS APPLICABLE)

☐ Conventional Fixed Rate   ☐ CHFA   ☐ FHA   ☐ Other (Describe)

☐ Conventional Variable Rate   ☐ VA   ☐ Seller (Attach Seller Financing Addendum)

     If Buyer cannot obtain a written commitment for the Mortgage (free of any conditions that are unacceptable to Buyer), Buyer may terminate this Agreement by providing Seller and Broker, not later than the Mortgage Contingency Date, with written notice of Buyer's inability to obtain such commitment. If Buyer does not elect to so terminate, then this Agreement will remain in full force and effect, unless Seller, within seven (7) days from the Mortgage Contingency Date, gives written notice to Buyer and Broker that Seller has elected to terminate this Agreement as a result of Buyer's inability to obtain such commitment. If either party so terminates this Agreement, then all deposits will be returned to Buyer, and the obligations of the parties under this Agreement shall end. If Buyer applies for a different type of mortgage than that checked above, Buyer shall provide Seller with prompt, written notice of such application. Seller shall have three (3) business days after receiving such written notice within which to elect to terminate this Agreement as a result of Buyer's application for a different type of mortgage than that checked above.

5.   **Combined Contingency Addendum.** ☐ If checked, the Combined Contingency Addendum attached is made a part of this Agreement.

6.   **Deposits.** The deposits specified in Paragraph 3 shall be made at the stated times. All deposits shall be made by

©1997-2002 Connecticut Association of REALTORS®, Inc.
Revised September 20, 2000
Revised July 25, 2002; March 24. 2003

_____   _____
Buyer Initials   Seller's Initials
                            Page 1 of 5

EQUAL HOUSING OPPORTUNITY   REALTOR®

check payable to the Listing Broker as escrow agent. Prior to the Closing of Title, the Listing Broker may pay the deposit funds to the Seller's attorney who shall hold them as escrow agent pending the Closing of Title. In the event any deposit funds payable pursuant to this Agreement are not so paid by Buyer, Seller may give written notice of such failure to Buyer(s) at the address specified in Paragraph 1 by certified mail, and if such notice is given and a period of five (5) days thereafter elapses without Buyer having corrected such failure, Seller may (1) declare Buyer to be in default, and (2) terminate this Agreement and the Seller shall be relieved of all obligations hereunder. In the event that this Agreement is terminated, Seller and Purchaser agree to provide such permissions for release of escrow monies as escrow agent may reasonably require. In the event of a dispute concerning the return of deposits held in escrow which results in court action, both the prevailing party and the escrow agent shall be entitled to reasonable attorney's fees from the losing party. In the event that the escrow agent commences a court action to determine the rights of the parties to deposits held in escrow, the escrow agent shall be entitled to attorney's fees, marshal's fees and docket fees to be paid out of the escrowed deposits. The parties agree that escrow agent will not be liable for the release of escrow monies in accordance with this Agreement or for errors of judgment in the release of escrowed deposits unless such errors are the result of gross or intentional misconduct.

7. **Property to be Maintained; Property Condition Disclosure.** Except as may be set forth elsewhere in this Agreement, Property is being sold "as is". Seller agrees to maintain Property with all buildings, landscaping and other improvements thereon, all appurtenances thereto, and any personal property included in the sale in the same condition, reasonable wear and tear excepted, as they were on the date of this Agreement. Buyer shall have the right to make a final inspection of the real property during a 48-hour period prior to closing. In the event Seller has failed to provide Buyer with a copy of the Uniform Property Condition Disclosure Report required by Public Act 95-311 and is not exempt from the Act, Seller shall credit Buyer with the sum of $300.00 at closing as required by law.

Buyer is notified that the Department of Environmental Protection is required pursuant to Section 22a-134f of the Connecticut General Statutes to furnish lists of hazardous waste facilities located within the town to the Town Clerk office. Buyer should refer to these lists and the Department of Environmental Protection for information on environmental questions concerning the Property and the lands surrounding the Property.

8. **Insurance/Risk of Loss.** The risk of loss or damage to Property by fire or other casualty until the delivery of the deed is assumed by the Seller. Seller shall keep the Property insured, at Seller's expense, against loss by fire and other casualties, with Extended Coverage provisions, in an amount equal to at least 80% of the Purchase Price, until the delivery of the deed. In case of any loss, the Seller shall pay over or assign to the Buyer upon payment of the balance of the Purchase Price all sums recovered on account of said insurance, or the Buyer may, at Buyer's option, terminate this Agreement and the Deposits shall be refunded to the Buyer, unless the Seller shall have restored the Property substantially to its former condition. This paragraph shall also apply to the items listed as fixtures in Paragraph 9 and the personal property set forth in Paragraph 2.

9. **Fixtures.** Included in this sale as part of the Property are the buildings, structures and improvements now thereon, and the fixtures belonging to the Seller and used in connection therewith, including, if any, all blinds, window shades, screens, doors, door and window hardware, storm windows, landscaping, awnings, shutters, electrical and lighting fixtures, door mirrors, pumps, mail boxes, sheds, plumbing fixtures, cabinetry, pool houses and outbuildings, mantles, flagpoles, alarm system and codes, swimming pool (if any) and swimming pool pumps and equipment, garbage disposal, automatic garage openers, central air conditioning equipment, and built-in dishwashers. (Any item crossed out and initialed from this paragraph is not included in the sale.)

10. **Title, Affidavits and Releases.** (A) Seller covenants and warrants that Seller is the fee title owner of the Property and has the authority and capacity to enter into this Agreement and consummate the transaction contemplated herein. The Property is to be conveyed by a good and sufficient Warranty Deed of the Seller (unless Seller is an executor, conservator, or administrator, in which case Buyer will receive a Fiduciary's Deed), conveying a good, insurable, and marketable title to the Property, free from all encumbrances, except as may be acceptable to Buyer and Buyer's Lender, if any, and except zoning and other municipal regulations, the Inland-Wetlands law and any state of facts that an accurate survey of the Property may reveal. Buyer shall at Buyer's own expense conduct a title examination of the Property within thirty (30) days of the date of acceptance of this Agreement. Buyer shall notify Seller of any defects in title that render title to the Property unmarketable, as defined by the Standards of Title of the Connecticut Bar Association, disclosed by such examination. If Seller is unable to remove such title defects within thirty (30) days of notification or the Closing of Title, whichever date is later, Buyer shall have the option to: (a) accept such title as Seller

Buyer Initials   Seller's Initials

EQUAL HOUSING
OPPORTUNITY

REALTOR®

FIGURE 7.1

Purchase and Sale Agreement (continued)

is able to convey without abatement or reduction of the Purchase Price, provided however, Seller shall pay any additional premium or post whatever bond and execute such affidavits and indemnity agreements as may be required by Buyer's title insurer to write title insurance over the defect or (b) cancel this Agreement and receive a return of all Deposits, and, in addition, Seller shall pay to Buyer any expenses actually incurred by Buyer for attorney fees, nonrefundable fees of lending institutions, survey costs and inspection fees. Seller shall pay any nonrefundable fee actually incurred by Buyer to extend, refresh or renew any mortgage commitment granted Buyer by Buyer's lender pursuant to the provisions of Paragraph 4 that expires while the Seller is attempting to remove such title defect.

(B) Seller agrees to furnish such affidavits concerning title, encroachments, mechanic's liens and other items and in such form as Buyer's title insurance company may require in order to obtain title insurance coverage on the Property or to waive exceptions to the title policy that are objectionable to Buyer's lender.

11.   Closing and Delivery of Possession. The closing will take place on _____ or at such other date as mutually agreed by the parties. The closing will be held at the offices of Seller's attorney unless Buyer has obtained a mortgage loan, in which event the closing will be held at the office of Buyer's lender's attorney. Upon the Closing of Title, Seller shall deliver occupancy, along with the keys, alarm codes and garage door transmitters, to the Property to the Buyer in a "broom clean" condition. "Broom clean" shall mean that the Property shall be empty of all personal property, except as may be included in the sale, free of all trash, garbage, junk, litter, broken or discarded items, and vacuumed or swept.

12.   Adjustments. The following are to be apportioned as of 11:59 pm of the day before closing:

(a) Taxes, special tax districts, municipal water taxes and sewer taxes using the uniform fiscal year method;
(b) Fuel oil (using the stated capacity of the storage tank);
(c) Rents as and when collected;
(d) Rental securities plus interest due thereon as provided by law; and
(e) Utilities (for those utilities for which a separate meter reading and final billing cannot be obtained at closing)   based on the usage for the previous billing period.

If the closing shall occur before a new tax rate is fixed, the apportionment of taxes shall be upon the basis of the old tax rate for the preceding period applied to the latest assessed valuation.

Special assessment liens shall be   paid by the Seller   assumed by the Buyer. Pending special assessment liens or special assessments that are pending but have not yet been fixed as to an amount shall be assumed by the Buyer, provided however, that if the improvement has been substantially completed as of the date of this Agreement, the Seller shall credit the Buyer at closing with an amount equal to the latest estimate by the public body charged with levying the special assessment for the improvement.

Any errors or omissions in computing apportionments at closing shall be corrected. This provision shall survive the closing.

13.   Seller's Representations. The Seller represents, to the best of the Seller's knowledge, information and belief that, at the time of Closing of Title: (1) Seller has good, marketable title to all personal property and fixtures included in the sale and there is no leased or rented personal property or fixtures located on the Property, except as may be noted below; (2) Seller is in material compliance with all State and municipal, zoning, environmental and health regulations affecting the Property and has no notice of any investigations, deficiencies, cease and desist orders, inspections or violations, actual or threatened, involving the Property, except as may be noted below; (3) Any buildings located on the Property are entirely within the boundary lines of the Property; (4) The subsurface sewage disposal and/or private water supply system, if any, and all utilities servicing the Property are located entirely within the boundary lines of the Property; (5) There is no violation of any restriction, covenant, agreement or condition affecting the Property; and (6) During the period of Seller's ownership, the Property has not been used for any commercial, industrial or other non-residential purpose and there has been no discharge, spillage, uncontrolled loss, seepage or filtration of oil, petroleum, or chemical liquids or other hazardous waste onto or emanating from the Property.

14.   Lead-Based Paint. If the Property is "target housing" under federal law (meaning, with some exceptions, housing built before 1978), Seller must permit Buyer a 10-day period (unless the parties mutually agree in writing to a different time period) to conduct a risk assessment or inspection of the Property for the presence of lead-based paint and

©1997-2002 Connecticut Association of REALTORS®, Inc.
Revised September 20, 2000
Revised July 25, 2002; March 24. 2003

_____   _____
Buyer Initials   Seller's Initials

EQUAL HOUSING
OPPORTUNITY   Page 3 of 5   REALTOR®

Purchase and Sale Agreement (continued)

lead-based paint hazards before Buyer is obligated under this Agreement. Buyer may waive this right of inspection in writing.

This Agreement is made subject to an inspection or risk assessment of the Property for the presence of lead-based paint or lead-based paint hazards at the Buyer's expense. This contingency shall be deemed waived unless Buyer provides the Seller or the Seller's attorney with written notice of the presence of defective lead-based paint or lead-based paint hazards along with a copy of the inspection and/or risk assessment within _____ days (insert "ten" or the number of days mutually agreed upon) of the date of acceptance of this Agreement. If such notice is given and Seller and Buyer cannot reach a mutually satisfactory agreement within fourteen (14) days of said notice regarding the defective lead-based paint or lead-based paint hazards, either party shall have the option of terminating this Agreement, and this Agreement shall be null and void. The Buyer may waive this contingency at any time without cause.

15.   **Default, Liquidated Damages.** If Buyer defaults under this Agreement and Seller is not in default, all initial and additional deposit funds provided in Paragraph 3 shall be paid over to and retained by Seller, less commissions due, if any, as liquidated damages, and both parties shall be relieved of further liability under this Agreement. If Seller defaults under this Agreement and Buyer is not in default, Buyer shall be entitled to any and all remedies provided by law including, without limitation, specific performance and recovery of amounts spent for mortgage application, appraisal, title search, and tests or inspections.

16.   **Assignment and Survivorship.** This Agreement may be assigned by either party without written consent of the other, and shall be binding upon the heirs, executors, administrators, successors and assigns of the parties hereto. However, if this Agreement contains a provision for Seller financing, it may not be assigned without the express written consent of the Seller.

17.   **Use of Electronic Record.** The parties agree that they may use an electronic record, including fax or e-mail, to make and keep this Agreement. Either party has the right to withdraw consent to have a record of this Agreement provided or made available to them in electronic form, but that does not permit that party to withdraw consent to the Agreement itself once it has been signed. A party's agreement to use an electronic record applies only to this particular real estate transaction and not to all real estate transactions.

For access to and retention of faxed records, there are no special hardware or software requirements beyond access to a fax machine or fax modem and accompanying software connected to a personal or laptop computer. For access to and retention of e-mail records, you will need a personal or laptop computer, Internet account and e-mail software.

Seller wishes to use (check one)   Fax machine. fax number is: _____
                                     E-mail. E-mail address is: _____
Buyer wishes to use (check one)   Fax machine. fax number is: _____
                                     E-mail. E-mail address is: _____

Each party will promptly inform the other of any change in E-mail address or fax number in writing.

18.   **Brokers Recognized.** The parties recognize _____ as   the Listing Broker and _____ as the Selling Broker in this transaction.

19.   **Additional Provisions.** _____
_____
_____
_____
_____

20.   **Acceptance. Date of Acceptance.** We, the parties hereto, each declare that this instrument contains the entire agreement between us, subject to no understandings, conditions, or representations other than those expressly stated herein. This Agreement may not be changed, modified or amended in whole or in part except in writing, signed by all parties. The "date of acceptance of this Agreement" shall be the latest date noted below on which a party accepts the Agreement.

_____   _____
Buyer Initials   Seller's Initials

EQUAL HOUSING OPPORTUNITY   REALTOR®

F I G U R E 7.1

Purchase and Sale Agreement (continued)

20.   Acceptance. Date of Acceptance. We, the parties hereto, each declare that this instrument contains the entire agreement between us, subject to no understandings, conditions, or representations other than those expressly stated herein. This Agreement may not be changed, modified or amended in whole or in part except in writing, signed by all parties.   The "date of acceptance of this Agreement" shall be the latest date noted below on which a party accepts the Agreement.

WITNESS the signatures of the parties below on the date(s) set forth beside their respective names.

Acceptance by Seller: **Acceptance by Buyer:**

Seller	Date	Buyer	Date

Seller	Date	Buyer	Date

Buyer Initials   Seller's Initials

Page 5 of 5

EQUAL HOUSING OPPORTUNITY

REALTOR®

Combined Contract Contingency Addendum to Purchase and Sale Agreement

---

COMBINED CONTINGENCY ADDENDUM TO PURCHASE AND SALE AGREEMENT

The following provisions and contingencies where so designated by Purchaser's initials are hereby made a part of the Purchase and Sale Agreement referred to hereunder (Purchaser and Seller are construed to be singular or plural as appropriate):

Purchaser: _____

Seller: _____

Property Address: _____

Purchaser has read the entire contents below and has indicated with initials whether each section is to be included or not included in the referenced Purchase and Sale Agreement. This Agreement is made subject to:

(1)   <u>Attorney Approval</u>
      Approval by Purchaser's and Seller's attorney within_____ days of the date of acceptance of the Agreement. The parties agree that such approval shall be deemed to have been given and this contingency is satisfied or waived unless a statement withholding approval is made in writing within the period set forth above.

      Included _____   Not included _____

(2)   <u>Home Inspection</u>
      A building inspection (by a licensed home inspector if the Department of Consumer Protection has issued such licenses) reporting the dwelling to be structurally sound and its mechanical systems (including but not limited to, plumbing, heating, central air conditioning, built-in swimming pools, and electrical) to be functioning properly. Individual repairs or replacements that cost less than $100.00 shall not be considered structural or mechanical defects unless the aggregate of such individual repairs or replacements exceeds $500.00. Failure of any component to comply with the building code in effect on the date of this Purchase and Sale Agreement shall not be considered a structural or mechanical defect if the component complied with the building code at the time of its installation and is grandfathered under the building code in effect on the date of this Purchase and Sale Agreement. This contingency shall be deemed satisfied unless Purchaser gives written notice of any structural and/or mechanical defects and a copy of the inspector's report to the Seller on or before_____ days from the Date of Acceptance of the Agreement. If such notice is given and Seller and Purchaser cannot reach a mutually satisfactory agreement within fourteen (14) days of said notice regarding said defects, either party shall have the option of terminating this Agreement, upon written notice of termination and this Agreement shall become null and void. Any redecorating is considered to be normal maintenance, and therefore, the responsibility of Purchaser and exempt from this contingency.

      Included _____   Not included _____   Inspection paid by: Seller ☐ Buyer ☐

(3)   <u>Pest Inspection</u>
      A report by a licensed pest control operator that all buildings on the property are free from infestation or damage by termites or any other wood-boring or wood-destroying insects. This contingency shall be deemed satisfied unless Purchaser gives written notice of infestation or damage and a copy of the pest control operator's report to Seller within___ days from the Date of Acceptance of the Agreement. If Seller and Purchaser cannot reach a mutually satisfactory agreement for the necessary extermination and/or repairs, either party has the option to terminate this Agreement upon written notice of termination and this Agreement shall become null and void.

      Included _____   Not included _____   Inspection paid by: Seller ☐ Buyer ☐

(4)   <u>Radon Concentration Test</u>
      A radon concentration test of the air and well water (if the source of domestic water for the property is by a private water well) indicating that, in the case of the air, the screening measurement is equal to or less than 4.0 pCi/l, and in the case of the well water, the average of at least two measurements is equal or less than 5,000 pCi/l. Seller shall grant Purchaser's testing company reasonable access to the property to perform the tests and agree to comply with all conditions necessary to obtain an accurate

©1997-2003 Connecticut Association of REALTORS®, Inc.
Revised: June 1, 1998
Revised May 22, 2000
Revised July 16, 2002
Revised March 11, 2003
Revised June 20, 2003; August 20, 2003

Page 1 of 4

REALTOR®

F I G U R E 7.2

Combined Contract Contingency Addendum to Purchase and Sale Agreement (continued)

reading. This contingency shall be deemed satisfied unless Purchaser gives written notice of a measurement in excess of 4.0 pci/l for the air or that the average of at least two measurements of radon in the well water exceeds 5,000 pCi/l and a copy of the test report to Seller within _____ from the Date of Acceptance of the Agreement. If Seller and Purchaser cannot reach a mutually satisfactory agreement for the measures necessary to reduce the concentration of radon gas to 4.0 pci/l or below in the case of the air and 5,000 pCi/l in the case of well water, either party has the option to terminate this Agreement upon written notice of termination and this Agreement shall become null and void. If measures are undertaken to reduce the concentration of radon gas in either the air or the well water, the reduction in concentration level shall be confirmed prior to closing by a radon measurements conducted in the same manner as the Buyer's measurements but to be paid for by Seller.

Included _____   Not included _____   Initial Inspection paid by: Seller ☐ Buyer ☐

(5)   Water Potability/Mineral and Chemical Analysis
A report of testing performed by a laboratory authorized to perform such test in the State of Connecticut demonstrating that the water supplied by the private water supply system meets Connecticut Department of Health Services guidelines, if any, for each of the following items: coliform bacteria, nitrate, nitrite, sodium, chloride, iron, manganese, sulfate, pH, hardness, turbidity and apparent color. In addition, if testing for herbicide or pesticide residues or volatile organic chemicals is required by the health district or municipal health department having jurisdiction over the private water supply system, the water supplied by the private water supply system shall also meet Connecticut Department of Health guidelines for those herbicide or pesticide residues or volatile organic chemicals for which testing is performed. Where no guideline or standard exists for private water supply systems for the item tested, the action level required by the Connecticut Health Department for public water supply systems shall be used as the guideline or standard. This contingency shall be deemed satisfied unless Purchaser gives written notice of test results not in conformance with the standards set forth in this paragraph and a copy of the test report to Seller within ____days from the Date of Acceptance of the Agreement. If Seller and Purchaser cannot reach a mutually satisfactory agreement for the measures necessary to treat the water so the water meets the Connecticut Health Department guidelines, either party has the option of terminating this Agreement upon written notice of termination and this Agreement shall become null and void. If measures are undertaken to treat the water, the effectiveness of treatment shall be confirmed prior to closing by a water test to be paid for by Seller.

Included _____   Not included _____   Analysis paid by: Seller ☐ Buyer ☐

(6)   Well Inspection
An inspection of the well system, including all components and/or a yield test, to be performed by a competent well inspector showing that the well system serving the property is satisfactory (based on recommendations published by the State of Connecticut or municipality in which the property is located). This contingency shall be deemed satisfied unless Purchaser gives written notice that the private well water system is unsatisfactory and a copy of the inspector's report to Seller on or before_____ days from the Date of Acceptance of this Agreement. If such notice is given and Seller and Purchaser cannot reach a mutually satisfactory agreement concerning any repairs of and/or defects of such well system, within fourteen (14) days of said notice, either party shall have the option of terminating this Agreement and this Agreement shall become null and void.

Included _____   Not included _____   Inspection paid by: Seller ☐ Buyer ☐

(7)   Septic Inspection
A report by a licensed septic installer, professional sanitary or civil engineer, registered sanitarian or a sanitarian certified by the Connecticut Department of Public Health to perform inspections, or an inspector accredited by the National Association of Waste Transporters (NAWT), National Small Flows Clearinghouse, National Sanitation Foundation (NSF) or any State of Connecticut-sponsored inspection certification program using the Connecticut Recommended Existing Septic System Inspection Report. The subsurface sewage disposal system shall be pumped at Seller's expense unless the system has been pumped within 6 months of the date of the inspection. Purchaser may withdraw from the Agreement by providing written notice along with a copy of the Report to Seller within _____ days from the Date of Acceptance of the Agreement if the Report notes any of the following conditions: (a) system operating at capacity under current usage levels; (b) need for component replacement due to structural damage; (c) further investigation of leaching system with machine digging is recommended; (d) evidence of prior high liquid levels

©1997-2003 Connecticut Association of REALTORS®, Inc.
Revised: June 1, 1998
Revised May 22, 2000
Revised July 16, 2002
Revised March 11, 2003
Revised June 20, 2003; August 20, 2003

Page 2 of 4

R REALTOR®

FIGURE 7.2

Combined Contract Contingency Addendum to Purchase and Sale Agreement (continued)

in system components; or (e) sewage overflow observed, repair required under permit of local health department. If the Report notes any of the following conditions: (a) plumbing leaks or wastewater routing problems in home; or (b) soil testing recommended to determine expansion/repair area, Seller may agree in writing to rectify leaks and routing problems and perform soil testing at Seller's expense, to be completed by the date of Closing, in which event the Agreement will remain in full force and effect.

Note: Purchaser acknowledges that: (a) there are many different types of septic system designs and construction; (b) Purchaser's experience with the septic system will depend on many factors (including intensity of use, materials disposed of in the system, family size) and may differ greatly from the previous user's experience; and (c) the Connecticut Department of Public Health, local Health District or Town Sanitarian may be able to provide an evaluation of the operation and design of the septic system serving the property and furnish further information regarding the construction, use, and maintenance of septic systems.

Included _____ Not included _____   Inspection paid by: Seller ☐ Buyer ☐

(8)   Septic System Cost Estimate
Purchaser's obtaining a price estimate not to exceed $_____ on or before _____, 20____ for the installation of a system suitable for Purchaser's intended use (including the number of bedrooms) of the property. If the price estimate exceeds the price noted above and Purchaser notifies Seller thereof on or before the above date, Purchaser shall have the option of terminating the Agreement and all sums paid as deposit shall be promptly returned to Purchaser and this Agreement shall become null and void.

Included _____ Not included _____

(9)   Condominium and Planned Unit Development
(a)   Purchaser understands that the property is a unit in a condominium or planned unit development and that the property will be conveyed subject to all of the terms, conditions, covenants, restrictions, agreements, obligations, assessments and lien rights as set forth in the declaration of condominium applicable to the property and the by-laws and exhibits recorded therewith, as they may be amended or supplemented, including, but not limited to, the obligations to make payment of common charges included therein, and all facts shown on the survey and floor plans filed with the declaration.

(b)   Seller agrees to comply with those requirements of the declaration or by-laws that create a right of first refusal, if any, in connection with the property. If any such right of first refusal is exercised, any sums paid hereunder shall be immediately returned to Purchaser and both parties shall be relieved of any further liability hereunder.

(c)   Purchaser will examine the Resale Certificate, if the unit owner's association is required by law to furnish a Resale Certificate, and if this Agreement is not voided within the rescission period permitted by statute, Purchaser agrees that Purchaser is then relying on the representations and disclosures appearing in the Resale Certificate if different or inconsistent with other representations or understandings given or inferred by Seller or Seller's agents.

(d)   Seller agrees that at the time of closing all installments of common expense assessments or other association assessments then due and payable will be paid.

(10)   Home Owners Insurance
Purchasers obtaining a binder for property/casualty insurance from an insurer licensed to do business in the State of Connecticut on such terms and conditions as may be acceptable to the Purchaser and the Purchaser's lender _____ days from the Date of Acceptance of the Agreement. If Purchaser cannot obtain such binder on or before the above date, Purchaser's shall have the option of terminating the Agreement and all sums paid as a deposit shall be promptly returned to Purchaser and this Agreement shall become null and void.

Included _____ Not included _____

When written notice is required by this Addendum, such notice may be made by one of the following methods: (1) first-class mail,

©1997-2003 Connecticut Association of REALTORS®, Inc.
Revised: June 1, 1998
Revised May 22, 2000
Revised July 16, 2002
Revised March 11, 2003
Revised June 20, 2003; August 20, 2003

REALTOR®

FIGURE 7.2

Combined Contract Contingency Addendum to Purchase and Sale Agreement (continued)

postage prepaid to the address set forth in the Agreement next to the recipient's name or to the recipient's attorney at the attorney's office address; (2) facsimile transmission to the recipient, the recipient's real estate agent or the recipient's attorney; or (3) hand delivered to the recipient or the recipient's attorney.

Seller shall grant reasonable access to the property to Purchaser and Purchaser's inspectors and laboratories for the purpose of conducting the inspections and tests required by this Addendum.

The term "days" as used throughout this Addendum shall mean "calendar days."

In the event that the Agreement is null and void for reasons as set forth in this Addendum, all monies paid as deposit(s) will be promptly returned to Purchaser. Seller and Purchaser agree to provide such permissions for release of escrow monies as escrow agent may reasonably require. The parties agree that escrow agent will not be liable for the release of escrow monies in accordance with this Agreement or for errors of judgment in the release of escrowed deposits unless such errors are the result of gross or intentional misconduct.

_____
Purchaser

_____
Date

_____
Purchaser

_____
Date

_____
Seller

_____
Date

_____
Seller

_____
Date

©1997-2003 Connecticut Association of REALTORS®, Inc.
Revised: June 1, 1998
Revised May 22, 2000
Revised July 16, 2002
Revised March 11, 2003
Revised June 20, 2003; August 20, 2003

Page 4 of 4

REALTOR®

F I G U R E   7.3

Contract Contingency Waiver

WAIVER OF CONTINGENCY FOR SALE OF BUYER'S REAL ESTATE

Property: _____

Sellers: _____

Buyers: _____

Buy/Sell Agreement Date: _____

The Buyers in the above-referenced buy/sell agreement hereby waive their rights under a certain Addendum for Sale of Buyer's Real Estate dated _____ which Addendum amends the Buy/Sell Agreement referenced above. In addition, the parties hereby agree that the Buy/Sell Agreement referenced above is amended as follows:

Amended Mortgage Commitment date: _____

Amended Closing Date: _____

Amended date for completion of all inspections and tests: _____

In all other respects the Buy/Sell Agreement referenced above remains in full force and effect.

Seller _____   Buyer _____

Seller _____   Buyer _____

Date _____   Date _____

©1998 Connecticut Association of REALTORS®, Inc.
May 26,1998

Reprinted with permission of the Connecticut Association of REALTORS®, Inc.

FIGURE 7.4

Hubbard Clause Contract Addendum

ADDENDUM FOR SALE OF BUYER'S REAL ESTATE

This Addendum is intended to amend a certain Purchase Agreement or Contract dated _____(the "Agreement") between the undersigned parties.

The parties each acknowledge that the Buyer owns real estate located at _____ _____(the "Buyer's Property") which must be sold in order for the Buyer to meet its obligations under the Agreement. If the Buyer notifies the Seller in writing on or before _____of the Buyer's failure to receive a purchase agreement or contract for the Buyer's real estate, which purchase agreement or contract is either without contingencies or has all the contingencies waived or fulfilled, then any deposit monies paid by the Buyer shall be returned to the Buyer and this Agreement shall be of no further force and effect.

It is also further agreed and understood that the Seller may continue to market Seller's Property by any means, including advertising and showing to prospective buyers with the following conditions:

1.   Seller shall cease marketing Seller's Property upon Seller's receipt of written notification by the Buyer that the Buyer is prepared to close in accordance with the terms of the Agreement.

2.   Seller shall provide Buyer or Buyer's attorney with written notice if Seller accepts any bona fide offer for the purchase of the Premises. Such written notice shall be signed by the Seller and contain a copy of the bona fide offer Seller intends to accept. Buyer shall then have until 7:00 pm on the third business day, time being of the essence, after the Buyer's or Buyer's attorney's receipt of Seller's notice in which to agree to close in accordance with the terms of the Agreement without any contingency for the sale of Buyer's real estate. If the Buyer does not notify the Seller in writing of the Buyer's agreement to close in accordance with the terms of the Agreement without any contingency for the sale of Buyer's real estate by 7:00 pm on the third business day after the Buyer's or Buyer's attorney's receipt of Seller's notice, time being of the essence, then any deposit monies paid by the Buyer shall be returned to the Buyer and this Agreement shall be of no further force and effect. An offer which contains a contingency for the sale of the offeror's real estate shall not be considered a "bona fide offer" for purposes of this paragraph.

_____   _____
Buyer   Date   Seller   Date

_____   _____
Buyer   Date   Seller   Date

©2001-2002 Connecticut Association of REALTORS®, Inc.
Revised July 15, 2002

IR
REALTOR®

F I G U R E 7.4

Hubbard Clause Contract Addendum (continued)

WAIVER OF CONTINGENCY FOR SALE OF BUYER'S REAL ESTATE

Property:_____

Sellers:_____

Buyers:_____

Purchase Agreement or Contract Date:_____

The Buyers in the above-referenced Purchase Agreement or contract hereby waive their rights under a certain Addendum for Sale of Buyer's Real Estate dated _____ _____which Addendum amends the Purchase Agreement or contract referenced above. In addition, the parties hereby agree that the Purchase Agreement or contract referenced above is amended as follows:

Amended Mortgage Commitment Date: _____

Amended Closing Date: _____

Amended date for completion of all inspections and tests: _____

In all other respects the Purchase Agreement or contract referenced above remains in full force and effect.

Seller _____   Buyer _____

Seller _____   Buyer _____

Date _____   Date _____

F I G U R E   7.5

Binder

The Greater Bridgeport Board of REALTORS®, Inc.

OFFER TO PURCHASE

RECEIVED OF _____
Address _____
the sum of $_____ as a deposit for the Purchase of the Property known as

at the Full Purchase Price of _____ Dollars.

This offer is given contingent upon the Purchaser's ability to obtain a _____ Mortgage
in the amount of_____ Dollars,
for a term of _____ years at the Prevailing Interest Rate by_____ (date).

THIS IS NOT A CONTRACT OF SALE, a Formal Contract shall be prepared by Seller's Attorney and shall be executed by Purchaser and the **Balance of Deposit $**_____ shall be paid on or before_____ to the Seller's Attorney and/or the Listing Agency, pursuant to Connecticut General Statutes 8-265F, to be held in trust until closing of title.

The Seller does not know and represents that he/she has no reason to believe that urea formaldehyde foam insulation has ever been installed on the premises of the Listed Property, and if it has that it is_____ (is not_____) still present.

The Sale to be consummated on or before _____

INSPECTIONS

If checked, this Offer to Purchase is subject to the following inspections and/or tests to be paid by the Purchaser:
☐ Wood Destroying Insects   ☐ Physical/Structural   ☐ Well   ☐ Septic   ☐ Radon
☐ Lead Substances/Paint   ☐ UFFI   ☐ Asbestos
☐ Other_____
a) Inspection to be completed on or before _____ 19_____
b) Notification of results to be within _____ business days after inspection date.

Included in the sale are the following: _____

Other terms: _____

Purchaser acknowledges that Seller has_____ (has not_____) furnished Purchaser with the Uniform Property Condition Disclosure Form required by Connecticut Public Act 95-311 prior to Purchaser's execution of this Agreement. If such Disclosure has been furnished, a copy is attached hereto. If such Disclosure has not been furnished, Seller shall give and Purchaser shall receive a credit of $300 against the purchase price at closing.

LEAD-BASED PAINT AND LEAD-BASED PAINT HAZARDS
[Required if Subject Real Property Consists of or Contains a Residential Unit Built Before 1978]

Lead Warning Statement
Every purchaser of any interest in residential real property on which a residential dwelling was built prior to 1978 is notified that such property may present exposure to lead from lead-based paint that may place young children at risk of developing lead poisoning. Lead poisoning in young children may produce permanent neurological damage, including learning disabilities, reduced intelligence quotient, behavioral problems, and impaired memory. Lead poisoning also poses a particular risk to pregnant women. The Seller of any interest in residential real property is required to provide the buyer with any information on lead-based paint hazards from risk assessments or inspection in the Seller's possession and notify the Buyer of any known lead-based paint hazards. A risk assessment or inspection for possible lead-based paint hazards is recommended prior to purchase.

☐ A completed *Disclosure of Information on Lead-Based Paint and Lead-Based Paint Hazards* is attached.
☐ This Offer to Purchase is contingent upon a risk assessment or inspection of the property for the presence of lead-based paint and/or lead-based paint hazards at the PURCHASER'S expense until 9 p.m. on:
☐ the tenth calendar-day after signing of the Offer to Purchase by all parties, -OR-
☐ the _____ calendar-day after signing of the Offer to Purchase by all parties, -OR-
☐ _____ (mutually agreed upon date).

(Intact lead-based paint that is in good condition is not necessarily a hazard. See EPA pamphlet *Protect Your Family From Lead in Your Home* for more information). This contingency will terminate at the above predetermined deadline unless the PURCHASER (or agent) delivers to the SELLER (or SELLER'S agent) a written contract addendum listing the specific existing deficiencies and corrections needed, together with a copy of the inspection and/or risk assessment report. The SELLER may, at the SELLER'S option, within ____ days after delivery of the addendum, elect in writing whether to correct the condition(s) prior to settlement. If the SELLER will correct the condition(s), the SELLER shall furnish the PURCHASER with certification from a risk assessor or inspector demonstrating that the condition has been remedied before the date of the settlement. If the SELLER does not elect to make the repairs, or if the SELLER makes a counter-offer, the PURCHASER shall have____ days to respond to the counter-offer or remove this contingency and take the property in an "as is" condition or this Offer to Purchase shall become void. The PURCHASER may remove this contingency at any time without cause.

SELLING AGENT   ACCEPTED BY PURCHASER(S)

Signed _____ Date _____   Signed _____ Date _____
Name _____   Name _____
Firm _____   Signed _____ Date _____
Address _____   Name _____
City/Town ____ State ____ Zip ____   Telephone _____
Telephone _____

ACCEPTANCE BY SELLER(S) - The foregoing terms and conditions are agreed to and accepted by Seller(s).
LISTING AGENT   SELLER(S)

Signed _____ Date _____   Signed _____ Date _____
Name _____   Name _____
Firm _____   Signed _____ Date _____
Address _____   Name _____
City/Town ____ State ____ Zip ____   Address _____
Telephone _____   City/Town ____ State ____ Zip ____ Telephone ____

© 1996 GBBR, Inc. (Form 3.2)

Reprinted with permission of the Greater Bridgeport Board of REALTORS®, Inc.

FIGURE 7.6

Residential Property Condition Disclosure Report

RE DISC Rev. 6/02

STATE OF CONNECTICUT
DEPARTMENT OF CONSUMER PROTECTION
165 Capitol Avenue ✦ Hartford, CT 06106

RESIDENTIAL PROPERTY CONDITION DISCLOSURE REPORT

Seller's Name:		
Property Street Address:		
Property City:	State:	Zip Code:

The Uniform Property Condition Disclosure Act <u>Connecticut General Statutes Section 20-327b</u> requires the seller of residential property to provide this disclosure to the prospective purchaser prior to the prospective purchaser's execution of any binder, contract to purchase, option or lease containing a purchase option. These provisions apply to the transfer of residential real property of four dwelling units or less made with or without the assistance of a licensed broker or salesperson. The seller will be required to credit the purchaser with the sum of $300.00 at closing if the seller fails to furnish this report as required by this act.

Please note that Connecticut law requires the owner of any dwelling in which children under the age of 6 reside to abate or manage materials containing toxic levels of lead

Pursuant to the Uniform Property Condition Disclosure Act, the seller is obligated to disclose here any knowledge of any problem regarding the following:

YES	NO	UNKN		I. GENERAL INFORMATION

1. How long have you occupied the property? _____ Age of structure _____

☐ ☐ ☐ 2. Does anybody other than yourself have any right to use any part of your property or does anybody else claim to own any part of your property? If yes, explain
_____

☐ ☐ ☐ 3. Is the property in a flood plain area or an area containing wetlands?
_____

☐ ☐ ☐ 4. Do you have any reason to believe that the municipality may impose any assessment for purposes such as sewer installation, sewer improvements, water main installation, water main improvements, sidewalks or other improvements?
_____

☐ ☐ ☐ 5. Is the property located in an historic village or special tax district?
Explain _____

Residential Property Condition Disclosure Report (continued)

YES	NO	UNKN		II. SYSTEM/UTILITIES	

☐ ☐ ☐ 6. HEATING SYSTEM problems? Explain_____
　　　　　　　　a. Heating System and Fuel Type_____
　　　　　　　　b. Is there an underground fuel tank? If yes, location and age_____
　　　　　　　　_____

☐ ☐ ☐ 7. HOT WATER HEATER problems? Explain
　　　　　　　　Type of hot water heater_____ Age _____

☐ ☐ ☐ 8. PLUMBING SYSTEM problems? Explain_____
　　　　　　　　_____

☐ ☐ ☐ 9. SEWAGE SYSTEM problems? Explain_____
　　　　　　　　a. Type of sewage disposal system
　　　　　　　　　　(central sewer, septic, cesspool, etc.)_____
　　　　　　　　b. If private: (a) Name of service company_____
　　　　　　　　　　　　　　　　(b) Date last pumped _____ Frequency _____
　　　　　　　　c. If public:
　　　　　　　　　　(1) Is there a separate charge made for sewer use? yes___ no _____
　　　　　　　　　　(2) If separate charge, is it a flat amount or metered? _____
　　　　　　　　　　(3) If flat amount, please state amount and payment dates
　　　　　　　　　　_____

　　　　　　　　　　(4) Are there any unpaid sewer charges, and if so state
　　　　　　　　　　　　the amount _____

☐ ☐ ☐ 10. AIR CONDITIONING problems? Explain_____
　　　　　　　　Air Conditioning type: Central _____Window _____ Other_____

☐ ☐ ☐ 11. ELECTRICAL SYSTEM problems? Explain_____

☐ ☐ ☐ 12. DRINKING WATER problems? Quality or Quantity? Explain_____
　　　　　　　　_____

　　　　　　　　If public drinking water:
　　　　　　　　a. Is there a separate charge made for water use? Yes_____ No_____
　　　　　　　　b. If separate charge, is it a flat amount or metered?_____
　　　　　　　　c. If flat amount, please state amount and payment dates

　　　　　　　　d. Are there any unpaid water charges, and if so state the amount _____

☐ ☐ ☐ 13. ELECTRONIC SECURITY SYSTEM problems? Explain_____

☐ ☐ ☐ 14. CARBON MONOXIDE OR SMOKE DETECTOR problems? Explain_____

☐ ☐ ☐ 15. FIRE SPRINKLER SYSTEM problems? Explain_____

FIGURE 7.6

Residential Property Condition Disclosure Report (continued)

YES	NO	UNKN	III. BUILDING/STRUCTURE/IMPROVEMENTS
☐	☐	☐	16. FOUNDATION/SLAB problems/settling? Explain_____
☐	☐	☐	17. BASEMENT Water/Seepage/Dampness? Explain amount, frequency and location. _____
☐	☐	☐	18. SUMP PUMP problems? If yes, explain_____
☐	☐	☐	19. ROOF leaks, problems? Explain _____ Roof type _____ Age _____
☐	☐	☐	20. INTERIOR WALLS/CEILING problems? Explain_____
☐	☐	☐	21. EXTERIOR SIDING problems? Explain_____
☐	☐	☐	22. FLOOR problems? Explain_____
☐	☐	☐	23. CHIMNEY/FIREPLACE/WOOD OR COAL STOVE problems? Explain:_____ _____
☐	☐	☐	24. Any knowledge of FIRE/SMOKE damage? Explain_____
☐	☐	☐	25. PATIO/DECK problems? _____ If made of wood, is wood treated or untreated?_____
☐	☐	☐	26. DRIVEWAY problems? Explain_____
☐	☐	☐	27. TERMITE/INSECT/RODENT/PEST INFESTATION problems? Explain_____ _____
☐	☐	☐	28. IS HOUSE INSULATED? Type _____ Location _____
☐	☐	☐	29. ROT AND WATER DAMAGE problems? Explain_____
☐	☐	☐	30. WATER DRAINAGE problems? Explain_____
☐	☐	☐	31. Are ASBESTOS CONTAINING INSULATION OR BUILDING MATERIALS present?____ If yes, location_____
☐	☐	☐	32. Is LEAD PAINT present? If yes, location_____
☐	☐	☐	33. Is LEAD PLUMBING present? If yes, location_____
☐	☐	☐	34. Has test for RADON been done? If yes, attach copy. State whether a radon control system is in place_____

Residential Property Condition Disclosure Report (continued)

The Seller should use this area to further explain any item above. Attach additional pages if necessary and indicate here _____ the number of additional pages attached.

I. Seller's Certification

To the extent of the Seller(s) knowledge as a property owner, the Seller acknowledges that the information contained above is true and accurate for those areas of the property listed. In the event a real estate broker or salesperson is utilized, the Seller authorizes the broker or salesperson to provide the above information to prospective buyers, selling agents or buyer's agents.

DATE _____ SELLER _____ SELLER _____
                                        (Signature)   (Type or Print)

DATE _____ SELLER _____ SELLER _____
                                        (Signature)   (Type or Print)

II. Responsibilities of Real Estate Brokers

This report in no way relieves a real estate broker of his or her obligation under the provisions of Section 20-328-5a of the Regulations of Connecticut State Agencies to disclose any material facts. Failure to do so could result in punitive action taken against the broker, such as fines, suspension or revocation of license.

III. Statements Not to Constitute a Warranty

Any representations made by the seller on this report shall not constitute a warranty to the buyer.

IV. Nature of Disclosure Report

This residential disclosure report is not a substitute for inspections, tests, and other methods of determining the physical condition of the property.

V. Information on the Residence of Convicted Felons

Information concerning the residence address of a person convicted of a crime may be available from law enforcement agencies or the department of public safety.

VI. Buyer's Certification

The buyer is urged to carefully inspect the property and, if desired, to have the property inspected by an expert. The buyer understands that there are areas of the property for which the seller has no knowledge and this disclosure statement does not encompass those areas.   The buyer also acknowledges that the buyer has read and received a signed copy of this statement from the seller or seller's agent.

DATE _____ BUYER _____ BUYER _____
                                        (Signature)   (Type or Print)

DATE _____ BUYER _____ BUYER _____
                                        (Signature)   (Type or Print)

Questions or Comments? Consumer Problems?
    Contact the Department of Consumer Protection at (860) 713-6150 or occprotrades@po.state.ct.us

If a mortgage is to be placed on the property conveyed and personal property items are to be included as additional security for the loan, a Uniform Commercial Code financing statement, indicating the nature of the security interest and identifying the items included, must be filed in the office of the secretary of state of Connecticut. Continuation statements must be filed on every fifth anniversary. These UCC provisions apply mainly to larger commercial or investment properties and rarely to the typical conveyance of a single-family residence.

Earnest money deposits—escrow accounts. Generally, the real estate sales contract provides that the broker will hold the earnest money deposited by the buyer. In such cases Connecticut laws regulating real estate brokers expressly forbid a commingling of personal funds with those held as deposits on listed properties. A salesperson must immediately assign or pay over directly to his or her broker *all funds* received from a real estate transaction. *Brokers must maintain a separate escrow or trust account for the deposit of all monies* received on behalf of their principals. These deposits must be made *within three banking days from the date of obtaining all signatures from all parties to the transaction.* The Real Estate Commission reserves the right to inspect these accounts at any time.

It is customary that the earnest money deposit be made payable to the brokerage, to be held in an escrow account. Under no circumstances can such deposit or interest benefit the broker. The amount of the deposit, however, is considered to be a debt to the buyer until the transaction closes. Interest earned on real estate broker accounts is paid to the Connecticut Housing Finance Authority to benefit a program for first-time homebuyers. A buyer and seller may decide, however, to allow the buyer's deposit to bear interest for the buyer or seller. In such case a separate account is maintained in the name of the parties involved. (See Chapter 10 for more details on escrow accounts for real estate deposits.)

Because the sales contract will generally identify the amount of money deposited with the broker or escrow agent, a receipt is not always required, though one may be drawn up on the buyer's request. Unless the deposit is made in cash, a canceled check will always serve as a receipt. Should a broker fail to comply with the statutory separate account regulations, he or she is subject to fines up to $1,000 and/or imprisonment for up to six months. The Real Estate Commission has the right to examine and audit a broker's escrow or trust account at any time.

Connecticut law provides for a procedure allowing brokers to hand over a deposit to a court when there is a dispute regarding the sale.

Destruction of the premises. In Connecticut, if the sales contract is silent on this point, it is presumed that the seller will carry the risk of loss and maintain fire insurance coverage until the date of closing. Most contracts do provide that the seller will bear the risk of loss if the premises are destroyed before the closing.

Defaults. If either the buyer or the seller breaches the contract in a realty transaction, the contract is said to be in default. The remedies for default in Connecticut are essentially the same as those mentioned in the principles texts. However, the nature of the default relates directly to a broker's right to collect a commission. The real estate broker's right to collect a commission is discussed in Chapter 1.

Leases

As previously discussed, the Connecticut statutes require that leases for terms of more than one year be in writing. To be valid, written lease contracts must describe the property leased, identify the parties, state the amount of rental and manner of payment, indicate dates, describe any other desirable terms and conditions, and contain the signatures of the parties to the contract. Leases are discussed in Chapter 12.

A broker who is entitled to a future commission for a commercial lease transaction can protect his or her right to receive that commission in the event the landlord sells the property by recording a Notice of Commission Rights in the municipal land records in the municipality where the leased property is located. A sample notice is provided in Chapter 1.

Escrow Agreements

Connecticut allows the conveyance of real property interests by way of the escrow procedure. The laws pertaining to such transactions are generally the same as those described in the basic text.

There has been some concern in Connecticut that an escrow agreement is not enforceable if the escrow holder is an attorney or agent for one or more of the parties due to a court case that basically came to that conclusion. Recent legislation has clarified this and confirmed that escrow agreements are valid in such a situation.

■ RESIDENTIAL PROPERTY CONDITION DISCLOSURE

Sellers are required to provide prospective purchasers with a property condition report in all residential real estate transactions (with few exceptions). The law applies to both FSBO (For Sale by Owner) and real estate agent–assisted transactions.

Covered property

- Residential real estate containing one to four dwelling units (including condominiums and cooperatives)
- Transfers by sale, exchange, or lease with an option to buy

Exclusions

- Transfers from co-owner to co-owner
- Transfers for no consideration to spouse, mother, father, brother, sister, child, grandparent, or grandchild
- Transfers pursuant to a court order
- Transfers of newly constructed residential real property that carries an implied warranty pursuant to CGS Chapter 827

- Transfers made by executors, administrators, trustees, or conservators
- Transfers by the federal government or federal quasi-governmental entity
- Transfers by deed in lieu of foreclosure
- Transfers by the state of Connecticut or any political subdivision
- Transfers by strict foreclosure, foreclosure by sale, or deed in lieu of foreclosure

Timing

- Disclosure reports must be delivered by the seller to a prospective purchaser at any time prior to the purchaser's signing a written offer to purchase, a binder, a contract, an option, or lease containing a purchase option.
- A photocopy, facsimile transmission, or duplicate original of the report signed by the purchaser must be attached to any written offers, binders, contracts, options, or leases containing a purchase option.
- A photocopy, facsimile transmission, or duplicate original of the report, containing both the seller's and purchaser's signatures, must be attached to any purchase agreement.

Role of seller. The responsibility for completing the form lies with the seller of the property. The disclosures are only required to be based on the seller's actual knowledge of the condition of the property. For each disclosure item on the form, the seller is required to respond yes, no, or, in some instances, unknown. For selected questions, the seller must explain certain conditions. If the seller fails to furnish the report as required, the seller must credit the buyer $300 at closing.

Role of real estate agent. Agents should advise the seller of the seller's responsibility to complete the form accurately. This law does not relieve agents of their obligation to disclose any material facts about the property.

Role of buyer. Seller's disclosures in the report do not constitute a warranty to the buyer. A buyer is urged to carefully inspect the property and to consider having the property inspected by an expert.

Obtaining forms. The required property disclosure report form has been developed by the Department of Consumer Protection. The form is shown as Figure 7.6. Copies of the form can be obtained by calling the department at 1-800-842-2649. Forms may also be obtained from local real estate agents. Also, Connecticut municipal town clerks and municipal libraries have copies of the form, which can be photocopied.

WWWeb.Link

The Connecticut Residential Property Disclosure Form is available online at *http://www.dcp.state.ct.us/licensing/PDFfiles/disclose.pdf.*

The Connecticut "Megan's Law" Sex Offender Registry is located at *www.state.ct.us/dps.sor.htm.*

■ DISCLOSURE OF OFF-SITE CONDITIONS

A residential seller and the seller's agent have satisfied their duty to disclose off-site waste conditions if the seller gives the buyer written notice of the availability of lists of hazardous waste facilities before entering into the contract. A sample notice is provided in Chapter 17; the Purchase and Sale Contract provided in this chapter also contains this notice provision.

■ BUILDING INSPECTION

In Connecticut, a buyer will typically negotiate for a building inspection contingency in the purchase and sale contract. Home inspectors are required to be licensed in Connecticut.

■ ENDNOTES

1. Several token exceptions, such as the purchase of life insurance, are exempted from these provisions.
2. *Cone v. Pedersen* (1945) 40 A. 2d 274, 131 Conn. 374.

QUESTIONS

1. The Uniform Commercial Code applies
   a. only to commercial real property.
   b. only to residential real property.
   c. primarily to personal property.
   d. primarily to real property.

2. In Connecticut, if personal property items are used as additional security for a mortgage on real property, a form must be filed with the secretary of state's office. This is required by the
   a. Law of Fixtures.
   b. Statute of Frauds.
   c. Uniform Commercial Code.
   d. Law of Agency.

3. In Connecticut, an individual may enter into legally enforceable contracts (with no exceptions) when he or she reaches the age of
   a. 16.   c. 19.
   b. 18.   d. 21.

4. Listing and buyer brokerage contracts are considered to be
   a. bilateral contracts.
   b. implied contracts.
   c. parol contracts.
   d. unilateral contracts.

5. Under a standard listing contract, a broker is considered to be a
   a. special agent.   c. procuring cause.
   b. general agent.   d. universal agent.

6. A seller is required to give a buyer a Property Condition Disclosure Report in all of the following transactions *except*
   a. when the seller is not assisted by a licensed real estate agent.
   b. if the seller has not resided on the property in the last year.
   c. a sale of commercial property.
   d. if the buyer has lived on the property as a tenant.

7. Property Condition Disclosure Reports must be delivered to the buyer
   a. prior to the buyer's making a written offer.
   b. at the time the buyer makes a written offer.
   c. prior to the buyer's signing a purchase and sale contract.
   d. at the time of the home inspection.

8. Seller has no knowledge of any plumbing system problems on the property he is selling. In actuality, however, the pipes are seriously corroded and will need to be replaced soon. In the Property Condition Disclosure Report, when responding to whether the seller has any knowledge of plumbing system problems, she should respond
   a. yes.
   b. no.
   c. unknown.
   d. Seller would not be required to respond to this question.

9. All funds received by a broker on behalf of his or her principal must be deposited in an escrow or trust account within
   a. three days of receiving the deposit.
   b. three days of obtaining all signatures.
   c. three banking days of receiving all signatures.
   d. three working days of receiving all signatures.

10. A lease must be in writing if it is for a period in excess of
    a. 60 days.   c. six months.
    b. 90 days.   d. one year.

TRANSFER OF TITLE

■ OVERVIEW

Title to real estate can be transferred in Connecticut in the following ways: voluntarily (by deed), involuntarily (by operation of law), and at the time of death (by will or intestate distribution).

■ DEEDS OF CONVEYANCE

In Connecticut the primary function of a deed is to convey or pass title (ownership) to land.[1] *The two most common forms of deeds of conveyance in Connecticut are the warranty and quitclaim deeds.* In instances where a deed is not constructed exactly according to statutory requirements, title may still be allowed to pass. The courts are generally liberal in their interpretations of deed construction and assign more importance to the passing of the estate than to the preciseness of the document through which it is passed.[2] Although the competent preparation of a deed and proper adherence to statutory provisions and requirements are important, minor errors will not generally void a deed. The court's intention is not to endorse shoddy document preparation; however, the courts recognize that the most important element in a deed is the actual conveyance, not the content of the conveyance document.

Requirements for a Valid Deed

In Connecticut the requirements for a valid conveyance are generally the same as the requirements described in the principles books. While any legal form of deed may be used, the Connecticut statutes also set forth statutory forms for deeds that may be used.[3] The deed must state the parties' full *legal names*. If the grantor has changed his or her name since acquiring the property to be conveyed, both names should be included. The deed usually is recorded by the attorney for the purchaser, but this may be handled by any other person. When a conveyance is executed by power of attorney, as described in the text, such power of attorney must be recorded with the deed unless it was previously on record and reference to it is made in the deed.

Other Types of Deeds

There are a variety of other types of deeds that surface from time to time under Connecticut statutes. Several of these are mentioned briefly below and will be discussed further in other chapters dealing with particular related circumstances.

Because Connecticut is a modified title-theory state with regard to mortgage financing, the *mortgage deed* is a common form of deed. Conveyances as a result of mortgage foreclosure require certificates of foreclosure executed by court order and essentially serve to convey full possession to the mortgage holders, who may subsequently convey title by warranty deed if they choose. Tax collector's deeds are given to the purchaser of property at a tax or sheriff's sale; such deeds are not recorded for a period of six months after the sale to provide the delinquent taxpayer a final opportunity to redeem his or her property before full legal title passes to the purchaser of the tax collector's deed. *Trust deeds*, while used in Connecticut, are used only as financing instruments to secure personal property and goods that fall within the jurisdiction of the Uniform Commercial Code, and therefore are of no particular importance to this text.

■ REAL ESTATE CONVEYANCE TAXES

Connecticut imposes a two-part tax on the sale or transfer of an interest in real property, which is payable at the time and place of recording the instrument of conveyance.[4] One part is for the benefit of the municipality. The *municipal conveyance tax rate* is .11 percent of the total selling price of the property. The second part of the tax is for the benefit of the state and is required to be forwarded to the State Commission of Revenue Services by the town clerk collecting the tax. The *state conveyance tax rate* is .5 percent of the first $800,000 of the selling price. The amount over $800,000 is taxed at the rate of 1 percent. (The state conveyance tax rate for all nonresidential property sales is a straight 1 percent of the total selling price.)

Note: The municipal conveyance tax rate has been temporarily increased to .25 percent through June 30, 2007. On and after July 1, 2007, the municipal conveyance tax rate will revert back to .11 percent (unless the legislature chooses to extend the temporary increase or to make it permanent).

In addition to the above state conveyance taxes, 18 "targeted investment communities" have the option of imposing an added .25 percent to the municipal conveyance tax, which would increase the total municipal conveyance tax in those communities to .50 percent. The municipalities that have the option of adding to the conveyance tax are Bloomfield, Bridgeport, Bristol, East Hartford, Groton, Hamden, Hartford, Meriden, Middletown, New Britain, New Haven, New London, Norwalk, Norwich, Southington, Stamford, Waterbury, and Windham.

For purposes of all examples and questions in this book, the .11 percent municipal tax rate is used. Adjustments would have to be made in real life accordingly if the town/time frame required one of the different rates.

The following are examples showing the calculation of the real estate conveyance tax:

■ **EXAMPLE** A residential property sells for $210,000. The conveyance tax is calculated as follows:

Municipal Conveyance Tax	= Selling Price × .0011
	= $210,000 × .0011
	= $231
State Conveyance Tax	= (Selling Price up to $800,000 × .005) + (Selling Price over $800,000 × .01)
	= ($210,000 × .005) + N/A
	= $1,050

■ **EXAMPLE** A residential property sells for $950,000. The conveyance tax is calculated as follows:

Municipal Conveyance Tax	= Selling Price × .0011
	= $950,000 × .0011
	= $1,045
State Conveyance Tax	= (Selling Price up to $800,000 × .005) + (Selling Price over $800,000 × .01)
	= ($800,000 × .005) + ($150,000 × .01)
	= $4,000 + $1,500
	= $5,500

■ **EXAMPLE** A commercial property sells for $375,000. The conveyance tax is calculated as follows:

Municipal Conveyance Tax	= Selling Price × .0011
	= $375,000 × .0011
	= $412.50
State Conveyance Tax	= Selling Price × .01
	= $375,000 × .01
	= $3,750

Taxes must be paid to the town clerk prior to recording, and the fact that they have been paid is noted by the town clerk on the deed.

Various categories of conveyances are exempted from the conveyance tax. These include deeds that secure debts or obligations (mortgage deeds), transfers to government agencies and divisions, gifts, dedications, condemnations, tax deeds, mortgage releases, partitions, mergers and deeds between a parent company and its subsidiaries involving no consideration other than cancellation of stock and land transfers of $2,000 or less, and transfers that make only a change of identity or a change in the form of ownership or organization rather than a change in beneficial ownership. Also exempt are employer and relocation company resales of residential property acquired through relocation plans, if the resale occurs within six months of the employee conveyance.

Calculation of Purchase Price Based on Conveyance Tax

Connecticut does not require that a deed state the actual consideration paid for property. Many times an agent may need this information to conduct a market study or better advise a buyer or seller. Because the amount of town conveyance tax paid is always stamped on a recorded deed, the purchase price can be calculated. This is done by dividing the town conveyance tax paid by the conveyance tax rate in effect at the time of conveyance. (Note that the rate is currently .11 percent, but it may be different in the past and future.)

■ **EXAMPLE**   A recently recorded deed does not state the actual purchase price, but the conveyance tax stamp indicates that $165 was paid for town conveyance tax. By dividing $165 by the current town conveyance tax rate of .11 percent (165 ÷ .0011), you can calculate that the purchase price was $150,000.

Conveyance of Farm, Forest, and Open-Space Land

As indicated in Chapter 6, various types of real property may be classified as farm, forest, or open-space land and are assessed and taxed at a lower rate than other properties.

The reason for this special classification and the resultant tax advantage is the state's desire to preserve such land and encourage agricultural and recreational land usage throughout the state. In recent years farm, forest, and open-space land has been difficult to preserve because of the burdens of high property taxes.

A special conveyance tax has also been instituted by the state for land under this classification. If the property is sold before ten years after the date the classification was obtained, a penalty conveyance tax must be paid in addition to the standard conveyance tax. The amount of the additional conveyance tax is based on a sliding scale of 0 to 10 percent of the total sales price. If the owner conveys within the first year of such classification, the penalty is 10 percent of the sales price. If he or she conveys within the second year, the penalty is 9 percent, and so on until, after the tenth year, no penalty taxes will be levied against the conveyance.

The obvious reason for this special conveyance tax is to discourage large landowners from applying for such classification merely to avoid paying higher taxes. This additional conveyance tax was challenged and upheld as constitutional.[5]

■ ADVERSE POSSESSION

Title to real property may be acquired by an individual through adverse possession of the property for a period of at least 15 years. The adverse user's possession of the property must be hostile and under claim of right, actual, open and notorious, exclusive, continuous, and uninterrupted. The procedure for acquiring title by adverse possession is very similar to the procedure for acquiring an easement by prescription, described in Chapter 3: a quiet title action is brought in civil court. The burden of proof rests with the person claiming right to the title, and the decision as to whether all the requirements for the acquisition of title by adverse possession have been met will be made by the court according to the facts of the case.[6] The courts adhere strictly to the statutory requirements necessary to acquire by adverse possession. The claimant's proof of the right to such title must be clear and positive.[7]

■ TRANSFER OF A DECEASED PERSON'S PROPERTY

When a joint tenant co-owner of real estate dies, the property automatically transfers to the other joint tenant(s). If a tenancy in common co-owner of real estate or an individual owner of real estate dies, the property transfers either (1) according to the will of the decedent or (2) if there is no will, according to the laws of the state.

Wills

In Connecticut a will may be prepared by anyone of sound mind who is at least 18 years of age. The document must be in writing and signed by at least two witnesses in the presence of the person making the will (the testator). The beneficiaries of a will may not sign as witnesses unless they are also heirs of the testator. A nonheir beneficiary runs the risk of being excluded from his or her devise if he or she signs as a witness.

On the death of the testator, the executor of the estate must submit the will to the probate court within 30 days. Once received by the court, notice of the hearing must be given to all interested parties. This is usually done by placing an announcement in the newspaper. Wills may be contested in court if they are felt to be illegal in their manner and order of distribution or statutory construction. Thus, if an heir, beneficiary, or other interested party feels that the will unfairly denies an inheritance or was prepared illegally, he or she has the right to contest the will in court.

Title to real property passes to the devisee(s) as of the date of the testator's death and is never really held by the executor or administrator of the estate.[8] If a specific devise of real property does not take place for any reason (such as the death of the devisee), the real estate passes to the devisee's heirs or assigns or is distributed with the balance of the testator's estate if the original heir died intestate and without heirs or assigns. In this latter situation, the real estate would first return to the estate for possible redistribution before the state would receive title by way of escheat.

Legalities of Descent

If the owner of real property interests dies without a will and is survived by his or her spouse, issue (children and their direct descendants), or other blood relatives, his or her interests pass to these individuals by descent. The distribution of such an estate may be determined in three distinct ways: (1) by a fiduciary (often an attorney), (2) by a committee of three disinterested parties appointed by the probate court, or (3) by mutual agreement of all the parties interested in the estate. When an estate is distributed by mutual agreement, all the interested parties who are legally capable execute and file with the court a mutual distribution agreement.[9] However, a regular probate decree ordering the distribution of an intestate estate stands above all others.[10] Thus, the court may override distributions occurring under any of the three traditional methods if it feels the situation calls for such action.

FIGURE 8.1

Intestate Distribution

Survivors	Distribution
Spouse and children* of both decedent and spouse	Spouse takes first $100,000 plus half of the remainder. Children take the other half.
Decedent's spouse and children,* one or more of whom is not the child of the spouse	Spouse takes half. All the children* share the other half equally.
Spouse and parent or parents (no children†)	Spouse takes the first $100,000 + three-fourths of the remainder. Parents take the other fourth.
Spouse only (no children†, no parents)	Spouse takes all.
Children* only (no spouse)	All goes to children.*
Parents (no spouse, no children†)	All goes to the parents.
Brothers* and sisters* (no spouse, no parents, no children†)	All goes to the brothers and sisters.
Next of kin (no spouse, no children†, no parents, no brothers† or sisters†)	All goes to next of kin.

If there is no next of kin, but there is a stepchild,* he or she will be the next in line to take. If there is no kin and no stepchild, all goes to the state of Connecticut.

* If this person(s) has died before the decedent, his or her descendants may take instead.
† or descendants.

Generally, intestate estates are distributed according to the order of descent outlined in Figure 8.1. The survivorship rights of a spouse in the property of his or her spouse take priority over the distribution mentioned in the figure. (See Chapter 4 on joint tenancy with right of survivorship

The Connecticut General Statutes also provide for the manner of distribution of an estate under a variety of unusual circumstances. In the event that no legal heirs or assigns can be identified *within 20 years of the decedent's demise, the estate of an individual passes to the state by escheat.* The statutes also pursue the inheritance problems related to absentee heirs, heirs from foreign countries, and a variety of other situations. In the event that a difficult inheritance problem is encountered, the wisest advice is to seek legal counsel specializing in inheritance cases.

■ ENDNOTES

1. *Preleski v. Farganiasz* (1922) 116 A. 593, 97 Conn. 345, 350.
2. *Barrett v. French* (1815) 1 Conn. 354.
3. Section 47-36c of the Connecticut General Statutes.
4. Sections 12-494, et seq., of Connecticut General Statutes.
5. *McKinney v. Town of Coventry* (1975) 339 A. 2d 480, 32 Conn. Supp. 82.
6. *Klein v. DeRosa* (1951) 79 A. 2d 773, 137 Conn. 586.
7. *Bridgeport Hydraulic Co. v. Sciortino* (1952) 88 A. 2d 379, 138 Conn. 690.
8. *Pigeon v. Hatheway* (1968) 239 A. 2d 523, 156 Conn. 175.
9. *Hotchkiss v. Goodno* (1915) 95 A. 26, 89 Conn. 420.
10. *Appeal of Dickinson* (1886) 6 A. 422, 54 Conn. 224.

QUESTIONS

1. A recently recorded deed states that the purchase price was "$10 and other good and valuable consideration." The conveyance tax stamp indicates that $192.50 was paid for town conveyance tax. What was the property sold for?
   a. $175,000
   b. $192,500
   c. $21,175
   d. $10

2. Carol and Charles are married. If Charles dies without a will, his entire estate would be taken by Carol if
   a. Charles has no previous spouses.
   b. Charles has no surviving children, grandchildren or parents.
   c. Charles's estate was valued at less than $100,000.
   d. Charles's estate was created after his marriage to Carol.

3. How old must a citizen of Connecticut be before he or she may prepare a legally binding will?
   a. 15 (as long as real property is not involved)
   b. 18
   c. 21
   d. Any age as long as the will is legally witnessed and recorded

4. How many witnesses must sign in the presence of the person making a will to fulfill the legal minimum?
   a. One
   b. Two
   c. Three
   d. Four

5. The prescriptive period in the state of Connecticut to acquire title to real property through adverse possession is
   a. 7 years.
   b. 10 years.
   c. 15 years.
   d. 20 years.

6. Since Arthur acquired a piece of property, he has legally changed his name. To convey that property to Henry by valid deed, Arthur should use
   a. the name as it appears in the deed.
   b. the present legal name.
   c. the name on the deed and the present legal name.
   d. whichever name he wishes.

7. Mark sold residential property to June for $450,000. The total municipal and state conveyance tax on the transaction would be
   a. $2,745.
   b. $4,995.
   c. $7,200.
   d. $7,245.

8. The state of Connecticut wishes to widen a highway; it has exercised its right of eminent domain and taken a portion of Alice Field's property through condemnation proceedings. The conveyance tax on Field's conveyance to the state of Connecticut would be
   a. one-half the usual.
   b. zero.
   c. the same as usual but picked up by the state.
   d. $250, regardless of the consideration amount.

9. Farmer Jones obtained a forest land classification on his rear 100-acre parcel on January 1, 1995, and thus reduced his tax assessment substantially. On June 30, 2001, Farmer Jones sold the property to a residential land developer for $2,250,000. In addition to the standard municipal and state conveyance tax, he would pay a "penalty" tax of
   a. $225,000.
   b. $90,000.
   c. $112,500.
   d. $135,000.

10. Unclaimed estates escheat to the state after a period of
   a. 5 years.
   b. 10 years.
   c. 15 years.
   d. 20 years.

CHAPTER NINE

TITLE RECORDS

■ OVERVIEW

Each of the 169 towns in Connecticut maintains extensive public records, which include deeds, mortgage deeds, notes, leases, mechanics' liens, and attachments. The town clerk is responsible for the maintenance of these records and will *stamp the date and time on a submitted document and apply his or her signature* to acknowledge official receipt and entry of the document into the public record.

Only certain types of notices of legal action, notary public commissions, and other miscellaneous data pertaining to real property transactions must be filed or recorded at the county courthouse. The classification of Connecticut's towns into counties is more a matter of judicial convenience than a serious attempt to provide an intermediate level of government between the local and state domains. The principal source of public records concerning real property conveyances remains at the local level and is duplicated nowhere else. It is common procedure for towns to maintain both original and microfilm copies of the public records to avoid the possible consequences of fire or other catastrophic loss.

WWWeb.Link

Links to Connecticut's municipalities, some of which have certain portions of their land records online, can be found at *www.munic.state.ct.us/townlist.htm.*

■ THE NECESSITY TO RECORD

In Connecticut the title to real property passes on delivery of the deed. While Connecticut statutes require that all conveyances and other documents affecting the title to real property be recorded,[1] the law will not generally void a conveyance simply because the deed was not recorded.[2] The recording requirement was enacted to create a reliable and accurate system of land registry and to prevent fraud in land title transactions, not to obstruct the passage of title by its arbitrary enforcement.[3] Note that recording a deed does not automatically validate it. To pass title (ownership) validly, the deed must first be delivered to the grantee. Recording land title conveyances gives *constructive notice* to subsequent purchasers and to the world of the condition of the title held and the manner in which it was conveyed.

The Connecticut policy requiring that realty conveyances be recorded is summed up well in the following quote from the case of *North v. Belden:*

> . . . *It has even been the policy of our law, that title to real estate should appear upon record, that it might be easily and accurately traced. This policy has added greatly to the security of our land titles, and has prevented much litigation, which would otherwise have arisen. And our courts have even considered it their duty to give as much construction to our statutes as will continue this salutary protection. It is true, there has been some diversity of opinion as to the precise extent of this doctrine; and cases will sometimes arise where there may be a doubt as to its application. One principle seems to be definitely settled, that the real nature of the transaction, so far as it can be disclosed, must appear upon the record, with reasonable certainty; and if the deed does not actually give notice of any condition or other circumstance, which might be important, it should at least point out a track, which the enquirer might pursue to obtain it.*[4]

Reasonable Time

The statutes state that deeds conveying title must be recorded within a reasonable time of delivery. Although no specific minimum or maximum of "reasonable time" has been set, the law provides for definite time schedules for recording the documents once the conveyance is presented to the city clerk's office.

Recording Fees

Connecticut towns charge a recording fee of $10 for the first page of a document and $5 for each additional page, plus an additional $3 per document (this additional fee is used for the preservation of historic documents). Thus, for example, the total recording fee for a four-page document would be $28 ($10 for first page, $15 for three additional pages, and $3 for document).

Grantor/Grantee Lists

The town clerk maintains lists separate from all other recorded documents, containing information on local real estate transactions indexed under the names of the grantors and grantees. Because the basic land records for any town are simply a chronological compilation of all types of documents received for recording, the grantor/grantee index makes it easier to trace a specific parcel's chain of title to pinpoint the volume and page number of a given transaction. While these lists may not seem important in a small hamlet recording only half a dozen documents a day, they are extremely valuable in a large city, where up to 1,000 or more documents may be entered in a single business day.

Day Book

There is sometimes a few days' time lapse between the recording of a document and the town clerk's indexing it in the grantor/grantee lists. Such documents are catalogued in a day book. When searching for information on real estate transactions, the day book should always be referred to, along with the grantor/grantee lists.

Change of Name or Status

If an individual or corporate owner of real estate undergoes a change of name or status—for example, a business merger—such change must be filed and recorded with the town clerk of the town where the real estate is located within 60 days from the date of such change.

Lost Titles

If a dispute arises over a land title and the person claiming rightful title has lost or misplaced his or her original deed, a copy of this deed from the public records will serve as prima facie evidence of the title.[5] This points out the importance and value of the recording requirement.

■ EVIDENCE OF TITLE

In Connecticut the purchaser assumes the responsibility to have title searches conducted or surveys completed. These searches are usually carried out by attorneys, and their cost is borne by the individual commissioning the search. However, there is no law requiring that the purchaser actually conduct a title search; it is merely in his or her best interest to have one done. If the purchaser finances the property, banking laws *do require* that a title search be conducted by an attorney.

Certificate of Title

The most common form of title search used in Connecticut is the attorney's certificate of title. The certificate of title generally includes a brief opinion about the marketability of the title and lists any encumbrances that the examining counsel has identified—utility easements, sewer liens, and so on. While not as detailed as an abstract, certificates of title are acceptable in the majority of real estate conveyances. A copy of a typical certificate of title appears in this chapter (Figure 9.1).

Abstract of Title

Quite obviously, if a particular conveyance involves a more intricate chain of title, the lender may require either an abstract or a title insurance policy. An abstract is a far more detailed summary of the chain of title and would be the preferred method of title search when there is some question about the "quality" of the title and the purchaser is seeking to remove this "cloud" on the title.

Title Search Preparation

If the purchaser is paying cash or the seller is providing any needed financing by taking back a purchase-money mortgage, the purchaser's attorney, at the purchaser's request, will conduct the title search. If the purchaser obtains a mortgage from a financial institution as a portion of his or her financing package, Connecticut statutes require that a title search (or at least a certificate of title) be prepared. The bank's closing attorney customarily conducts this search.[6] Note that the bank's closing attorney and the purchaser's attorney are usually the same person. In the first instance, where the purchaser is paying cash, the search would be conducted exclusively on behalf of the purchaser. In the second case, where the purchaser has a mortgage from a bank, the search would benefit both the purchaser and the bank.

Regardless of whether a certificate of title or complete abstract is prepared, such searches are not absolute guarantees of clear title. The complexity of real estate conveyances often leaves room for error in the most diligent title searches.

F I G U R E 9.1

Certificate of Title

TITLE RECORD S13-5

CERTIFICATE OF TITLE

Storrs, Connecticut
October 11, 2004

To: Mansfield Federal Savings and Loan Association
33 Storrs Road
Storrs, CT 06268

THIS IS TO CERTIFY that I have examined the title to the premises situated on the southerly side of Merrow Road in Mansfield, Connecticut, and being known as Lot No. 19 in the "GLENWOOD ACRES" Subdivision, and being more particularly described in a certain Mortgage Deed from Samuel L. and Patricia D. Jones to the Mansfield Federal Savings and Loan Association, Storrs, CT, dated October 9, 1990, and recorded in Volume 120, Page 89 of the Mansfield Land Records, and I am of the opinion that said mortgagors have a good and sufficient title thereto of record, free and clear of all recorded and property indexed encumbrances, except:

1. Any and all provisions of any ordinance, municipal regulations, and public or private law.

2. Taxes to become due the Town of Mansfield on the List of October 1, 2003.

3. A possible pole line easement in favor of the Connecticut Light and Power Company more fully appearing of record.

4. A mortgage in the original principal amount of $182,000 from Samuel L. and Patricia D. Jones to the Mansfield Federal Savings and Loan Association, Storrs, CT, dated October 9, 1990, and recorded on October 11, 1990, in Volume 120, Page 89 of the Mansfield Land Records.

5. Any statement of facts that an accurate survey may disclose.

Clarence Darrow
Attorney at Law

Title Searching

Searching a title is a complicated procedure that involves not only knowing what public records to look to but also the legal implication of many real estate–related documents. A full title search should be performed only by someone experienced and qualified to do so.

In general, title searching involves looking up the records of transactions in the grantor/grantee indexes and referring to copies of actual documents in the volumes. To begin a title search, one would look up the name of the current owner of the property (this can be obtained from the street cards in the tax assessor's office if it is not known) under the grantee index for the time of conveyance. The seller to the current owner would be referred to as the *grantor*. You would then find the seller's immediate predecessor in title by looking up the seller's name in the grantee index. This process of searching back in time would be continued until the original owner of the property was found. You would then need to search forward through the grantor indexes for each owner of the property for the time he or she held the property to find any mortgages, liens, and recorded interests of others. The last step would be to check the day book for any documents affecting the title to the property that are not yet indexed in the grantor/grantee indexes.

Title Insurance

Title insurance is used when certificates of title or abstracts are insufficient to offset the risks of potentially faulty titles. In Connecticut financial institutions are the largest users of title insurance. Title insurance usually is required on all real estate title transfers, including single-family conveyances. Lending institutions set their own requirements regarding the need for title insurance and its coverage. Many national title insurance companies, as well as a statewide attorney's title guaranty fund, operate within the state.

Torrens System

Connecticut does not recognize or employ the Torrens system or any other system of land title registration.

■ MARKETABLE RECORD TITLE ACT

A marketable record title is one that is unbroken for a period of 40 years.[7] However, this does not mean that an owner must possess the property for 40 years before he or she has marketable record title. Instead it means that the chain of title must be traced back at least 40 years without encountering a "break," for example, some unverified conveyance, encumbrance, or other interest. Establishing a marketable record title does not extinguish other valid recorded interests or those arising out of transactions that occurred before the root of title, such as mortgages, restrictions, and so on. (*Example:* A mortgage with a 50-year term is recorded 41 years ago. A deed conveying the property free of the mortgage is recorded 40 years ago. Under the Marketable Record Title Act, the mortgage would be extinguished.) Certain interests are excepted from the act's operation (i.e., government entities, certain easements).

Marketable record title is, however, the best and most desirable form of title. Notice of claim to an interest in land must be recorded within the 40-year period to remain effective against the property. If an individual has held a parcel of land for 40 years, during which time no transactions involving the parcel have taken place and no claims of interest have been filed and recorded against it, the owner's period of possession is enough to establish marketable record title in most cases if the owner's root of title is clear. An attorney's title search generally indicates the degree to which a title is considered marketable or the limitations to its marketability if it is not completely free of encumbrances.

Native American land claims.   Since the Mashantucket Native Americans have struck it rich with a casino in Ledyard, many recognized and unrecognized Indian tribes throughout the state have been making legal claims to old tribal lands. Many of these lands were conveyed by the Native Americans or governing bodies back in the 1700s and 1800s and have for many years been owned by private individuals. Obviously, the Native Americans' claims to lands have sent shivers of fear into the hearts of many private property owners and have resulted in questions as to why the Marketable Record Title Act or adverse possession would not defeat the Native Americans' claims. Basically, this is because Native American title is a matter of federal law and cannot be extinguished without federal consent (even by a conveyance by the Native Americans).[8] State statutes dealing with the marketable title, adverse possession, or the like cannot be enforced against the federal law mandates.

■ ENDNOTES

1. Section 47-10 of the Connecticut General Statutes.
2. *French v. Gray* (1816) 2 Conn. 92; and *Smith v. Starkweather* (1811) S Day 207.
3. *Sadd v. Heim* (1956) 124 A. 2d 522, 143 Conn. 582; and *Ashley Realty Company v. Metropolitan District* (1944) 13 Conn. Supp. 91, error on other grounds 46 A. 2d 13, 1323. Conn. 551.
4. 13 Conn. 376, 35 Am. Dec. 83 (1840).
5. *Kelsey v. Hanmer* (1847) 18 Conn. 311.
6. See *Connecticut General Statutes Title 36, Sections 99 and 178* for more information regarding these underwriting requirements.
7. See Section 47-33b et seq. of the Connecticut General Statutes.
8. See the Indian Nonintercourse Act, 25 USCA Section 177.

QUESTIONS

1. Max has recorded his deed to 180 Shore Drive in the land records. The primary purpose of this recording is to
   a. enforce the transfer.
   b. give others constructive notice of the transfer.
   c. give others actual notice of the transfer.
   d. give notice to the town clerk of the transfer.

2. Dana enters into a purchase and sale contract to buy a house on October 15. The closing occurs on November 15, at which time the seller delivers the deed. The deed is recorded on November 17. Dana moves into the property on November 18. In Connecticut, title would have passed from the seller to Dana on
   a. October 15.
   b. November 15.
   c. November 17.
   d. November 18.

3. What types of documents are required to be recorded in the land records?
   a. Only deeds
   b. Only deeds and mortgages
   c. All documents affecting the title to real property
   d. All legal documents

4. Deeds must be recorded in the land records within _____ of the date of conveyance.
   a. a reasonable time
   b. one business day
   c. three business days
   d. one month

5. The local official who records deeds and maintains the grantor/grantee lists in Connecticut is the
   a. first selectman.
   b. assessor.
   c. tax collector.
   d. town clerk.

6. A certificate of title is a
   a. brief opinion about the marketability of the title.
   b. guarantee of clear title.
   c. guarantee of marketable title.
   d. summary of the chain of title.

7. To establish a "marketable record title," an unbroken chain of title must be established for a period of at least
   a. 15 years.   c. 40 years.
   b. 20 years.   d. 60 years.

8. In the event of a lost or misplaced title, a copy of the recorded title document from the public records
   a. is inadmissible in a court of law.
   b. indicates only equitable title.
   c. is prima facie evidence of title.
   d. is deemed useless.

9. Any change of name or status of an individual or corporate owner of real estate must be recorded with the town clerk in the town where the real estate is located within
   a. 30 days.   c. 90 days.
   b. 60 days.   d. 180 days.

10. Connecticut land records are indexed through
    a. a Torrens system.
    b. lot, block, map numbers.
    c. the location of the property.
    d. grantor/grantee indexes.

CHAPTER TEN

REAL ESTATE LICENSE LAWS

■ OVERVIEW

The Connecticut law governing the licensing and conduct of real estate brokers and salespeople is Title 20, Chapter 392 of the Connecticut General Statutes. These laws are enforced by the Connecticut Real Estate Commission, which is part of the Department of Consumer Protection. The Commission also enacts and enforces regulations relating to the interpretation of these laws.

WWWeb.Link

Connecticut real estate licensing laws, updated through January 1, 2003, can be found at *www.cga.state.ct.us/2003/pub/Chap392.htm.* Connecticut offers an online, searchable database of licensing requirements, information, and forms, including real estate and appraisal licensing at *www.ct-clic.com.* Additionally, Connecticut intends to provide an online licensing site to renew licenses, check the status of an application for new license, download rosters of current license holders, and verify the status, complaint, and discipline history of all active licenses at *www.dcpaccess.state.ct.us.*

Connecticut also requires licensure or certification of real estate appraisers. Real estate brokers and salespersons are allowed to estimate the value of real estate as part of a market analysis for the owner, as long as the value estimate is not referred to as an appraisal and any fee paid in valuing a one- to four-family residence is credited against future compensation owed the salesperson or broker. The law governing licensure, certification, and conduct of appraisers, as well as this exemption for real estate brokers and salespersons, is discussed in Chapter 13.

Real property securities dealers must hold a real estate broker's license in Connecticut. The license law contains specific provisions covering their operations and licensing. Details of the law in this area can be found in Appendix A.

In Connecticut, the validity of the real estate license law has been challenged on the basis of its constitutionality and alleged denial of due process. However, the courts have held the license law to be a legitimate exercise of police power when utilized to promote the general welfare of the citizenry. In two landmark cases, the license law was contested and proven to be constitutionally valid on the premise of police power.[1] Although the licensing requirement excludes some people from acting as brokers and salespeople, such exclusion does protect the general public from incompetent and unscrupulous operators.

■ WHO MUST BE LICENSED (SECTIONS 20-312 AND 20-325)

Any person, partnership, association, limited liability company, or corporation *engaging in the real estate business* must have a license to do so, and any person who engages in the business of a real estate broker or salesperson without a license may be fined and/or imprisoned.

**Definitions
(Section 20-311)**

Real Estate Broker—A real estate broker is any person who, for another and for a fee, commission, or other valuable consideration, performs, offers to perform, or attempts to perform any of the following activities pertaining to an estate or interest in real property:

- Lists real estate for sale
- Sells real estate
- Exchanges real estate
- Buys real estate
- Rents or collects rent for the use of real estate
- Resells a mobile home

Any person *acting for another and for a fee*, commission, or other valuable consideration, who performs or offers or attempts to perform any of these activities is *engaging in the real estate business*.

Real Estate Salesperson—A real estate salesperson is defined as any person *employed* by a real estate broker or *affiliated* with a real estate broker as an independent contractor who performs or offers or attempts to perform any of the aforesaid activities on behalf of a real estate broker. The broker must be licensed in all cases, and the activity must pertain to estates or interests in real property. Any person performing the activities described for properties owned by the broker is considered to be a real estate salesperson.

Person—A person includes individuals, partnerships, associations, limited liability companies, or corporations.

**Exceptions
(Section 20-329)**

The following persons are exempted from the licensing requirement:

- The clerical or custodial employees of a real estate broker (Section 20-311 of the Connecticut General Statutes)
- Owners/lessors of real property who are not primarily in the real estate business, or their employees who are employed as on-site residential superintendents or custodians when any real estate activities are

conducted in the regular course of their business (the Commission has interpreted this law as requiring all of the following conditions for the exception to apply: the individual must (1) be a regular employee, (2) be employed as a superintendent or custodian, (3) work on a residential site where he or she engages in licensed activities, and (4) reside at the location where he or she works and engages in those licensed activities)[2]

- Attorneys at law when serving as legal counsel to their clients
- Receivers, trustees in bankruptcy, administrators, executors, or other fiduciaries, while acting as such
- Persons selling real estate under court order
- Trustees acting under a trust agreement, deed of trust, or will and their regular salaried employees
- Witnesses in court attesting to the value of real estate, who are exempt from brokerage license but must be licensed as appraisers
- Government employees acting within the scope of their regular employment responsibilities
- Any employee of any nonprofit housing corporation that manages a housing project assisted in whole or in part by the federal government pursuant to Section 8 of the United States Housing Act of 1937, as amended, while performing such duties

CONNECTICUT REAL ESTATE COMMISSION (SECTION 20-311a)

The Connecticut Real Estate Commission exists within the Department of Consumer Protection. The commission makeup is as follows:

- eight members—five in real estate business (three licensed brokers and two licensed salespersons); and three members of the public;
- at least one member from each congressional district; and
- not more than a bare majority from same political party.

Commission members are not paid for their services but are reimbursed for necessary expenses incurred in the performance of their duties.

Members of the commission

- are appointed by the governor;
- take an oath to perform faithfully the prescribed duties; and
- may be removed from office for cause by the governor after being given an opportunity to be heard.

Seats vacated through resignation, death, or removal are filled by appointees of the governor.

Duties of the Real Estate Commission (Sections 20-311b and 20-326)

The commission's foremost duty is to apply and enforce the license law pertaining to the real estate business. Within 30 days after the appointment of the members, the commission must meet and select a chairperson and any other officers needed to accomplish its obligations. A majority of the members constitutes a quorum.

The commission, under the aegis of the Department of Consumer Protection, issues licenses, arbitrates disputes between brokers and salespersons, formulates and enforces rules and regulations, and administers all the provisions of real estate business. It must also keep records of all its activities and submit an annual report to the governor.

Approval of Schools (Section 20-314a)

The commission also evaluates schools offering real estate courses and real estate–related subjects and approves schools offering courses that fulfill the prelicensing educational requirement and continuing education requirements discussed later in this chapter. Students taking nonapproved courses may not be considered for licensing.

Bonding (Section 20-311d)

The chairperson of the commission must be bonded in accordance with the requirements of the State Insurance Purchasing Board.

Deposit of Fees (Section 20-311e)

All fees collected by the commission must be deposited with the state treasurer (except the portion of license fees payable to the University of Connecticut in conjunction with the operation of the Center for Real Estate and Urban Economic Studies).

■ LICENSING PROCEDURE

A summary of the licensing requirements can be found at Table 10.1. The following text goes into a little greater detail on the requirements.

Applications (Sections 20-313 and 20-314)

Application for a real estate license must be made in writing on forms prescribed by the commission. The commission may request information to assure itself of the applicant's honesty, truthfulness, integrity, and competency. Applications for a broker's license must be accompanied by a nonrefundable $60 application fee, and those for a salesperson's license by a $40 application fee.

Any individual who willfully misrepresents any facts required to be disclosed on the application or in any other document to be filed with the commission in connection with the application for a license may be fined up to $500, imprisoned up to six months, or both.

Examinations (Section 20-314)

The license law states that applicants for either a broker's or salesperson's license must pass a written examination before a license can be issued. While the statute does not prescribe the topics to be covered or the nature of the examination, the information packet sent to all applicants indicates the following areas of study for persons taking either the broker's or salesperson's examination:

■ *Real Estate Contracts, Ownership, and Other Legal Aspects*—Essential elements of contracts and specific contracts used, including leases, listing agreements, sales contracts, and options; deeds, interests in property,

Connecticut Real Estate Brokers and Salespersons Requirements Summary

	Broker	Salesperson
Education	30 hours—Real Estate Principles and Practices (this changes to 60 hours on October 1, 2004) 30 hours—Real Estate Appraisal 30 hours—Other Real Estate Course	30 hours—Real Estate Principles and Practices (this changes to 60 hours on October 1, 2004)
Experience	2 years experience as a Real Estate Salesperson	None
Testing	Broker's Licensing Exam (score of 75% or better)	Salesperson's Licensing Exam (score of 70% or better)
Sponsor	No	Yes (by a broker)
Minimum Age	18	18
Renewal	March 31, annually	May 31, annually
Continuing Education	12 hours every two years including 3 hours in Real Estate Law/Fair Housing	12 hours every two years including 3 hours in Real Estate Law/Fair Housing
FEES Application	$60	$40
Testing	$65	$65
Initial Year	$450	$225
Renewal	$300	$225
Continuing Education Processing Fee (Biennial)	$8	$8
Guaranty Fee (One time)		$20
Change of Employment	n/a	$25

condominiums, and fair housing acts; land-use controls, public powers, and property ownership

■ *Real Estate Valuation and Mathematics*—Principles of value and approaches to estimating value; appraisal terminology; property descriptions, taxes, and assessments; ability to work with numbers in calculating real estate issues

■ *Real Estate Finance and Investment*—Financial institutions; sources of financing, including governmental agencies; financing instruments and financing arrangements; loans and mortgages; tax ramifications

■ *Real Estate Brokerage*—Law of agency and fiduciary responsibilities; property management, including property maintenance, collecting rents, and general scope and functions; settlement procedures, including the Real Estate Settlement Procedures Act (RESPA); listing and showing property; compliance with the federal Fair Housing Act

Connecticut real estate licensing examinations are administered by PSI Real Estate Licensing Examination Services, Glendale, California. The uniform portion of the examination consists of 80 questions on both the broker's and salesperson's examinations. The Connecticut portion of the licensing examination consists of 30 questions on the salesperson's examination and 40 questions on the broker's examination. The Connecticut portion of the examination includes questions based on the Connecticut Real Estate Licensing Law and Regulations, Guaranty Fund, Fair Housing, Escrow Account Responsibilities, Real Properties Securities/Syndication, Interstate Land Sales Disclosure Act, Common Interest Ownership Act, and Landlord/Tenant Regulations. Applicants taking the examination administered by PSI are required to pay fees covering the cost of the examination directly to the testing service. This fee is separate from the application fee.

As soon as the prospective licensee's application has been approved by the commission and the applicant has received a certificate of Examination Eligibility, the applicant may register with PSI to sit for the exam. PSI has exam sites in West Hartford and Norwalk. Only applicants who have received a Certificate of Examination Eligibility from the Real Estate Commission may take the exam.

WWWeb.Link

A PSI Connecticut candidate information bulletin can be found at *www.psiexams.com.*

Failures (Section 20-314(c))

Applicants are notified on site of the examination results from PSI. If an applicant fails, he or she is eligible to retake the examination. Each payment of the $60 for brokers or $40 for salespeople *license application fee entitles the applicant to take the Real Estate Licensing Examination four times within a one-year period.* After taking the examination for the first time, however, the applicant *must pay an additional sum for a retake examination.*

Fees (Sections 20-314(f), 20-319(b), and 20-319(a))

Initial license applications must be submitted with nonrefundable application fees of $60 for brokers and $40 for salespersons. The fee for taking the examination is paid directly to PSI. In addition, every new licensee must make a one-time payment of *$20 to the Real Estate Guaranty Fund,* which is discussed later in the chapter. Initial licensee fees may be prorated by the commission if issued midyear (based on the license renewal year).

The commission pays a portion of both brokers' and salespersons' license fees to the University of Connecticut to operate the Center for Real Estate and Urban Economic Studies. The Center was established in 1965 at the university to

- conduct studies in real estate and urban economics and publish and disseminate the findings and results of these studies;
- support the degree-oriented teaching programs in real estate and urban economics offered by the university;
- assist the Connecticut Real Estate Commission in its licensing and educational programming; and
- assist the noncredit programs in real estate at the university.

License Issued (Sections 20-314, 20-316, and 20-318)

Once an individual meets all the commission's requirements and passes the license examination, he or she is issued a license on payment of the appropriate fees. Once licensed, the applicant is entitled to perform all the acts of a real estate broker or salesperson as described earlier in this chapter.

For a fee of $25, the commission will issue a certificate to each licensee stating the licensee is licensed. Although a licensee may be asked to produce a certificate, the law does not require that it be publicly displayed.

Grounds for Refusal of a License (Section 20-316)

Even though an applicant has passed the license examination and produced the required character references, there are still circumstances under which the application could be refused or the license withheld. The commission will generally refuse to issue a license to any applicant who

- has been refused a real estate broker's or salesperson's license in any state within the year preceding the current application;
- has had a real estate broker's or salesperson's license revoked in any state within the year preceding the current application; and
- is not yet 18 years old.

Any applicant who is refused a license will be notified and given an opportunity for a hearing according to regulations established by the Commissioner of the Department of Consumer Protection.

Convicted felons.   In 1973 the state amended its statutes barring convicted felons from either state employment or licensure. For this reason, the commission will not automatically refuse to issue a license to any applicant who has been convicted of forgery, embezzlement, extortion, obtaining money under false pretenses, criminal conspiracy to defraud, or any similar offenses. The commission also will not automatically deny a license to any partnership or corporation of which a person convicted of such crimes is a member or stockholder with a controlling interest.

Section 46a-80 of the Connecticut General Statutes provides that the commission must take into consideration all of the following points in the case of any such applicant:

- the nature of the crime and its relationship to the job for which the person applied;
- information pertaining to the degree of rehabilitation of the convicted person;
- the amount of time that has elapsed since the applicant's conviction or release;

After considering these points, the commission may determine the applicant's suitability for a real estate license.

Note that these provisions relating to the grounds for refusing a license apply to all applicants, including those who were actively engaged in the real estate business before the license law and regulations were enacted.

Licensing Corporations and Other Entities (Section 20-312)

Any business firm—corporation, partnership, or association—applying for a broker's license must designate one individual to serve as the firm's broker under the license. A firm must submit two applications to the commission, one in the firm's name and the second in the firm designee's name. Both the designee's and the firm's applications must be accompanied by an application fee and a guaranty fund fee. The firm must also submit a certified copy of its articles of incorporation.

Once the firm's designee has met all of the licensure requirements, the commission will issue a license to the firm. This license entitles the individual designated in the application to perform all the acts of a real estate broker on behalf of the firm. The firm's license does not entitle other members or officers to engage in the brokerage business. *Every member or officer of the firm who actively participates in the brokerage business must qualify for and obtain a broker's license, and every employee or independent contractor who acts as salesperson for the firm must have a salesperson's license.* The designated broker also has the option of holding an individual license as well as serving as the designated broker for the firm.

Licensing Nonresidents (Section 20-317)

Any nonresident may obtain a Connecticut real estate broker's or salesperson's license by meeting all the requirements of Chapter 392. The commission does, however, recognize a *reciprocal licensing agreement* with certain other states. As of the writing of this edition, those states were Alabama, Colorado, Georgia, Illinois, Massachusetts, Mississippi, Nebraska, New York, North Carolina, Ohio, Oklahoma, and Rhode Island.

Under this agreement the commission may grant a license to a licensed broker or salesperson from a state that *requires license applicants to pass a written examination and grants the same reciprocity to Connecticut real estate licensees.* However, the licensure requirements of the reciprocal state must be substantially similar to or higher than the requirements in Connecticut. A nonresident licensee/applicant from a state that does NOT have reciprocity with Connecticut is required to pass the Connecticut portion of the real estate examination.

All nonresident applicants must file with the commission an *irrevocable consent to suit.* This consent enables suits and actions to be brought against the nonresident licensee in Connecticut as though he or she were a resident licensee. Notice of process may be served on the commission chairperson (against the nonresident licensee) only if a duplicate copy is provided to be forwarded by registered or certified mail to the nonresident licensee's last-known address. No judgment by default (because the nonresident has not appeared) can be brought until 20 days after the process was mailed.

Nonresident holders of license-by-reciprocity who become Connecticut residents have a valid Connecticut license and are not required to qualify with course, experience, and examination requirements in order to maintain the validity of their license.[3]

■ GENERAL OPERATION OF A REAL ESTATE BUSINESS

The Connecticut license law and regulations *do not* require that a real estate licensee maintain a definite place of business or display either a license or a sign indicating that the licensee is a real estate broker or salesperson.

Care of Licenses (Sections 20-314, 20-319, 20-319a, 20-322, and 20-328-10a)

License renewal.   All real estate licenses expire annually and are renewable on payment of the appropriate fee. Brokers' licenses expire on March 31; salespersons' licenses expire on May 31. The commission has the authority to change the expiration date.[4]

If, for any reason, the license is not renewed on request, the fee is returned. All renewal refusals by the commission are written and may be challenged on the licensee's written request for a hearing or appeal according to the regulations established by the commissioner of the Department of Consumer Protection.

As long as a licensee has all the qualifications specified by the law and has complied with all the regulations of Chapter 392, his or her license must be renewed. Even inactive members of the brokerage community may not be denied renewal.

Continuing education requirements.   To renew a license in even-numbered years, the licensee must show that

■ he or she successfully completed a course or courses, approved by the commission, of continuing education in current real estate practices and licensing laws consisting of not less than 12 hours of classroom study during the two-year period preceding renewal (the Connecticut Real Estate Commission specifies that one 3-hour module on Connecticut Real Estate License Law/Fair Housing is required as part of the 12-hour continuing education courses, and for the 2003-2004 CE cycle one 3-hour module must be in Real Estate Agency); *or*

■ he or she passed a personal written examination during the two-year period preceding such renewal (this examination may be prepared by the commission or a national testing service); *or*

■ he or she has equivalent continuing education experience or study as determined by the commissioner of the Department of Consumer Protection.

Continuing education courses may be offered and taken in a distance education/online format. The continuing education renewal requirement creates a uniform level of expertise among licensed real estate practitioners. The main purpose for the continuing education requirements is to ensure that the general public is receiving the highest level of service possible.

Change of employment.   A licensed real estate salesperson who transfers employment from one broker to another must register this change with the commission and pay a $25 transfer fee. Furthermore, upon any termination of a salesperson's employment (or broker working for a broker), he or she must return to the broker all records and information collected during such employment. Within ten days of the return of such information (or within 45 days of the termination of the relationship), the broker shall give the salesperson a written account of all active listing agreements, agency agreements, transactions, and commissions and compensation involving the salesperson. The accounting must include a statement of the commission or compensation that the broker intends to pay the salesperson.

■ REGULATIONS

Regulations for Conduct of Brokers and Salespeople (Sections 20-328-1a through 10a)

The license law empowers the commissioner of the Department of Consumer Protection with advice and assistance from the commission to make any reasonable regulations necessary relating to the form and manner of filing applications for licenses and the manner in which licensees conduct the brokerage business. The regulations are summarized here and organized according to topic.

Definitions (Sections 20-328-1a through 10a)

Blockbusting—To induce or attempt to induce a person to sell or rent a dwelling because a minority group member (based on a protected classification) is moving in.

Broker—Same as defined in Section 20-311(1).

Licensee—Real estate broker or salesperson licensed in Connecticut.

Net Listing—A listing contract in which the broker receives whatever exceeds the net price agreed on between the seller and broker.

Salesperson—Same as defined in Section 20-311(2).

Steering—To restrict or attempt to restrict the choices of a person by word or action when seeking, negotiating for, buying, or renting a dwelling because of a protected classification.

Duties to Parties (Section 20-328-2a)

- A licensee shall disclose to all parties concerned his or her present or contemplated interest in a property.
- The licensee shall disclose to the buyer or seller any relationship that exists to the seller or buyer, such as immediate family member or member of the same real estate firm.
- All exclusive-right-to-sell and exclusive-agency agreements require that the agent *make a diligent effort to sell the property*.
- An exclusive buyer or lessee agency agreement requires that the agent *make a diligent offer to find a property* within the prospective buyer's or lessee's specifications.
- All offers must include essential terms and conditions, including the manner in which the purchase is to be financed or a clause conditioned on later execution of a bond for deed or a complete agreement for sale.
- Offers received shall be submitted to the licensee's client as quickly as possible.

- Unless agreed otherwise, the listing broker or buyer's broker is not obligated to market the property after an offer or counteroffer has been accepted.
- A licensee cannot negotiate directly with another licensee's client, unless the other licensee consents or *a diligent effort is made to contact the other licensee without success.*
- No sign shall be placed on the property without the written consent of the owner.
- All brokers shall cooperate with all other brokers when it is in the best interest of the client.

Duty To Cooperate (Section 20-328-3a)

A licensee shall cooperate truthfully with the Department of Consumer Protection, Real Estate Division, staff personnel in investigating a possible violation of the statutes.

Discrimination and Fair Housing (Section 20-328-4a)

A licensee shall neither deny equal professional services to any person nor be party to any plan to discriminate against a person on the basis of race, color, creed, sex, age, physical, mental or learning disability, ethnic or national origin, marital status, sexual orientation, lawful source of income, or familial status. No licensee shall participate in blockbusting or steering. All representation agreements must include the statement: "This agreement is subject to the Connecticut General Statutes prohibiting discrimination in commercial and residential real estate transactions (CGS Title 46a, Chapter 814c)."

"Psychologically impacted property" (Section 20-329cc through Section 20-329ee).

Brokers, salespeople (including buyer agents), and owners are not liable to buyers or tenants for failure to disclose that a property was occupied by a person who was HIV-positive or had AIDS or that a suicide, murder, or other felony occurred on the property. However, if a purchaser/tenant advises the owner or licensee in writing that psychological information is important to their decision, then the owner or licensee does have a duty to disclose in writing any knowledge about whether a suicide, murder, or other felony occurred on the property (but not HIV-status of persons that have lived there). The owner and licensee never has a duty to disclose the HIV-status of previous occupants, and in fact such disclosure may be in violation of state and federal fair housing law.

Effective October 1, 2004, this law changes. Sellers, landlords, and licensees will not be liable for failure to disclose a "nonmaterial fact," which is a fact related to whether a property occupant has or had a disease listed by the Public Health Commissioner, or the fact that there was a death or felony on the property.

Misrepresentation, Disclosure, and Advertising (Section 20-328-5a)

Real estate advertising is broadly defined to include all forms of identification, representation, promotion, and solicitation disseminated in any manner and by any means of communication to the public for any purpose related to licensed real estate activity. A licensee must abide by the following rules.

- A licensee shall not misrepresent or conceal *any material fact.*
- The actual selling price must be properly and accurately represented.

- A licensee is required to diligently obtain and present accurate information in advertisements and other representations to the public. No blind ads are allowed. Full disclosure of the broker's name is required.
- An agent of the seller, buyer, lessor, or lessee shall make a written disclosure of whom he or she represents in the transaction to prospective purchasers. This disclosure is attached to any offer or agreement to purchase or lease. See Chapter 1 for a complete discussion of these disclosure requirements.
- To advertise property listed with another broker, the licensee must get permission of the other broker. That listing information can't be changed in any way without the permission of the other broker, and must be updated at least every 72 hours.
- Internet advertising must include, on every page of the site, the licensee's name and office address, the name of the real estate broker the licensee is affiliated with, all states where the licensee is licensed, and the last date when the site property information has been updated.
- Any electronic communication, including e-mail and bulletin board postings, must contain the following information on the first or last page of the communication: licensee's name and office address, the name of the real estate broker the licensee is affiliated with, and all states where the licensee is licensed.

**Agreements
(Section 20-328-6a)**

A written contract between the licensee and party the licensee is representing is required before any attempt can be made to negotiate a sale, exchange, purchase, or lease. This written agreement shall correctly identify the property and contain all terms and conditions including compensation to be paid, beginning and expiration dates, and signatures and addresses of all parties concerned. If the contract is with the owner, the type of listing must be clearly disclosed in writing. Refer to Chapter 2 for further information on agency representation agreements.

**Deposits, Escrow
and Trust Account
(Sections 20-328-7a
and 20-324k)**

When a licensee receives deposits or other monies as part of the transaction, that licensee shall pay them *promptly* over to the broker. All monies accepted or held by a licensed broker on behalf of a principal or client must be placed in a trust or an escrow account. The account must be distinct and separate from the broker's personal account and maintained in a bank doing business in Connecticut.

Any funds accepted by the broker from a principal, client, or some other person to which the broker is not personally or legally entitled (including such items as down payment, earnest money, deposit, rental money, and rental security deposit) *must be deposited within three banking days from the date the agreement evidencing such transaction is signed by all necessary parties thereto.* Any broker who violates this section of the licensing law can be fined up to $2,000 or imprisoned up to six months or both. The commission reserves the right to inspect these accounts at any time.

Connecticut law provides for a procedure allowing a broker to hand over a deposit to a court when there is a dispute regarding the sale.

Interest Earned on Real Estate Deposits (Section 8-265f)

There is a program for the use of interest earned on real estate broker escrow or trust accounts. All brokers are required to participate and deposit down payment money in interest-bearing accounts specifically established for use in this program. The interest earned from these amounts shall be paid to the Connecticut Housing Finance Authority. This interest is used for mortgage assistance for first-time homebuyers and low-income and moderate-income families. A client *may request* that his or her deposit not be part of this program (regardless of amount of deposit or duration), in which case the deposit is to be put in a separate interest-bearing account.

Commissions and Compensation (Sections 20-325a, 20-325b, and 20-328-8a)

Compensation (either in the form of a commission or other type of fee) may not be shared with unlicensed persons engaging in the real estate business for another person, and no compensation may be demanded unless the licensee has reasonable cause for payment. Each written agreement that sets a compensation for the real estate broker for the consummated real estate transaction must contain the following statement in not less than ten-point boldface type (or in some manner that stands out significantly from the text preceding it):

NOTICE: THE AMOUNT OR RATE OF REAL ESTATE BROKER COMPENSATION IS NOT FIXED BY LAW. IT IS SET BY EACH BROKER INDIVIDUALLY AND MAY BE NEGOTIABLE BETWEEN YOU AND THE BROKER.

Additionally, the regulations specify the following about broker compensation:

■ A licensee shall receive compensation only when reasonable cause for such exists.
■ When a party fails to proceed with a transaction, the real estate broker has no right to any funds deposited with the broker, even though compensation may have been earned.
■ A licensee shall receive no compensation for expenditures made for his or her client without the knowledge and consent of the client.
■ Compensation from more than one party to a transaction cannot be accepted without all parties to the transaction agreeing to it prior to the closing.
■ No part of any real estate compensation can be given to a person who was nonlicensed at the time services were rendered.
■ A licensee must assign or pay over directly to his or her real estate broker all funds received from a transaction.
■ Real estate brokers cannot compensate another broker's salespersons directly. All compensations are paid to the real estate broker of the cooperating agency.

Agreements with Out-of-State Brokers

In general, an unlicensed person cannot engage in the real estate business in Connecticut, and a Connecticut licensee cannot share compensation with an unlicensed person engaging in the real estate business on behalf of another person. This means that a Connecticut licensee cannot share compensation with an out-of-state broker or salesperson that is licensed in another state, but not Connecticut. As of October 1, 2004, however, compensation can be shared with agents that are licensed in another state, but not Connecticut, in a commercial real estate transaction if various conditions are met, including that the out-of-state agent affiliate with a Connecticut licensed broker.

Referral Fees

Connecticut prohibits a broker from paying a referral fee to an unlicensed person or entity if that person or entity is engaging in the real estate business. To meet this license requirement, the person receiving the fee can be licensed in either Connecticut or another state.

A licensee cannot demand a referral fee, unless a reasonable cause for payment exists. Through policy guidance, the commission has stated that a reasonable cause for payment (which would allow a licensee to demand a referral fee) means that either:

- an actual introduction of business has been made;
- a subagency relationship exists;
- a contractual referral fee relationship exists; or
- a contractual cooperative brokerage relationship exists.

Interfering with Agency Relationships (Section 20-328-9a)

Connecticut prohibits a licensee from interfering with the agency relationship of another licensee. Further, a licensee is prohibited from advising a client of another licensee to break his or her agency contract with the other licensee. When interpreting these mandates, the commission has stated that an agency relationship is not established until a written agency agreement (either a listing or buyer agency agreement) is entered into.

The commission has defined interference with the agency relationship of another licensee to include

- demanding a referral fee from another licensee without reasonable cause;
- threatening to take harmful actions against the client of another licensee because of the agency relationship; and
- counseling a client of another licensee on how to terminate or amend an existing agency contract.

While relocation companies have to follow these rules also, the communication of corporate relocation policies or benefits to a transferring employee is not considered interference, provided that the communication does not involve advice or encouragement on how to terminate or amend an existing agency contract.

■ SUSPENSION OR REVOCATION OF A LICENSE (SECTION 20-320)

The commission has the power to suspend temporarily or revoke permanently the license of any broker or salesperson and/or impose a fine of up to $2,000, if it finds that the licensee (or person fraudulently obtaining a license) is guilty of any of the following activities:

- Making any material misrepresentation
- Making any false promise of a character likely to influence, persuade, or induce
- Acting for more than one party in a transaction without the knowledge of all parties for whom the licensee acts
- Representing or attempting to represent a real estate broker other than the licensee's employer or the broker with whom the licensee is affiliated, without the express knowledge and consent of the licensee's employer or affiliated broker
- Failing to account for or remit within a reasonable time any monies coming into the licensee's possession that belong to others
- Entering into an exclusive-listing contract or buyer-agency contract that provides for an automatic extension of the contract beyond the stated termination date
- Failing to deliver immediately a copy of any instrument to any party executing it, when the licensee has prepared or supervised the preparation of the instrument and the instrument relates to the licensee's employment or to any real estate transaction with which the licensee is involved
- Being convicted in a court of competent jurisdiction in any state of forgery, embezzlement, obtaining money under false pretenses, larceny, extortion, conspiracy to defraud, or other like offense (In such cases the commission must consider the circumstances as provided by Section 46a-80, which is discussed earlier in this chapter under "Convicted felons.")
- Collecting compensation in advance of services to be performed and failing, on the demand of the person paying the compensation or the commission, to account for this money
- Commingling funds of others with the licensee's own, or failing to keep these funds in an escrow or a trust account
- Performing any act or conduct that constitutes dishonest, fraudulent, or improper dealings
- Failing to provide agency disclosures as required by Section 20-325c
- Violating any provision of the license law or any of the commission's regulations

The commission may suspend or revoke a license on its own initiative or in response to a verified written complaint that supplies evidence and documentation to warrant the commission's action.

Prior Notice and Hearing (Section 20-321)

Before refusing, suspending, or revoking a license or imposing any fine, the commission must notify the licensee of the charges. The licensee will be given the opportunity of a hearing as provided in the regulations established by the commissioner of the Department of Consumer Protection.

Appeals to Commission Rulings (Section 20-322)

Any person who feels that the commission's decisions, orders, or regulations are unfair or unjust may appeal to the superior court for the New Britain judicial district or the judicial district in which he or she resides. Any corporation aggrieved by such decisions, orders, or regulations must appeal to the superior court for the New Britain judicial district or the judicial district in which it maintains its principal place of business. For additional information see Title 4, Section 4-183 of the Connecticut General Statutes on "Appeal to the Superior Court."

License Revocation on Conviction of Crime (Section 20-323)

Any licensee who is convicted of any of the offenses (forgery, embezzlement, and so on) listed in the preceding section, "Suspension or Revocation of a License," forfeits his or her license and all fees paid in connection with it. The clerk of the court in which the conviction takes place must forward a certified copy of the conviction to the commission. Within ten days after receiving this notice, the commission will notify the licensee in writing that his or her license has been revoked. Any application for reinstatement must conform to the requirements of Section 46a-80, which is discussed earlier in this chapter under "Convicted felons."

■ REAL ESTATE GUARANTY FUND (SECTION 20-324a)

The license law directs and authorizes the commission to maintain a Real Estate Guaranty Fund from which persons may recover compensation if they are aggrieved by the following actions of licensed real estate brokers, salespeople, or unlicensed employees of any broker:

- The embezzlement of money or property
- Obtaining money or property from persons by false pretenses, trickery, or forgery
- Fraud, misrepresentation, or deceit by or on the part of the licensed broker, salesperson, or unlicensed employee of the broker

The maximum compensation paid in connection with any single claim or transaction is $25,000, regardless of the number of persons aggrieved or parcels of real estate involved.

Maintaining the Fund (Sections 20-324b and 20-324c)

Any person who obtains a real estate broker's or salesperson's license for the first time must pay a one-time fee to the Real Estate Guaranty Fund in the amount of $20. By state law, this fee as well as $3 of each annual license renewal fee and all fines imposed against licensees for certain unethical or illegal acts must be credited to the fund. The level of this fund shall not exceed $500,000.

Recovery from the Fund

Time limitations on actions to recover (Section 20-324d). Any actions that might involve subsequent recovery from the guaranty fund must be initiated *no later than two years from the date of the final judgment or on expiration of time for an appeal.*

Procedure for recovery (Section 20-324e). To collect from the fund, an aggrieved person must sue the licensee or unlicensed employee and obtain a judgment against him or her. Any person commencing legal action that might involve a subsequent recovery from the guaranty fund must notify the commission, in writing, at the time the action is initiated. Once notified, the commission has the right to enter an appearance or intervene in or defend an action.

Recovery of a valid judgment.   Once the aggrieved person obtains a final judgment in court against the broker, salesperson, or unlicensed employee of the broker due to any of the misdeeds cited above, and the appeal period expires, the aggrieved person applies to the Real Estate Commission for an order directing payment from the Guaranty Fund. The commission then holds a hearing where the aggrieved person will be required to show certain matters, particularly that he has unsuccessfully tried to collect the judgment. If the aggrieved person makes a showing that is satisfactory to the commission, the commission will approve payment from the fund.

Revocation of License on Payment from Fund

When the commission makes a payment from the fund to satisfy a judgment claim, the license of the broker or salesperson whose actions were the cause of claim will automatically be revoked. The license will not be reissued until the person has repaid the entire sum, plus interest at a rate determined by the commission, to the guaranty fund. Bankruptcy does not extinguish this penalty.

Insufficient Money in the Guaranty Fund

In the event that the Real Estate Guaranty Fund does not contain sufficient money to honor a claim made against it, the commission will pay the claim to the extent of the existing money and satisfy the unpaid portion of the claim, plus 4 percent annual interest, as soon as sufficient money becomes available. Should there be more than one unsatisfied claim, they are paid in order of their filing dates.

Subrogation of the Judgment Creditor Rights (Section 20-324h)

Once it has made any payment from the guaranty fund, the commission is subrogated to (acquires by substitution) all the rights of the judgment creditor up to the amount that was paid from the fund. Any monies, including interest, subsequently recovered by the commission from the debtor must be deposited in the guaranty fund.

Penalties for False or Untrue Claims (Section 20-324f)

Any person who makes a false or untrue claim in the course of filing a notice, statement, or document relating to an action involving subsequent recovery from the guaranty fund may be fined $200 or more.

Procedure for the Commission (Section 20-324g)

As discussed in the paragraph on "Procedure for Recovery," when the commission receives a notice of actions involving the Real Estate Guaranty Fund, it may take whatever actions it deems necessary or appropriate on behalf of and in defense of the defendant named by the aggrieved party. These actions extend to any appeals or other appropriate methods of review employed in the case.

Additional Regulations Concerning Recovery (Sections 20-324i and j)

The commission has the authority to make and enforce any necessary regulations for the efficient administration of the sections of the license law pertaining to the Real Estate Guaranty Fund.

The appeals process discussed earlier in this chapter pertaining to the suspension or revocation of a license also applies to the commission's decisions, orders, or regulations concerning the guaranty fund (see Section 20-322).

■ ENDNOTES

1. *United Interchange, Inc. v. Spellacy* (1957) 136 A. 2d 801, 144 Conn. 647; and *Cyphers v. Allyn* (1955) 118 A. 2d 318, 142 Conn. 699.
2. Declaratory Ruling, Connecticut Real Estate Commission, April 1, 1999.
3. Legal Opinion, Connecticut Attorney General's Office, June 11, 1999.
4. PA 94-36, Section 40(b).

QUESTIONS

1. The real estate license law is administered by the
   a. Council on Housing Matters.
   b. Real Estate Commission.
   c. Connecticut Association of REALTORS®.
   d. Department of Housing.

2. A person must be licensed as a real estate broker or salesperson if that person is
   a. selling her house.
   b. buying a house for her personal use.
   c. engaging in the real estate business.
   d. constructing houses.

3. "Engaging in the real estate business" consists of acting for another and for a fee in all of the following activities *except*
   a. managing real estate.
   b. reselling a mobile home.
   c. selling real estate.
   d. collecting rent for the use of real estate.

4. Which of the following persons are sometimes exempt from the real estate licensing requirement?
   a. Attorneys at law
   b. Appraisers
   c. Associations, partnerships, corporations
   d. Real property securities dealers

5. Joyce is an office manager for a local real estate firm. Her primary responsibilities include coordinating the flow of paperwork through the office, preparing forms and advertising copy, and hiring and supervising clerical personnel. Joyce
   a. is violating the license law.
   b. is required to have a broker's license.
   c. is required to have a salesperson's license.
   d. does not need a real estate license for this job.

6. Applications for any real estate license in Connecticut must
   a. be completed before taking the written exam.
   b. contain a picture of the applicant.
   c. be made before May 31 of each year.
   d. be accompanied by a sworn statement attesting to the applicant's character.

7. You are employed by Acme Apartments as a residential on-site property custodian. Part of your duties involves negotiating leases for the apartments. In this position you
   a. must have a salesperson's license.
   b. must have a broker's license.
   c. are exempt from the licensing requirements if you reside at Acme Apartments.
   d. are violating the license law.

8. In addition to a course in real estate principles and practices, the broker applicant must also take a course in
   a. real estate law.
   b. the law of contracts.
   c. real estate finance.
   d. real estate appraisal.

9. Applicants who fail a license examination
   a. are notified of the results at the examination site.
   b. must wait 180 days before a retake.
   c. are scheduled for a review session by the commission.
   d. must score 80 percent on a subsequent retake to pass.

10. The initial salesperson's license fee is presently _____, and annual renewals are _____.
    a. $225/$225   c. $225/$75
    b. $300/$225   d. $450/$300

11. The license law stipulates that the commission will issue to each licensee a(n)
    a. license certificate for a fee of $25.
    b. approved seal to be used on all contracts signed by the licensee.
    c. designation.
    d. title.

12. After moving to Connecticut, Alan applies for a real estate salesperson's license. The commission discovers from his application that he was refused a license in his former state because he was not yet 18 years old. Alan is now 18 and possesses all the other qualifications. How long from the date of the earlier refusal must Alan wait to be issued a Connecticut license?
    a. He must wait one year.
    b. He must wait five years.
    c. He can be issued a license immediately.
    d. He is ineligible until he has been a resident of Connecticut for one year.

13. A nonresident license applicant must file with the commission a(n)
    a. certificate of specific performance.
    b. irrevocable consent to suit.
    c. copy of his or her birth certificate.
    d. corpus delicti.

14. All real estate salespersons' licenses
    a. are granted in perpetuity.
    b. do not need to be renewed unless previously revoked.
    c. expire annually on April 30.
    d. expire annually on May 31.

15. All listings in Connecticut must include all of the following *except*
    a. written confirmation.
    b. date of expiration.
    c. signatures of owners and brokers.
    d. certificate of title insurance.

16. Listings based on a "net price" are
    a. always more profitable because no minimum is set on the amount of commission collectible.
    b. legal in Connecticut as long as the seller agrees.
    c. illegal in Connecticut at any time.
    d. permissible with approval of the commission.

17. Kathleen accompanies a young couple during an open house on a property listed with her agency. The couple is so impressed with the house and Kathleen's response to their questions that they decide to make an offer. Before the offer is presented to the principal, they ask Kathleen's personal opinion as to whether they should insist on a bond for deed or simply accept a standard sales contract. Kathleen should
    a. make a decision and support it with facts.
    b. refer the couple to an attorney for legal advice.
    c. assure the couple that either is acceptable.
    d. admit she does not know.

18. If a broker tells a lender that the sales price on a property is something above its actual sales price,
    a. the broker has done nothing wrong as long as the appraisal substantiates this price.
    b. the buyer is likely to receive an interest rate break.
    c. the broker can lose his or her license and be fined and imprisoned.
    d. the buyer can receive a higher mortgage amount.

19. The commission has the power to revoke a salesperson's license, if the salesperson
    a. attempts to represent a real estate broker other than her employer, after obtaining her employer's consent.
    b. attempts to represent a buyer.
    c. enters into an exclusive listing contract.
    d. deposits a buyer's down payment in her own bank account.

20. To renew a license in even-numbered years, a salesperson or broker must
    a. pay a fee of $225 only.
    b. be actively participating in the real estate business.
    c. have completed six hours of continuing education in the last two years, three hours in real estate law and three hours in fair housing.
    d. have completed 12 hours of continuing education in the last two years.

21. Who may receive compensation from the Real Estate Guaranty Fund?
    a. A broker who does not receive an earned commission
    b. A seller who pays a commission to a broker under false pretenses
    c. A buyer who pays a fee to a broker under a buyer agency agreement
    d. A cooperating broker who does not receive a commission split

22. The maximum compensation that will be paid from the Real Estate Guaranty Fund for any single transaction is
    a. $5,000.
    b. $10,000.
    c. $25,000.
    d. $50,000.

23. In Connecticut, how old must an individual be to qualify for a real estate license?
    a. 15
    b. 16
    c. 18
    d. 20

REAL ESTATE FINANCING: PRINCIPLES/PRACTICE

■ OVERVIEW

Legally, Connecticut is a title theory state, but in practice it holds a *modified* position with respect to mortgages. Although the lender receives a mortgage deed that ostensibly conveys title to the property, the lender permits the borrower to continue in possession of the property and to retain title as long as the terms of the mortgage are complied with (e.g., payment of principal, interest, tax, insurance). *The lender's right to exercise ownership through possession is defeated as long as the monthly payments are made on time and all the conditions of the mortgage are met.*

■ THE MORTGAGE DEED AND NOTE

The standard clauses included in mortgage deeds and notes used in Connecticut relate primarily to the rights and obligations of both the mortgagee/lender and mortgagor/borrower (such as prepayment privileges, assignments, and defaults). There may be subtle variations in these clauses from institution to institution.

Usury

Mortgage loans for more than $15,000 are automatically exempted from usury regulations. Thus, there is no ceiling on the interest rates that may be charged on these real estate loans in Connecticut.

Recording

Mortgages in Connecticut are recorded for at least two reasons. First, the application of title theory gives rise to mortgage deeds, and all deeds must be recorded under state law. Second, in the event of a default on the part of the mortgagor, the date of recording generally establishes the order of priority for the satisfaction of claims. This second point is particularly significant for lenders who rewrite or refinance existing first mortgages without paying off an existing second mortgage (or equivalent junior financing). If the lender who rewrites the existing first mortgage is unaware of the secondary financing or fails to obtain a subordination agreement from the second mortgagee, its mortgage will stand second in line to be satisfied in the event of a default and/or subsequent foreclosure action because the newly refinanced mortgage was recorded after the existing secondary financing. Thus, it is important for lenders to be aware of the necessity to record notes and deeds and to conduct proper title searches to ascertain the existence of prior liens (particularly those still outstanding).

Releases

Once the mortgage has been satisfied, the lender is required by law to execute and deliver a release. This would be the case whether the mortgage was paid off in cash or the property was appropriated to satisfy the debt. Releases are then recorded and indexed by the town clerk under the names of the mortgagor and releasor. In addition, a marginal entry is made on the record of the original mortgage referring to the release. Releases drawn up in the following form are considered sufficient:

■ **EXAMPLE**

Know all persons by these presents, that _____ of _____ in the county of _____ and state of _____ do hereby release and discharge a certain (mortgage, mechanic's lien, or power of attorney for the conveyance of land) from _____ to _____ dated _____ and recorded in the records of the town of _____ in the county of _____ and state of Connecticut, in book _____ at page _____. In witness whereof _____ have hereunto set _____ hand and seal, this _____ day of _____ , A.D. Signed, sealed, and delivered in the presence of _____.

(Seal)

(Acknowledgment)

This is a general release form and can be used in a number of circumstances.

In the case of partial releases from a construction loan, the instrument must clearly identify the extent (dollar amount) to which the mortgage is released and the portion of the property being released from the mortgage.

Assignments

A lender may assign its interests in a mortgage to another party by completing an instrument of assignment, such as the following:

■ **EXAMPLE**

Know all persons by these presents, that _____ of _____ in the county of _____ and state of _____ does hereby grant, bargain, sell, assign, transfer and set over a certain (mortgage, assignment of rents and leases or assignment of interest in a lease) from _____ to _____ dated _____ and recorded in the records of the town of _____ county of _____ and state of Connecticut, in book _____ at page _____ in witness whereof _____ have hereunto set _____ hand and seal, this _____ day of _____ , A.D. Signed, sealed, and delivered in the presence of _____.

(Seal)

(Acknowledgment)

This is a general form that may be used to assign a number of different interests in real estate. Instruments of assignment are recorded in the same manner as mortgages and releases.

■ MORTGAGE BROKERAGE

Any company acting as a mortgage broker for first mortgage loans must have a license to do so.[1] A mortgage broker is defined as a person who for a fee or other valuable consideration negotiates, solicits, arranges, places, or finds a first mortgage loan that is to be made by a mortgage lender. There is no exception for real estate brokers and salespersons.

Licensed mortgage brokers must maintain adequate records of the loan transaction, including a statement signed by the borrower acknowledging receipt of the statement and disclosing the fee to be paid. The commissioner of banking may suspend or revoke a license if the mortgage broker violates this law. A $40,000 surety bond is required of first mortgage brokers.

Secondary mortgage brokers must also be licensed in Connecticut.[2] A secondary mortgage broker is defined as a person who, for a fee or other consideration, negotiates, solicits, places, or finds a secondary mortgage loan that is to be made by a lender. A licensed real estate broker does not need a secondary mortgage brokerage license to negotiate secondary mortgage loans if such negotiation is done in the course of his or her business as a broker (such as when a buyer broker helps a buyer secure a second mortgage loan from a seller).

WWWeb.Link

A list of Connecticut first mortgage brokers can be found at *www.state.ct.us/dob/pages/1stmtg.htm* and a list of second mortgage brokers can be found at *www.state.ct.us/dob/pages/2ndmtg.htm*. Inquiries, complaints, and licensure information can also be accessed at those sites.

■ REAL ESTATE BROKER ACTING AS MORTGAGE BROKER

A real estate broker or salesperson who receives a fee or commission for the sale of one- to four-family residential real estate *cannot* receive a fee or commission for assisting the buyer in the sale in obtaining a mortgage loan *unless* there is a written agreement between the broker or salesperson and buyer, and certain *disclosures* are made.[3] The disclosure must be in writing (in at least ten-point boldface capital letters) and given to the buyer before the buyer signs the contract for mortgage brokerage services. The disclosure must be as follows:

> I UNDERSTAND THAT THE REAL ESTATE BROKER OR SALES-
> PERSON IN THIS TRANSACTION HAS OFFERED TO ASSIST ME
> IN FINDING A MORTGAGE LOAN. ADDITIONALLY, I UNDER-
> STAND THAT THIS REAL ESTATE BROKER OR SALESPERSON
> DOES NOT REPRESENT ANY PARTICULAR MORTGAGE

LENDER AND WILL ATTEMPT TO OBTAIN THE BEST TERMS AVAILABLE WITHIN THE MORTGAGE LOAN MARKET FOR MY SPECIFIC HOME FINANCING NEEDS. IF THE REAL ESTATE BROKER OR SALESPERSON DOES NOT FULFILL HIS FIDU-CIARY OBLIGATION, I MAY FILE A COMPLAINT WITH THE DEPARTMENT OF BANKING. I ALSO UNDERSTAND THAT I MAY ATTEMPT TO FIND A MORTGAGE LOAN TO FINANCE THE PURCHASE OF MY HOME WITHOUT THE ASSISTANCE OF THE REAL ESTATE BROKER OR SALESPERSON, IN WHICH CASE I WILL NOT BE OBLIGATED TO PAY A FEE TO THE REAL ESTATE BROKER OR SALESPERSON.

Any fee or commission received by a broker or salesperson for assisting the buyer in a first mortgage loan must be related to the services actually performed based on reasonable hourly rates. The compensation cannot be imposed for the mere referral of the buyer to the mortgage lender and must be paid directly to the broker or salesperson by the buyer rather than from the mortgage loan proceeds at the time of closing.

■ PREDATORY LENDING

Connecticut places limits on "high cost loans," including mandatory disclo-sures and prohibited practices and provisions. Provisions limiting prepaid finance charges apply even if a loan is not high cost.

WWWeb.Link   The Mortgage Bankers Association has an informative site on Connecticut and other state predatory lending requirements at *www.mba.org/resources/prelend/.*

■ MORTGAGE FORECLOSURE

When a mortgage falls into default due to the borrower's failure to make required payments or other violations of the terms of the mortgage contract, foreclosure is the usual result. If a lender agrees, a mortgagor may avoid a foreclosure action by granting the lender a *deed in lieu of foreclosure* (a voluntary deed). This presumes, however, that the mortgagee is agreeable to this alter-native. In this case, the defaulting mortgagor would convey the title to the property to the lender outright rather than face the prospects of a strict fore-closure and its attendant costs. These costs would range from the incidental expenses associated with court and legal fees to the long-term penalty of the poor credit rating almost certain to accompany a foreclosure action. In general, however, strict foreclosures and foreclosures by sale represent the most common methods by which real property interests are foreclosed on in Connecticut.

Strict Foreclosure   Under a strict foreclosure, the mortgagee first files a suit to foreclose. As part of the suit, the lender is required to submit a current real estate appraisal on the property to be foreclosed, prepared by a Connecticut licensed or certified appraiser. Notice, in the form of a summons, of the impending foreclosure is delivered to all parties having a recorded interest in the property. Such notice directs them to appear in court on a specified date set by the court. A notice of the foreclosure action, *lis pendens* (litigation pending), is also recorded in the land records of the town in which the property is located. On the court date, any arguments for and against the foreclosure action will be heard, and the appraisal will be entered into the proceedings to establish the value estimate of the court-appointed appraisers.

If the parties to the foreclosure suit take no action to extend the date on which a foreclosure judgment will be effective, the court will enter a judgment of foreclosure, set a law day on which the property will pass to the foreclosing creditor if no one redeems the property, and establish a day in court on which each of the intervening creditors will have the opportunity to redeem the mortgage and take over the property. If neither the defaulted mortgagor nor any of the other creditors has the capacity or desire to redeem the property, it goes to the foreclosing mortgagee and the slate is wiped clean, that is, all other claims except delinquent taxes, valid mechanics' liens, and liens that were recorded before the mortgage are extinguished.

Thus, if First National Bank, the first mortgagee, forecloses on property on which Home Finance holds a second mortgage, Home Finance may redeem the bank's mortgage and take title by paying off the first mortgage and whatever other costs might have resulted from the foreclosure action. If there are any intervening creditors (debts that are recorded and stand ahead of the redeeming creditor), the redeeming creditor must also pay them before acquiring title.

Certificate of satisfaction. Once either the defendant (defaulted mortgagor) or another creditor redeems the property from foreclosure, the plaintiff (mortgagee initiating the suit) must execute and deliver to the defendant a certificate of satisfaction. This certificate is signed by the plaintiff and evidences the fact that the debt and costs of foreclosure have been satisfied. It must be filed by the defendant with the court in which the original foreclosure judgment was entered and recorded in the records of the town in which the property is located, as discussed earlier in this chapter.

Modifying judgments of foreclosure. As discussed above, if no one redeems the property within the time period established by the court, title will rest in the foreclosing creditor. After a judgment of foreclosure has been rendered by the court, the judgment may be reopened at the court's discretion at any time before the title to the property passes to the foreclosing creditor. The court may reopen the judgment to make any modifications it feels are equitable on the written motion of any person having a legitimate interest in the foreclosure action. Once title has passed, the judgment cannot be reopened. Note, however, that judgments are not reopened at the whim and fancy of the party who makes such a request before the court. Because it is at the court's discretion to reopen judgment, the reasons for doing so must be substantial, such as fraud, misrepresentation, or an error of the court. The court will not reopen judgment merely to give the defendant another shot at redeeming the property.

Foreclosure certificates.   Once title to a property foreclosed rests in the person(s) who initiated the suit, that person(s) must record a foreclosure certificate in the land records of the town in which the property is located. The certificate must contain at least the following information:

- A description of the property foreclosed
- The mortgage deed on which the foreclosure took place
- The volume and page number where the above deed was recorded
- The time at which the title became absolute in the foreclosing party
- The signature of the person taking title (or his or her agent)

Ejectment and possession.   Under any foreclosure judgment, the foreclosing party may issue a complaint to the court demanding possession of the property he or she is foreclosing. If the court upholds the plaintiff's request, the defendant may be ejected from the property. Note that tenants of the property who are not involved in the foreclosure suit generally are protected from ejectment.

Foreclosure by Sale   A foreclosure by sale typically is requested by a creditor whose claim is subordinate to that of the foreclosing mortgagee. Under a strict foreclosure, this creditor would be compelled to redeem the foreclosing mortgage and debts to all other intervening creditors to take the property. Under a foreclosure by sale, he or she need only be the highest bidder. Thus, the sale offers a junior lienholder the opportunity to acquire the property at a lesser cost than under strict foreclosure. Any deficiencies would be the problem of the original debtor—not the purchaser at the sale.

A foreclosure by sale would begin in essentially the same manner as a strict foreclosure and would follow all the steps identified above up to the point of notifying the parties to the foreclosure suit. Under Connecticut mortgage law, any party to the foreclosure suit may request that the court order a foreclosure by sale instead of a strict foreclosure. If the court so orders, it will appoint a committee to conduct the sale and require that notice of the sale be advertised (in accordance with specific notice requirements). The date of the sale is decided on by the court on the advisement of the parties to the suit and their respective counsel.

The sale is conducted by the court-appointed committee and is similar to an auction. *Anyone* may bid on the property, including the party being foreclosed and the junior lienholders. The purchasing bidder on the property is required to post a deposit on the property and is given a period of time to procure the additional funds to complete the sale. Both the amount of the deposit and the time allowed are determined by the court or its appointed committee. The proceeds of a foreclosure by sale would be used to satisfy the claims against the property in order of court-established priority (date of recording), with any excess returned to the mortgagor. If the sale fails to yield sufficient funds to satisfy the mortgage or lien foreclosed on, the court may order a *deficiency judgment* against the party liable for this mortgage or lien. The other creditors would be squeezed out and would receive nothing. At the sale the purchaser would receive a sheriff's deed and would acquire the same title that would have passed to the foreclosing creditor under a strict foreclosure.

Deed in Lieu of Foreclosure

As discussed earlier in this chapter, there are some instances in which a debtor/mortgagor may wish to simply deed the property over to the potentially foreclosing mortgagee rather than face the costs and trial of a foreclosure suit. The mortgagee, however, should exercise caution in agreeing to such a deed in lieu of foreclosure, particularly if there are other delinquent loans on the property. Other creditors, clamoring that the conveyance was effected to squeeze them out, could make life very difficult for the mortgagee accepting the deed. Typically, a lender would agree to such an arrangement only if it were the sole (or at least principal) creditor. The presumed advantages of this method or alternative to foreclosure are found in the time and expense saved by both parties.

Redemption

The defaulted mortgagor has only two opportunities to redeem the property. Under strict foreclosure he or she may redeem the property on the law day provided by the court. Under a foreclosure by sale, he or she may redeem by bidding successfully on the property. In most foreclosure cases there is no other redemption period. The only exception is in the case of property foreclosed for delinquent taxes; in such case the property owner has six months to redeem the property (unless the property was abandoned, in which case the redemption period is reduced to 60 days).

Deficiency Judgments

Should a *foreclosure by sale* not produce enough funds from a sale to satisfy the foreclosing creditor, the court may order a deficiency judgment against the debtor liable for the debt or lien. This becomes a general lien.

If, however, a foreclosure by sale produces a sales price below the value established by the court-ordered appraisal, the court requires that the debt(s) outstanding as of the date of sale be reduced (credited) by one-half the difference between the appraisal value and the sales price before it will grant a deficiency judgment. Thus, if a property foreclosed by sale yields a $400,000 sales price and has a court appraisal indicating a value of $420,000, the foreclosing creditor must credit $10,000 to the money owed before obtaining a deficiency judgment.[4]

Under a *strict foreclosure*, the plaintiff (foreclosing mortgagee) may be awarded a deficiency judgment based on the difference between the amount of its claim and the court appraisal. The idea behind allowing deficiency judgments is to prevent waste on the part of the defaulted borrower by making him or her liable for the difference between the appraisal and the claim of the mortgagee. It serves to prevent these borrowers from walking away from their investments when they experience problems. In the case of a strict foreclosure, the plaintiff must make an application for a deficiency judgment within 90 days of the end of the time period allowed for redemption.

Deficiency judgments must be recorded within four months from the time they are awarded to become valid liens on the property of the debtor. When and if the lien is satisfied, a discharge of lien must be prepared and recorded in the appropriate town land records (generally in the town in which the property is located).

■ SOURCES OF MORTGAGE FUNDS

The funds available for financing the purchase of or investment in real estate flow from a variety of sources in the mortgage market. The principal sources of mortgage financing are financial institutions. Individuals and other private sources make up the remainder of the mortgage market. Different financial institutions came into being over the years to meet different credit or savings needs. This helps to explain the great diversity that exists in the mortgage market. Because of these differences, some lending institutions are better equipped than others to make certain types of real estate loans. Depending on the regulatory limitations placed on them and their methods of operation, investment policies, and organizational structures, the different types of institutions provide mortgage funds to different categories of borrowers or market segments.

It is important that real estate brokers and salespersons have a thorough knowledge of the mortgage market to effectively counsel their clients and customers. The following discussion provides a brief analysis of some of the different types of loan programs in Connecticut.

Connecticut Housing Programs

The Connecticut Department of Economic and Community Development offers many different programs to provide loans and grants for the development and purchase of low-income housing.

The *Home Investment Partnerships Program* provides grants to localities to build, buy, and/or rehabilitate affordable housing for rent or home ownership. It also provides direct rental assistance to low-income people.

The *Federal Section 8 Housing Payment Assistance Program* and the *State Rental Assistance Program* each provide rent subsidies to low-income and moderate-income persons. They provide an opportunity to afford quality housing. There are prescribed income levels and property rental levels applicable to this program.

Financial services are readily available to business firms and homeowners. Tax credit vouchers are available to business firms that make contributions to nonprofit organizations to develop, sponsor, and manage housing programs for low-income and moderate-income families.

WWWeb.Link

Details of these and other programs are available online at *www.state.ct.us/ecd/housing/index.htm*.

Connecticut Housing Finance Authority (CHFA)

For the past several years, the state of Connecticut has provided an additional source of mortgage financing for low-income and moderate-income families through the Connecticut Housing Finance Authority. The CHFA offers a below-market interest rate (BMIR) program through approved lenders to qualified applicants. To become an approved lender, an institution is required to submit an application to the CHFA detailing its ability to handle the program and service any loans it makes under the program. In general, the approved lender must also be willing to write FHA and VA loans. The CHFA provides specific amounts of funds to its approved lenders to originate mortgages. When the lender's allocated funds are depleted, the lender may apply for an additional allocation.

Qualification for the program is based on a sliding income scale related to family size that stipulates a maximum sales price for properties that can be financed through the program. Both incomes and sales prices are modified by geographic areas within the state to reflect differences in the cost of living.

Applicants register their loan applications with an approved CHFA lender. Once the loan is approved by both the lender and CHFA and the papers are signed, the loan is assigned to the CHFA (the lender retains the service fee). The funds for the program are provided through bond issues of the CHFA. A CHFA program also exists to finance development projects of housing for low-income and moderate-income families.

It is important that brokers and salespersons be aware of programs like the CHFA (and the FHA and VA as well) to assist their clients in obtaining mortgage loan financing.

WWWeb.Link

A list of the currently applicable income limits and sales prices can be obtained from the CHFA Web site at *www.chfa.org*.

Following is a sampling of the CHFA programs. Borrower income limits apply to most programs.

Homebuyer Mortgage Program. Below-market-interest-rate 30-year mortgage loans (as much as 1 percent below comparable rates) for first-time homebuyers (persons who have not owned their own residence within the last three years).

Homeownership Program. Below-market interest rates on 30-year mortgage loans for police and public school teachers who are first-time homebuyers. Local police must buy in the community they serve. State police must buy in one of Connecticut's 20 most populous cities. Teachers have some location restrictions and must be teaching in certain priority school districts.

Rehabilitation Mortgage Loan. Below-market-interest-rate loans to finance the purchase and rehabilitation (or refinance) of homes in need of repair. Available to first-time homebuyers and any homebuyer in certain targeted areas.

Alternative Mortgage Loans

Section 36a-265 of the Connecticut General Statutes grants authority to state-chartered financial institutions to extend alternative mortgage loans. The law states that financial institutions must disclose alternative mortgage information to loan applicants at the same time that information on all types of mortgage loans is disclosed. Mortgage loan applicants have the choice of applying for conventional mortgage loans or alternative mortgage loans offered by the institutions.

Before a state-chartered financial institution makes an alternative mortgage loan available, the Connecticut Banking Department must approve a prototype plan. Many alternative mortgage instruments are offered in Connecticut, such as graduated payment mortgage (GPM), reverse annuity mortgage (RAM), growing equity mortgage (GEM), and variable rate mortgage (VRM).

■ HOME MORTGAGE DISCLOSURE ACT (HMDA)

The Home Mortgage Disclosure Act (HMDA) of 1975 requires that all depository institutions with assets in excess of $10 million and with one or more offices in a Standard Metropolitan Statistical Area (SMSA) disclose where they made their mortgage loans. The purpose of HMDA is to aid in the identification of *redlining* practices, which accelerate the decline of our inner cities and other neighborhoods. *Redlining* is defined as *the process of denying loans in specific geographic locations.* This practice is usually, if not always, associated with the decline in property values and the deterioration of housing in certain areas of a city.

Title III of HMDA requires that lenders covered by this act disclose where residential loans were made during the year by census tract number. The act pertains to all types of residential loans—conventional, FHA, FNMA, DVA, multifamily, and home improvement loans. Disclosures are made on an annual basis. Connecticut General Statutes Section 36-466 also requires that lenders disclose the reason for denial of each mortgage loan application on the HMDA forms.

As reported, information will be broken down into major categories: loans made by the lender and loans purchased by the lender (including participations). Each of these categories will be further broken down into loans within the relevant SMSA and those outside. The relevant SMSA is defined as an SMSA within which the lender maintains the home or a branch office. Loans made outside the relevant SMSA need only be disclosed by number and amount, rather than by census tract number.

■ ENDNOTES

1. Chapter 660A of the Connecticut General Statutes.
2. Chapter 646A of the Connecticut General Statutes.
3. Section 20-325c of the Connecticut General Statutes.
4. *North End Bank and Trust Company v. Mandell* (1931) 155 A. 80, 113 Conn. 241.

QUESTIONS

1. Generally, what establishes the priority of claims if the mortgagor defaults and a foreclosure suit is initiated?
   a. The date of recording
   b. The dollar amount
   c. The party initiating the action
   d. The order of redemption

2. A property owner wants to refinance his or her existing first mortgage on a building that is also subject to a recorded home improvement loan. The lender on the refinanced mortgage does not realize that the home improvement loan exists and undertakes the refinancing proposal. The lender on the improvement loan
   a. now stands first in line.
   b. should seek a subordination agreement.
   c. is squeezed out.
   d. still stands behind the *first* mortgage.

3. Any person acting as a mortgage broker for a first mortgage loan must
   a. be a licensed real estate broker.
   b. be a licensed mortgage broker.
   c. not accept consideration for his/her services.
   d. negotiate such loan in the course of business as a real estate salesperson or broker.

4. Which of the following documents must be recorded?
   a. A mortgage release
   b. A mortgage commitment
   c. A listing contract
   d. A sales contract

5. Harry owes $200,000 mortgage on a house worth $150,000, so he hands the keys to the bank and walks away. After the foreclosure sale fails to cover the outstanding loan owed, the lender can
   a. collect only the proceeds from the sale.
   b. have Harry arrested.
   c. do nothing to Harry.
   d. collect a deficiency judgment against Harry.

6. Before title passes under a strict foreclosure of a first mortgage, other creditors have an opportunity to
   a. redeem the foreclosing mortgage interest.
   b. refinance the foreclosing mortgage interest.
   c. rewrite the foreclosing mortgage interest.
   d. do nothing in regard to the foreclosing mortgage interest.

7. A court-ordered appraisal in conjunction with a foreclosure must be completed by
   a. a licensed broker.
   b. three disinterested parties, including an appraiser.
   c. no fewer than three persons, one of whom must be a licensed broker.
   d. a committee of court referees.

8. Once a judgment has been rendered by the court in a strict foreclosure action, the court may reopen the judgment
   a. at any time.
   b. at any time prior to the passing of title.
   c. within 60 days from the passing of title.
   d. The court cannot reopen judgments under strict foreclosure.

9. A bank has acquired title to a defaulted mortgagor's property through a strict foreclosure action. What must the bank now record?
   a. A mortgage deed
   b. A dissolution certificate
   c. An irrevocable consent of subrogation
   d. A foreclosure certificate

10. Homeowner's property is being foreclosed on through a strict foreclosure process. Homeowner has the right to redeem the property by
    a. redeeming the property before title passes to the foreclosing creditor.
    b. being the successful bidder at the foreclosure sale.
    c. redeeming the property within one year of title's passing to the foreclosing creditor.
    d. matching the successful bidder's bid within one year of the foreclosure sale.

CHAPTER TWELVE

LEASES

■ OVERVIEW

Connecticut has comprehensive statutory laws regarding residential landlord-tenant matters governing rights and responsibilities, habitability, rental payments, security deposits, and remedies. Tenants who intentionally damage leased property may be prosecuted criminally. The statutory law can be found under Title 47a of the Connecticut General Statutes, entitled "Landlord and Tenant."

 WWWeb.Link

Information on Connecticut's rental housing industry can be found at *www.ctlandlord.com* and *www.cses.com/RENTAL/ct/Connecticut.asp.*

■ LEASE

In Connecticut, the statute of frauds requires that *leases for a term of more than one year be in writing.*[1] However, inasmuch as Connecticut law requires that all contracts be in writing and it considers leases as contracts, all leases regardless of term should be in writing (although this is not a legal requirement and does not affect the validity of the lease). This includes leases that are month-to-month, week-to-week, and less than one year.

Connecticut law also requires that leases for more than one year be *recorded* in the local land records to give constructive notice to a third party (future purchaser of the property, future recourse to a landlord's action, etc.) in a manner similar to recording deeds.[2] Alternatively, a *notice of lease* may be recorded in lieu of the lease itself, provided that the notice of lease discloses at least the following pertinent information:

■ The names and addresses of the parties to the lease
■ The lease term with beginning and termination dates
■ A description of the property
■ Reference to the lease, including its date of execution
■ Notice of any right of extension or renewal
■ Date by which an option to purchase (if any) must be exercised
■ Reference to the place where the lease is kept on file

Leases and leasehold estates are considered to be personal property under Connecticut statutes, even though the operation of long-term leases, such as a 99-year lease, gives rise to possession that is tantamount to ownership.

It is advisable to remember that a lease is a tool to create a harmonious relationship between landlord and tenant. The completeness and full understanding of its clauses by both landlord and tenant can accomplish this. Without this clear understanding and cooperation, problems are inevitable. A lease form in plain language is shown in Figure 12.1.

■ LEASEHOLD ESTATES

Connecticut recognizes all the tenancies and methods of termination discussed in the text. However, in Connecticut *landlords must provide tenants with a notice to quit possession at least three days prior to the lease expiration date.*[3] (This notice requirement may be waived in the lease.) If a tenant holds over after the expiration of his or her lease, the law construes the tenancy as a month-to-month occupancy and not an agreement for a further lease. In all cases where a tenancy is not subject to an agreed-on term or expiration date, it is construed as a month-to-month tenancy. Unless the rental agreement fixes a definite term, the tenancy is month-to-month, except in the case of a tenant who pays weekly rent; then the tenancy is week-to-week.

■ LANDLORD AND TENANT ACT

Connecticut has a comprehensive statute relating to the rights and responsibilities of landlords and tenants, rental payments, security deposits, and summary process (evictions). The legislation relates primarily to residential dwelling units. The current law is found under Title 47a—"Landlord and Tenant"—of the Connecticut General Statutes and includes several important provisions.

Lease Provisions

Leases and other rental agreements may contain any terms and conditions agreeable to both parties that are not in violation of state laws. These terms and conditions may include the rent payable, the length of the term of the agreement, and any other provisions that would act to govern the rights and obligations of each party.

Prohibited clauses.   The lease agreement may not contain clauses by which the tenant (lessee)

■ agrees to waive his or her legal rights under the Connecticut General Statutes;
■ allows the landlord to automatically obtain a judgment in court against the tenant without the tenant's knowledge (see discussion of judgment clauses in the text);
■ agrees to excuse the landlord from any damages that the tenant suffers that would normally be the legal responsibilities of the landlord;
■ agrees to waive his or her right to interest on the security deposit;

F I G U R E **12.1**

Residential Lease

LEASE

1. Date of Lease; Parties

This Lease is made on _____ , 20___ , between _____ , Landlord, and _____ and _____ , Tenant(s). The parties shall be referred to as "Landlord" and "Tenant" in the remaining provisions of this Lease.

2. Lease

Landlord hereby leases to Tenant the ☐ house and grounds ☐ apartment located at _____ , Connecticut 06____ , referred to in this Lease as "the Premises."

3. Term of Lease

The term of this Lease is one year. It begins on _____ , 20_____ and ends on _____ , 20____ at 11:59 p.m.

4. Rent; Time and Manner of Payment of Rent

The total rent for the term of this Lease is $_____ . The rent must be paid in equal monthly installments of $_____ on the first day of each month of the term of the Lease. Tenant has paid the sum of $_____ , receipt of which is acknowledged, as a deposit in order to hold the Premises open for rental. Tenant shall pay the additional sum of $_____ as an additional deposit upon the execution of this Lease. Any deposits in excess of the first monthly installment of rent shall be applied to Security (see Paragraph 16).

5. Use of The Premises

The Premises must be used and occupied only and solely as a private dwelling for Tenant and Tenant's children, if any, to live in. It may not be used for any other purpose. Any full-time occupancy by any other party who has not signed this Lease is prohibited.

Tenant will not store any unregistered automobiles, motorized contrivances, building materials, hazardous materials, or other personal property on or upon the outside grounds of the Premises.

☐ If checked, Tenant may keep _____ as pet(s) on the Premises and outside grounds. Tenant shall keep the pet(s) healthy and well groomed. Tenant shall also keep the Premises and outside grounds free from animal waste, litter and other noxious or unhealthy animal byproducts.

Page 1 of 5

FIGURE 12.1

Residential Lease (continued)

6. Condition of The Premises

It is understood that Tenant will take possession of the Premises in its present condition.

Any appliances located in the Premises on the date of this Lease are furnished solely for the convenience of Tenant and are not a part of this Lease unless otherwise noted in the Lease. Tenant shall perform, at Tenant's sole expense, any maintenance required on the appliances.

☐ *(Applicable if checked)* Tenant shall keep the outside driveways, sidewalks and walkways free from snow and ice and accumulations of litter and debris and shall mow the lawn when necessary to maintain a neat appearance to the outside grounds.

Tenant acknowledges that there are smoke detectors present at the Premises. Tenant will not do any act which serves to disable or damage the smoke detectors. In the event that a smoke detector malfunctions, Tenant will promptly notify Landlord of the malfunction.

7. Requirements of Law

Tenant is to comply with all the sanitary laws, ordinances and rules, and all orders of the Health Department or Health District or other authorities, including zoning authorities, affecting the cleanliness, occupancy, use and preservation thereof for the Premises and the sidewalks and walkways to the Premises during the term of the Lease.

8. Access to The Premises

Tenant agrees that Landlord, Landlord's agents, servants and contractors shall have the right to enter into and upon the Premises, or any part of the Premises, at all reasonable hours for the purpose of examining same, or making emergency repairs or alterations as may be necessary for the safety and preservation thereof.

9. Fuel, Heat, Gas, Electricity, Telephone and other Utilities

Tenant shall pay all charges for the following:

☐ fuel (including fireplace wood, propane, oil, and gas) needed to heat the Premises

☐ hot water	☐ electricity
☐ cable services	☐ municipal water
☐ telephone	☐ other (specify) _____
☐ snow removal	☐ lawn care including mowing

☐ *(Applicable if checked)* Tenant shall light and maintain the furnace which heats the Premises, including cleaning and lighting the furnace.

F I G U R E　12.1

Residential Lease (continued)

10. Damage by Fire or Other Casualty

If the Premises, or any part thereof, shall be slightly damaged by fire or other casualty during said term, the Premises shall be promptly repaired by Landlord and an abatement will be made for the rent corresponding with the time during which and the extent to which said Premises may have been untenantable, but if the building should be so damaged that Landlord shall decide to rebuild, the term of this Lease shall cease and the rent be paid up to the time of the fire or other casualty.

11. Alterations by Tenant

Tenant shall not make any alterations, additions, or improvements to the Premises without the written consent of Landlord. The kinds of alterations, additions or improvements referred to are those which are of a more or less permanent nature, such as new floors, partitions, wallpaper and paneling. If consent of Landlord is given, then any or all of such alterations, additions or improvements, may, if Landlord wishes, become the property of Landlord at the end of the term of the Lease. However, if Landlord wishes, Landlord may require Tenant to remove any or all of such alterations, additions or improvements at the end of the term of the Lease and restore the Premises to the condition it was in when the term of this Lease began.

12. Liability of Landlord; Reimbursement by Tenant; Insurance

If Landlord must pay any damages for a claim arising from the fault of Tenant, then Tenant must reimburse Landlord for any such sums paid. In addition, Tenant must reimburse Landlord for any expense Landlord incurred in defending against such claim, whether or not Landlord has to pay any damages.

During the term of this Lease, Tenant, at Tenant's expense, shall carry public liability insurance not less than the following limits: Bodily injury - $_____,000; property damage - $_____,000. Tenant agrees to furnish Landlord, prior to occupancy, with a certificate of insurance evidencing that Tenant has secured the insurance required by this paragraph and that Landlord is named as an additional insured or loss payee of such insurance. Tenant also agrees to insure his/her own personal property located in the Premises.

13. Assignment and Sublease

This Lease may not be assigned, nor may the Premises be sublet, without the advance written consent of Landlord. Such consent shall not be unreasonably withheld. Any such assignment or sublease does not relieve Tenant of any of Tenant's obligations or liability under this Lease. The subtenant shall be bound by and subject to all the terms of this Lease.

14. Quiet Enjoyment by Tenant

As long as Tenant pays the rent and is not in default on any of the conditions of this Lease, Tenant shall peaceably and quietly have, hold and enjoy the Premises during the term of the Lease.

15. Warranty of Habitability

Landlord represents and states that the Premises and all areas used in connection with it are fit for human life and for the use reasonably intended by the parties and there are no conditions dangerous, hazardous or detrimental to life, health and safety.

16. Security

Tenant, prior to occupancy, shall deposit with Landlord the sum of $_____ _____ Dollars ($ .00) as security for the performance of Tenant's obligations under the Lease. Landlord shall hold such sum or deposit the same in a bank as may be required by law. Under the law, Tenant may be entitled to interest on such security deposit at interest rates determined yearly by the Connecticut Banking Department.

If Tenant fails to make any payments of rent or defaults under any other obligations of this Lease, Landlord may use the security in payment of such rent or in payment of any sums Landlord may be forced to spend because of Tenant's default. If Landlord does so use the security, then he shall notify Tenant in writing of the amount so used, and Tenant shall immediately forward a like amount to Landlord. There shall always be deposited with Landlord a sum not less than the amount originally deposited as security.

If at the end of the term of the Lease Tenant has made all payments of rent required and fully complied with all the other obligations under the Lease, then Landlord shall return the security to Tenant together with any interest that may be required by law.

17. Waiver by Landlord or Tenant Limited

If either Landlord or Tenant waives or fails to enforce any of their rights under the Lease, this does not mean that any other rights under the Lease are waived. Further, if Landlord or Tenant waives or fails to enforce any of their rights under a specific paragraph of the Lease, such waiver or failure to enforce such rights is limited to the specific instance in question and is not a waiver of any later breaches of such paragraph.

18. Invalidity or Illegality of Part of Lease

If any part of this Lease is invalid or illegal, then only that part shall be void and have no effect. All other parts of the Lease shall remain in full force and effect.

19. Modification or Change of Lease

The only way in which any of the provisions of this Lease can be changed or modified is by a written agreement signed by both parties.

Residential Lease (continued)

20. Persons Bound by Lease

It is the intent of the parties that this Lease shall be binding upon Landlord and Tenant and upon any parties who may in the future succeed to their interests.

21. Surrender of The Premises

At the expiration of the term of this Lease, Tenant will surrender the Premises in as good a state and condition as they were in when the term began, reasonable use and wear excepted.

22. Captions for Paragraphs of Lease

The captions of the various paragraphs of this Lease are for convenience and reference purposes only. They are of no other effect.

23. Amendment of Listing

☐ *(Applicable if checked)* The parties recognize _____ as the listing real estate broker and _____ as the cooperating real estate broker. Landlord agrees that the listing agreement dated _____ for the rental of the Premises is hereby amended to provide that in the event this Tenant purchases the Premises during the term of this Lease or within _____ days after the termination of this Lease, the Landlord will pay compensation to the listing real estate broker calculated as follows _____ _____ and the term of the listing shall be extended to _____ days after the term of this Lease.

_____   _____
Landlord   Landlord

_____   _____
Tenant   Tenant

- agrees to allow the landlord to evict or dispossess him or her without court order;
- consents to the seizure of property as security for rent; or
- agrees to pay the landlord's attorney's fee in excess of 15 percent of any judgment against the tenant in the event the landlord must take the tenant to court.

Nonallowable clauses in a lease are unenforceable.

Security Deposits

Legislation regulating security deposits is found in Sections 47a-21 through 47a-22a (Advanced Rental Payments, Security Deposits) of the Connecticut General Statutes. A landlord is not required to charge a security deposit. The maximum security deposit a landlord can demand is two months' rent. In the case of tenants 62 years old or older, however, landlords can require only one month's rent.

Security deposits must be kept in an escrow account and separate from the other funds of the landlord. The escrow account must be maintained in a financial institution. The Banking Commission has enforcement powers over this portion of the Landlord and Tenant Act. The landlord must pay the tenant the earned interest on the deposit at the anniversary of the lease. The penalty for not doing so is a fine of $100. A landlord who knowingly and willfully neglects to return the security deposit to the tenant on termination of the lease will be fined $250, unless there is evidence that the landlord was entitled to the funds for damages created by the tenant. A fine of $500 and/or 30 days of imprisonment is levied on a landlord who does not hold the security deposit in escrow.

Interest on Security Deposits

The current law stipulates that landlords must pay tenants interest on their security deposits only in residential units. The rate of interest payable is a floating rate tied to the average savings deposit rate as published in the Federal Reserve Bulletin. The rate is set annually on the first of the year and published by the commissioner of banking. It can never go lower than 1.5 percent.[4] Exemptions to this regulation are for residential units owned or controlled by an educational institution for housing its students and their families, for mobile homes, or for space, lots, or parks for mobile homes.

The interest must be paid on every anniversary of the lease (typically each year). It may be paid directly to the tenant or subtracted from the next monthly rent payment at the option of the lessor. If any rental payment is received later than ten days after the scheduled due date, the tenant forfeits the interest for the month he or she is late in paying the rent. If the lease (rental agreement) is terminated prior to an anniversary, the lessor is required to pay interest up to a date within 30 days of actual termination.

Returning the security deposit. Within 30 days of the date the tenancy ends, the landlord must return the deposit (and applicable accrued interest) to the tenant, unless there have been damages to the property by the tenant. The landlord can deduct from the security deposit any amount of damages caused by the tenant through violation of the rental agreement if the landlord provides the tenant with a written notification of the nature of the damages within 30 days of the date the tenancy ends. In the case of such notification, the balance of any security deposit and interest due and an itemized statement of damages must be delivered to the tenant at his or her forwarding address within 30 days after termination of the tenancy. Should the landlord fail to observe any of these requirements and provisions, the tenant may recover up to twice the security deposit due the tenant (except if the landlord fails to deliver only the interest, in which case the tenant can recover up to twice the interest due). In addition, there is a $250 penalty for each failure of the landlord to return a security deposit plus interest due.

Security deposits can be held by the landlord for rent owed. Any person may bring an action for repossession of confiscated property or for money damages in any court of competent jurisdiction to reclaim any part of the security deposit. This does not preclude the landlord or tenant from recovering other damages.

WWWeb.Link   The Connecticut Department of Banking Web site provides valuable information on rental housing security deposit questions and complaints, as well as current year security deposit interest requirements—*www.state.ct.us/dob/pages/renting.htm.*

Landlord's Rules

The landlord may adopt and enforce rules and regulations regarding a tenant's use and occupancy of the property only if such rules or regulations

- promote the convenience, safety, or welfare of the tenants; equitably distribute services to all the tenants; or protect the property from abusive use;
- are related reasonably to the purpose for which they were adopted;
- apply to all tenants equally and fairly;
- are clear enough to be understood by the tenants; and
- are made known to the tenant when he or she enters into the rental agreement or at the time a new rule or regulation is adopted.

Any new rule or regulation that substantially modifies a current tenant's agreement is invalid unless the tenant consents to it in writing.

If the rental unit is in a condominium, the condominium association has the right to change rules at any time and to bind the owner (landlord) to such new rules and fine the owner for any violations committed by the tenant. Therefore the language of the lease should state that the "tenant shall abide by all the rules, including any that may be hereafter adopted by the condominium association."

Landlord's Right To Enter

The landlord has the right to enter the dwelling unit of a lessee to make inspections, repairs, alterations, and so on when entry is made at reasonable times. The landlord's entry must be made after giving the tenant reasonable notice and in a manner that does not constitute harassment of the tenant (such as repeated entries). Entry in the case of emergency may be made by the landlord without the tenant's consent. The landlord may also enter the unit if the tenant has surrendered or abandoned it. Either party may seek a judgment or injunctive relief if the tenant refuses to allow entry or if the landlord makes repeated, supposedly legal, entries that have the effect of harassment.

Landlord's Obligations

Landlords must provide tenants with a written notice indicating the name and address of the manager of the property and the name of the person on whom any legal process may be served. In lieu of such a notice, the person who, under the landlord's authorization, entered into the lease agreement with the tenant will be considered the manager and person on whom legal process may be served.

It is also the duty of the landlord to comply with all applicable laws and ordinances in his or her operation of the property. These duties extend but are not necessarily limited to the following:

- Adhering to applicable building and housing codes
- Keeping the property in *fit and habitable* condition (unless the property is intentionally made unfit for occupancy by the tenant, his or her family, or others on the property without the landlord's consent—in which case the repair becomes the tenant's responsibility) (property containing defective lead-based paint is considered uninhabitable)
- Keeping all common areas in clean and safe condition
- Maintaining in good and safe working condition all equipment supplied by the landlord, used by the tenant, and necessary to permit occupancy, including appliances, heating and ventilating equipment, sanitary facilities, and so on
- Providing and maintaining trash receptacles as needed
- Supplying heat, running water, and reasonable amounts of hot water at all times (unless the law does not require it or the unit occupied is constructed so that the tenant has a direct public utility connection and controls these amenities)

The landlord and tenant may make a good-faith written agreement that provides that the tenant perform specified maintenance or repairs, as long as the agreement does not cover or diminish the obligations of the landlord under the six items listed above.

If a landlord sells the property to another person, he or she is relieved of liabilities under the rental agreements concerning the property as soon as written notice of the new owner is sent to the tenant.

Managers of rental properties represent the landlord and are not personally liable for violations of rental agreements.

Unlawful occupancy.   A certificate of occupancy is issued by the local building inspector and certifies that a structure is habitable for the purpose intended. If a landlord allows or permits a tenant to occupy a building that has not received a *certificate of occupancy* (where required), he or she is prohibited from recovering rent during the period of this unlawful occupancy. If the tenant voluntarily pays rent during this period, the landlord is obligated to put it in an escrow account and not withdraw it until a certificate of occupancy has been issued.

Receipt of payment of rent. A landlord must provide a tenant with a receipt for a cash payment, even if no receipt is requested.

Tenant's Obligations

In using property, tenants are generally obligated to conduct themselves and to use the property in accordance with both state and local laws and ordinances and without infringing on the rights of others, particularly those occupying other portions of the same property. State law further provides that a tenant

- comply with all building, housing, or fire codes materially affecting health and safety;
- keep his or her unit as clean and safe as the general condition of the premises permits;
- remove all trash and rubbish to places and/or receptacles provided by the landlord;
- keep all plumbing fixtures and appliances as clean as the condition of such fixtures and appliances permits;
- use all equipment and appliances in a reasonable manner;
- not willfully destroy, damage, impair, or remove any part of the property or permit another person to do so;
- not disturb his or her neighbors' peaceful enjoyment of the property;
- occupy a dwelling unit only as a dwelling unit; and
- notify the landlord of anticipated extended absences from the premises.

Criminal damage. A tenant who intentionally damages leased property (including damage due to reckless action) is considered to have committed a crime and can be criminally prosecuted. If damage to the property exceeds $1,500, the crime is criminal damage to the landlord's property in the first degree, which is a class D felony. If the damage exceeds $250, the crime is criminal damage of a landlord's property in the second degree, a misdemeanor.

Landlord's Recourse (Remedies)

If a tenant fails to pay rent within nine days of the due date, the landlord may terminate the lease and evict the tenant under the procedures described later in this chapter.

With respect to breaches of the lease by the tenant that do not involve nonpayment of rent, the landlord may deliver a written notice to the tenant citing the breaches and notifying the tenant that unless these breaches are remedied, the lease will terminate in 15 days. The tenant has 15 days from the date of the notice to cure the breaches by repair or payment to the landlord. At the end of this 15-day period, if the tenant takes no action to correct the breach, the lease is effectively terminated.

Actions by the landlord. The landlord may initiate or maintain legal actions against the tenant in a variety of different circumstances. The landlord may maintain an action to recover possession of a dwelling unit under the eviction procedure (summary process) discussed later in this chapter if

- the tenant is using the unit in an illegal manner, or in a way that is prohibited by the lease agreement;
- the tenant has not paid the rent;
- the landlord is making a good-faith attempt to recover possession to use the unit as his or her own home;
- the tenant's guests or family, with his or her consent, have willfully damaged the property or otherwise violated his or her legal obligations; or
- the landlord is seeking to recover possession after giving proper notice to terminate the tenant's periodic tenancy, especially when this notice was given to the tenant prior to any complaints made by the tenant.

Tenant's protection. Landlords are barred from initiating or maintaining any legal actions against a tenant to recover possession, increase rent, or decrease services to which the tenant was entitled within six months after

- the tenant made a good-faith attempt to legally remedy the landlord's violations of his or her legal obligations or of any other state or local laws and ordinances;
- any municipal agency or official has filed a notice, order, or complaint regarding any violations by the landlord;
- the tenant has made a request in good faith that the landlord make needed repairs; or
- the tenant has organized or become a member of a tenants' association or union.

Raising rents would not be deemed retaliatory and will be allowed when costs due to the tenant's lack of care of the property or property taxes or other operating expenses have increased substantially at least four months before the landlord's request for the additional rent. Any increase cannot exceed each unit's pro rata share of the higher tax or cost.

Abandonment of property (and landlord's duty to mitigate damages). In the event that a tenant abandons the property, the landlord is required to make a reasonable effort to rent the property to minimize the tenant's liabilities. The landlord must begin efforts as soon as he or she receives notice of the abandonment and must seek to obtain a fair market rent for it. Thus, if a tenant on a 12-month lease abandons the property after three months, the landlord cannot merely sit back and allow the overdue rent to pile up under the assumption that he or she can eventually sue the abandoning tenant for the full amount. The landlord must make a reasonable effort to rent the abandoned unit to keep the loss, the amount for which he or she could sue the previous tenant, to a minimum.

Tenant's Recourse (Remedies)

If the landlord breaches the rental agreement or fails to fulfill any of his or her legal obligations, the tenant may terminate the agreement. To terminate the lease agreement, the tenant must give the landlord 15 days from the receipt of written notice of the acts and/or omissions that provoked the breach. If the landlord has not taken any action at the end of the 15-day period, the lease is effectively terminated.

In the event that the same problem giving rise to a current breach has occurred within the previous six months, for example, a leaking ceiling, the tenant can terminate the agreement on 14 days' written notice, as long as the notice specifies the date on which the breach, the leak in this case, occurred and the date on which the tenant intends to vacate. This must still be within 30 days of the breach. Note, however, that if the breach is the result of the *tenant's* (or member of the tenant's family, or another person on the leased property with the tenant's consent) *willful or negligent act or omission,* he or she may not terminate the agreement by the means indicated above.

Supplying essential services.   If a landlord fails, for reasons *not* beyond his or her control, to supply such essential services as heat, water, or electricity, the tenant(s) may give notice to him or her by identifying the breach and may subsequently elect to provide for the services in the following manner:

- The tenant may provide the service at his or her own expense and then deduct this amount from the scheduled rental payment.
- If the lack of any services makes the occupancy of the premises impossible, the tenant may procure substitute housing until the services are restored. Note that the landlord must be given two days to remedy the breach before this alternative may be used. If the same breach has occurred within the previous six months, the two-day period is eliminated and substitute housing may be procured immediately. Under this alternative, the tenant is not liable for rent and may recover any costs exceeding the regular rent, if the substitute housing is more expensive.
- If the failure was willful, the tenant can terminate the rental agreement as described above and recover an amount equal to the greater of two months' rent or twice actual damages.

In all the cases above, the tenant may recover reasonable attorney's fees if incurred in defense of an action relating to the landlord's failure to provide essential services. Prepaid rent, security deposits, and interest are recoverable under any of the above actions, in addition to other damages.

Damage or destruction of property.   If property is damaged or destroyed so that the tenant can no longer occupy or enjoy occupancy of the unit, and the damage is the result of the landlord's willful act or negligence, the tenant is not liable to pay rent. At the option of the tenant, he or she may vacate the premises and notify the landlord of intention to terminate the lease agreement within 15 days. In this case, the landlord must return all prepaid rent and security deposits to the tenant. The tenant's other alternative is to adjust his or her rental payment to reflect the reduction in fair market rental value caused by damage to the premises.

Action to enforce landlord's responsibilities.   If a landlord has failed to perform any of his or her legal duties, a tenant may institute an action in superior court to enforce those responsibilities. The court may grant the following types of relief:

- Order the landlord to comply with his duties

- Appoint a receiver to collect rent and correct defective conditions
- Stop other proceedings concerning the property
- Award the tenant money damages, which may include a retroactive abatement of rent
- Other appropriate relief

After a tenant has filed such an action, the tenant pays to the court all rent when due.

■ SUMMARY PROCESS (ACTUAL EVICTION)

Suits to recover possession of property that is illegally occupied by a tenant due to termination of a lease, violation of its terms, nonpayment of rent, and so on generally fall under the provisions of *summary process*. Summary process is usually equated with actual eviction proceedings. This section will provide you with a discussion of the basic elements of Connecticut's laws regarding summary process. Because the legal nature of summary process is so complex, you are advised to consult the statutes and competent legal advice whenever you have a question about it.

Notice To Quit Possession

The first step in a residential eviction is the service of a Notice to Quit. This is a written notice given by the landlord to the tenant calling for the tenant to quit possession. The landlord must have a valid reason to ask the tenant to quit possession, such as nonpayment of rent or violation of the rental agreement. Service of this Notice to Quit has the effect of terminating the tenant's right to occupy the property.

If a tenant or a person occupying property uses the property illegally (for example, as a betting parlor or in violation of vice laws), this automatically serves to void any lease that might be in effect and precludes the necessity for the landlord to provide a notice to quit possession.

Court Action

If the tenant does not leave after the time to quit possession has passed, the landlord can file a complaint in Superior Court for immediate possession. If the tenant fails to appear in court, the court will file a judgment and award the landlord possession and his or her court costs. If the tenant appears in court, a hearing is conducted, and the court will order the tenant to deposit with the court an amount equal to the fair market rental value of the property for the court proceeding period. The court will then make a determination as to possession of the property.

Appeals

The court requires that tenants making appeals in an eviction action post a bond for all rents accrued and those that will become due during the appeal. If there is no lease in effect that identifies the rental amount, the bond will be based on fair market rental value.

Appeals must be made within five business days after court judgment is rendered. As long as the court does not feel that the appeal is being made solely to delay execution, it will accept the application for appeal, and the execution of the judgment (eviction) will be *stayed,* or put off.

Stay of Execution

Unless the landlord is evicting the tenant for nonpayment of rent, nuisance, the use of the property for immoral or illegal purposes, or no initial right to occupy the property, there will be a five-day stay of execution. In addition to this stay of execution, a tenant may, upon application to court, be granted additional time to vacate the premises if the court finds the reasons valid and acceptable and his or her application for this additional time is made before the expiration of the basic five-day period.

Ejection and the Removal and Sale of Personal Effects

On the expiration of any stay(s) of execution or the date on which a judgment is permitted to be executed, the tenant/occupant/defendant must remove himself or herself and all belongings from the property. If the tenant does not do this, the landlord may request an execution of the summary process judgment and have the tenant's goods and belongings removed by a state marshal and placed on the adjacent sidewalk, street, or highway.

The state marshal must make a reasonable effort to locate the tenant and inform him or her of the action to be taken and of the possibility of a sale of the belongings if they are not claimed within 10 days.

If the tenant does not claim the goods removed from the property immediately, they will be removed and stored for a period of 15 days. The storage expense will be borne by the tenant. Assuming no claim is made, the property will be sold at public auction. Once the sale has been effected, the tenant may claim the proceeds (less expenses) within 30 days. After 30 days, all the proceeds are turned over to the town treasury.

Actions of Summary Process by Other Parties

Landlords are not the only parties who may bring actions of summary process to recover possession. Assignees, mortgagees, and reversioners/remaindermen are also permitted by the statutes to bring such actions. The selectmen of a town owning property may also initiate and maintain actions against tenants occupying the town's property in the same manner as illustrated for landlords.

Eviction of Elderly, Blind, or Disabled

Landlords are prohibited from evicting these protected classes from five-or-more-unit dwellings *except* for nonpayment of rent, refusal to pay a fair and equitable rent increase, noncompliance with adopted rules and regulations, voiding of the rental agreement, permanent removal from the dwelling, or landlord's bona fide intention to use that unit as his or her own principal residence. This law also covers those tenants who have as permanent residents in their household a spouse, sibling, parent, or grandparent over 62 years of age, as well as a member of the family who is blind or physically disabled.

■ FAIR RENT COMMISSION

Municipalities where renter-occupied dwellings exceed 5,000 units are required to have a fair rent commission unless a municipality voted against it. Two or more towns not subject to this requirement may form a joint fair rent commission.

The fair rent commission regulates and eliminates excessive charges for residential rental property. Other housing problems are also considered by the commission. It is a forum for both tenants and landlords.

The commission cannot accept complaints from any tenant who owes back rent or who currently is being evicted by a landlord. The tenant is required to pay the "last agreed-on rent" on time each and every month pending the results of the hearing. As a result of a formal hearing, the commission's decision may require that the tenant pay any rent increase retroactive to its effective date.

■ ENDNOTES

1. Section 47-19 of the Connecticut General Statutes.
2. Section 47-19 of the Connecticut General Statutes.
3. Section 47a-23 of the Connecticut General Statutes.
4. Section 47a-21(i) of the Connecticut General Statutes.

QUESTIONS

1. With respect to leases for terms in excess of one year, the landlord may record, instead of the actual lease, a
   a. *lis pendens*.
   b. rent supplement notice.
   c. notice of constructive occupancy.
   d. notice of lease.

2. In Connecticut when there is no agreement on the part of the landlord and tenant as to the term or expiration date of the tenancy, the tenancy is construed to be
   a. ad limbonium.
   b. month-to-month.
   c. constructive occupancy.
   d. illegal.

3. Jack and Jill have an agreement to lease a unit at Hilltop Wells. There is a provision in the lease to waive their rights to the interest earned from the security deposit. This provision is
   a. unenforceable, thus making the lease invalid.
   b. unenforceable, but the lease is still valid.
   c. enforceable because all parties agreed to it.
   d. enforceable only for the term of the lease.

4. Rules and regulations for tenants of leased property must be presented initially to the tenants by the landlord
   a. at the time the tenant first violates them.
   b. at the time the tenant requests such.
   c. at any time during the rental agreement.
   d. at the time the tenant enters into the rental agreement or at the time the rules or regulations are adopted.

5. Through the landlord's negligence and inaction, the heat in an apartment complex is shut off, and a tenant moves into a furnished apartment until repairs are completed. The most the tenant can recover for the cost of this substitute housing is
   a. its actual cost plus regular rent.
   b. the excess of its cost over regular rent.
   c. nothing.
   d. an amount up to, but not over, the regular rent.

6. The landlord may terminate the rental agreement if a tenant fails to pay rent within how many days of the scheduled due date?
   a. 7 days   c. 10 days
   b. 9 days   d. 30 days

7. How long must a landlord wait before he or she can raise rents to reflect a substantial increase in property taxes without being deemed to have taken retaliatory action?
   a. Forever, because this is illegal
   b. Until all the leases expire
   c. Four months
   d. Six months

8. Ruth leased space in a warehouse and put down a two-month security deposit. What percent interest does her security deposit earn as long as she does not pay her rent late?
   a. 2 percent
   b. 4 percent
   c. 5¼ percent
   d. A rate tied to the average savings deposit rate

9. If a monthly rental payment is made more than ten days after the due date, how much must the tenant forfeit on his or her security deposit?
   a. One month's interest
   b. The whole year's interest
   c. No interest
   d. One-half the interest

10. A tenant skips out on his last scheduled monthly payment on a one-year lease. The landlord may
   a. keep the tenant's belongings.
   b. sue the tenant for the back rent.
   c. do nothing because the lease is terminated.
   d. extend the lease automatically because the tenant gave no notice.

11. If an evicted tenant does not move his or her belongings, under summary process the belongings of the evicted tenant may be
   a. used by the landlord.
   b. sold by the landlord.
   c. placed on the street by the sheriff.
   d. brought to the town dump.

12. If no one claims the proceeds of sale resulting from the sale at public auction of the belongings of an evicted tenant within 30 days from such sale, these proceeds are turned over to the
   a. landlord, to offset the judgment.
   b. sheriff who executed the eviction.
   c. town treasury.
   d. state's general fund.

13. Which of the following statements about security deposits is false?
   a. Security deposits are required for residential units.
   b. Landlords must pay tenants interest on their security deposits.
   c. At the end of the lease, the landlord can apply the security deposit to rent owed by the tenant.
   d. Unless there have been damages, the landlord must return the security deposit to the tenant within 30 days of the end of the lease.

14. In a fit of rage, a tenant intentionally punches a wall, causing approximately $500 in damage to the leased property. The tenant may
   a. be arrested (tenant committed a crime).
   b. lose his or her entire security deposit of $1,000.
   c. be subject to a rent increase to cover the damage.
   d. abandon the property because it is no longer fit for living.

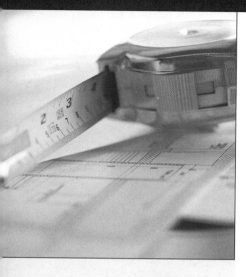

REAL ESTATE APPRAISAL

■ OVERVIEW

Connecticut requires state licensure of real estate appraisers. Licensure falls into five different categories (two of which are scheduled to be eliminated), which include certifications, limited licenses, and provisional licenses. There are various educational, experience, and examination requirements for each category. Once licensed, appraisers must take mandatory continuing education.

The Connecticut law governing the licensing and conduct of real estate appraisers is codified at Title 20, Chapter 400g of the Connecticut General Statutes. Appraisal Regulations begins at Section 20-504-1; Appraisal Regulations Concerning Approval of Schools begins at Section 20-512-1.

WWWeb.Link

Connecticut real estate appraisal licensing laws, updated through January 1, 2003, can be found at *www.cga.state.ct.us/2003/pub/Chap400g.htm*. Connecticut offers an online, searchable database of licensing requirements, information, and forms, including appraisal licensing at *www.ct-clic.com*. Additionally, Connecticut intends to provide an online licensing site to renew licenses, check the status of an application for new license, download rosters of current license holders, and verify the status, complaint, and discipline history of all active licenses at *www.dcpaccess.state.ct.us*.

■ WHO MUST BE LICENSED (SECTION 20-501)

Any person who acts as a real estate appraiser or provisional appraiser or who engages in the real estate appraisal business must have the appropriate certification or license to do so. *Engaging in the real estate appraisal business* is defined as *the act or process of estimating the value of real estate for a fee or other valuable consideration*.

**Exception
to Licensure
(Section 20-526)**

The following persons are exempted from the licensing requirements:

- Any person under contract with the municipality to perform a revaluation of real estate for tax assessment purposes.
- Any licensed real estate broker or real estate salesperson estimating the value of real estate as part of a market analysis. This value estimate must
  - be for the property owner of the real estate being valued;
  - be for the purpose of a prospective listing or sale of the real estate, providing information to the owner under a listing agreement, or providing information to a prospective buyer or tenant under a buyer or tenant agency agreement; and
  - not be referred to or construed to be an appraisal.
  - For one- to four-family residences, if the owner enters into a listing with the broker or salesperson, any fee paid for the value estimate must be credited against compensation owed under the listing.

Connecticut is a mandatory appraisal state. This means that exemptions to licensure or certification requirements pursuant to FDIC regulations are not recognized in Connecticut.

**Fines and Penalties
(Section 20-523)**

Any person who engages in the real estate appraisal business without obtaining a license or certification shall be fined not more than $1,000 or imprisoned for six months or both, and will be ineligible to obtain a license or certification for one year from conviction of the offense.

Any firm or person not licensed or certified to conduct the business of appraisal but who represents itself or himself as being licensed or certified shall be fined up to $1,000 or imprisoned for six months or both.

■ CONNECTICUT REAL ESTATE APPRAISAL COMMISSION (SECTION 20-502)

The Connecticut Real Estate Appraisal Commission exists within the Department of Consumer Protection and consists of eight members. Five of these members must be either certified general appraisers or certified residential appraisers, and three are public members. No more than a bare majority are to be members of the same political party, and there must be at least one member from each congressional district.

Members of the commission are appointed by the governor. Each member must take an oath to perform the prescribed duties faithfully; members may be removed from office for cause by the governor after being given an opportunity to be heard. Seats vacated through resignation, death, or removal are filled by appointees of the governor.

**Duties of the Real
Estate Appraisal
Commission**

The Real Estate Appraisal Commission must meet 30 days after the members have been appointed for the purpose of organizing and selecting officers other than the chairperson, as the commission deems appropriate. A majority of its members constitutes a quorum. The commission authorizes the Department of Consumer Protection to issue certification, licenses, tenured licenses, and provisional licenses to real estate appraisers, as well as to administer provisions of the law concerning the appraisal business. The commission meets quarterly; it can convene more frequently at the discretion of the chairperson or a majority of the commission members.

Approval of schools (Section 20-512-1 et seq. of the Appraisal Regulations). The commission evaluates schools offering real estate appraisal courses and related subjects and approves course offerings that fulfill the prelicensing/precertification and continuing education requirements discussed later in this chapter. Students taking nonapproved courses may not be considered for licensing/certification.

■ DEFINITIONS (SECTION 20-504-1 OF THE APPRAISAL REGULATIONS)

Appraisal—The act or process of developing an opinion of value or an opinion of value.

Appraisal Experience—Appraisal-related experience obtained by performing fee and staff appraisals, ad valorem tax appraisals, mass appraisals, review appraisals, appraisal analyses, and feasibility analyses or studies and by teaching appraisal courses.

Complex Residential Property—Residential property where the property itself, the form of ownership, or the market conditions are atypical.

Federally Related Transaction—Any real estate–related financial transaction that (a) a federal financial institutions regulatory agency of the Resolution Trust Corporation engages in, contracts for, or regulates and (b) requires the service of an appraiser pursuant to the Financial Institutions Reform, Recovery and Enforcement Act of 1989 (FIRREA). A real estate–related financial transaction means a transaction involving the

- sale, lease, purchase, investment in, or exchange of real property, including interests in property or the financing thereof;
- refinancing of real property or interests in real property; and
- use of real property or interests in property as security for a loan or investment, including mortgage-backed securities.

Residential Real Estate—Property improved with one-unit to four-unit residential structures and vacant or unimproved land where the highest and best use analysis is for one-unit to four-unit residential purposes. This does not include land where a development analysis/appraisal, such as a subdivision development analysis or condominium development analysis, is necessary or utilized.

Transaction Value—With regard to federally related transactions: (a) for loans or other extensions of credit, the amount of the loan or extension of credit; (b) for sales, leases, purchases, and investments in or exchanges of real property, the market value of the real property interest involved; and (c) for the pooling of loans or interests in real property for resale or purchase, the amount of the loan or the market value of the real property calculated with respect to each such loan or interest in real property.

■ LICENSURE CATEGORIES (SECTION 20-504-3 OF THE APPRAISAL REGULATIONS)

The appraisal law establishes the following categories of appraiser licensure:

- State certified general appraiser
- State certified residential appraiser
- Limited general appraiser*
- Limited residential appraiser*
- State provisional licensed appraiser

Note that the asterisked (*) categories will be eliminated as of September 30, 2006. The commission is not issuing any new licenses for these categories, but until that date will be accepting renewals of existing licenses.

No appraiser is permitted to perform appraisal work that is beyond the scope of practice for his or her category of licensure.

State Certified General Appraiser

A state certified general appraiser is allowed to appraise all types of real estate, without regard to transaction value, for all types of transactions, including federally related transactions.

State Certified Residential Appraiser

A state certified residential appraiser is allowed to appraise all residential real estate, without regard to transaction value, for all types of transactions, including federally related transactions.

Limited General Appraiser

A limited general appraiser (formerly referred to as a *tenured general appraiser*) is a person who holds a valid general appraiser license as of April 30, 1994, which is the renewal of an original license issued on or before December 31, 1990, and which was issued without the appraiser having passed an examination requirement, and who properly applied and qualified for a May 1, 1994, renewal.

An appraiser in this category is allowed to appraise all types of real estate, without regard to transaction value, for transactions other than federally related transactions.

Limited Residential Appraiser

A limited residential appraiser (formerly referred to as a *tenured residential appraiser*) is a person who holds a valid residential appraiser license as of April 30, 1994, which is the renewal of an original license issued on or before December 31, 1990, and which was issued without the appraiser having passed an examination requirement, and who properly applied and qualified for a May 1, 1994, renewal.

In this category, an appraiser is allowed to appraise residential real estate, without regard to transaction value, for transactions other than federally related transactions.

**State Provisional
Licensed Appraiser**

The purpose of this category is to provide an entry level that will allow appraisers to develop the appraisal experience needed to qualify for a category of certified or licensed appraiser. A person can be a provisional licensed appraiser for only four years.

A provisional licensed appraiser is allowed to appraise real estate while under the direct supervision of a certified appraiser or licensed appraiser, for the types of property and in the types of transactions the supervising appraiser is permitted to appraise.

■ LICENSING PROCEDURES (SECTIONS 20-509 AND 20-504-5 OF THE APPRAISAL REGULATIONS)

All applications for certifications and licenses must be in writing on forms prescribed by the Department of Consumer Protection and accompanied with information that attests to the applicant's honesty, truthfulness, integrity and competency.

Certification and license requirements are summarized in Table 13.1. The application fee for certification is $45; for initial issuance of the license it is $300; and for renewal, it is $225.

A written examination is required for a certification or license. To pass the exam, an applicant must obtain a score of at least 75 percent.

**Licensing Corporations,
Partnerships,
and Associations
(Section 20-501)**

Partnerships, associations, or corporations may be granted a license or certification to engage in the *real estate appraisal business* only if every member or officer who actively participates in the business is a licensed or certified appraiser.

■ FEDERAL REGISTRY (SECTION 20-504-10 OF THE APPRAISAL REGULATIONS)

The Appraisal Subcommittee of the Federal Financial Institutions Examination Council requires that each state submit a roster of certified and licensed appraisers to it along with an annual registry fee of $25 from each appraiser. (Limited and provisional licensed appraisers are not listed.)

■ LICENSURE RENEWAL (SECTION 20-504-7 OF THE APPRAISAL REGULATIONS)

Appraisal certifications and licenses expire on April 30 of each year. Appraisers must apply each year for renewal of their certifications or licenses. Renewal fees for each category are listed in Table 13.1.

Continuing Education

In every even-numbered year, appraisers must submit proof of compliance with continuing education requirements with their renewal applications. The continuing education requirements vary with licensure category. See Table 13.1 for a list of requirements.

TABLE 13.1

Connecticut Real Estate Appraisal Certification/Licensing Requirements Summary

		Minimum Requirements		
	Qualified For Appraisal Of	**Education**	**Experience**	**Testing**
State Certified General Appraiser	All property types for all types of transactions	180 hours, concentrating on income-producing properties and including 15 hours USPAP (2) (3)	3,000 hours over at least 30 months with 50% minimum spent on appraising income properties	General Appraiser Examination (7)
State Certified Residential Appraiser	All 1-4 family properties for all types of transactions	120 hours, including 15 hours USPAP (2) (3)	2,500 hours over at least 2 years	Residential Appraiser Examination (7)
Limited General Appraiser ˙Renewals Only	All property types for non-federally related transactions (10)	N/A	N/A	N/A
Limited Residential Appraiser ˙Renewals Only	Residential properties for non-federally related transactions (10)	N/A	N/A	N/A
State Provisional Licensed Appraiser	Must be under supervision of certified or licensed appraiser. Practice limited to the types of properties and transactions for which supervising appraiser is qualified	75 hours, of Real Estate Appraisal including 15 hours of USPAP (2) (3)	None, but time spent as a provisional licensed appraiser is limited to 4 years	None

Keep Summary Sheet for Future Reference. NOTE: This is a summary intended to give an overview. For specific questions consult statutes and regulations.

(1) For federally related transactions. Dollar limits and complex/non-complex criteria do not apply in non-federally related transactions.
(2) Courses must be a minimum of 15 hours including an examination. No time limit on education, except USPAP. Principles and Practices of R.E. taken after 9/1/00 does not qualify for prelicensing or license upgrade.
(3) The 15 hour with exam USPAP course must have been successfully completed within the six (6) year period preceding the date of application.
(4) N.A.
(5) Continuing education offerings must be at least 2 hours in length.
(6) Submission for continuing education credit is in even-numbered years.

■ APPRAISAL STANDARDS (SECTION 20-504-2 OF THE APPRAISAL REGULATIONS)

An appraiser is required to follow the Uniform Standards of Professional Appraisal Practice (USPAP) adopted by the Appraisal Standards Review Board of the Appraisal Foundation that are in effect at the time the services are performed. Copies of USPAP are available upon request from the Appraisal Commission.

	Fees				
Continuing Education	**Application**	**Testing**	**Initial Year**	**Renewal**	**Continuing Education**
28 hours every 2 years, including 3 hours on Appraisal legislation, USPAP and 7 hours National USPAP (5) (6) (11)	$45.00	$65.00 (7)	$300.00 plus $25.00 annual registry fee (10)	$225.00 plus $25.00 annual registry fee	$8.00
28 hours every 2 years, including 3 hours on Appraisal legislation, USPAP and equal opportunity laws and 7 hours National USPAP (5) (6) (11)	$45.00 (8)	$65.00 (7)	$300.00 plus $25.00 annual registry fee (10)	$225.00 plus $25.00 annual registry fee	$8.00
15 hours every 2 years, including 3 hours on Appraisal legislation, USPAP and equal opportunity laws (5) (6) (9) (11)	N/A	N/A	N/A	$225.00	$8.00
15 hours every 2 years, including 3 hours on Appraisal legislation, USPAP and equal opportunity laws (5) (6) (9) (11)	N/A	N/A	N/A	$225.00	$8.00
28 hours every 2 years, including 3 hours on Appraisal legislation, USPAP and equal opportunity laws and 7 hours National USPAP (5) (6) (8) (11)	$40.00	N/A	$50.00	$50.00	$8.00

(7) The applicant may take exam up to four times in a one-year period.

(8) No continuing education requirement for first renewal of provisional license.

(9) Limited appraisers are not qualified to perform appraisals for federally related transactions not even if co-signed by a licensed or certified appraiser.

(10) Initial (first license only) license fee is prorated on a quarterly basis.

(11) Effective January 1, 2003, the 7 hour National USPAP course must be taken every two years and taught by an AQB Certified Instructor.

Rec. 04/09/2003

An appraiser who wishes to enter in or on any real estate not the subject of appraisal to conduct a market comparison must obtain permission from the owner or occupier of the real estate and must identify himself or herself as an appraiser.

Each appraisal, review appraisal, or consulting report must contain (for each appraiser signing the report) the appraiser's name, either printed or typed; the category of licensure held and license number; the state of issuance; and the expiration date of the license.

■ APPRAISERS LICENSED IN ANOTHER STATE (SECTION 20-504-9 OF THE APPRAISAL REGULATIONS)

A person licensed as an appraiser in another state may become an appraiser in Connecticut by meeting all the requirements for a category of licensure as described above. The Connecticut Appraisal Commission has developed some reciprocity agreements with other states so that an appraiser from another state who holds a valid certification or license from that other state could obtain the same level of licensure in Connecticut without going through the full qualifying process. This would also work for an appraiser from Connecticut who wants to obtain a category of licensure to work in another state. Information about specific state reciprocity can be obtained through the Appraisal Commission.

As of the time of the writing of this text edition, Connecticut recognized reciprocity with Maine, Massachusetts, Missouri, New Hampshire, New York, Rhode Island, Tennessee, and Wyoming.

Connecticut has a temporary certification, license, and provisional license that allows nonresident appraisers to conduct appraisal work on a temporary basis within the state. The nonresident appraiser must hold a valid certification or license from another state and submit an application to the commission with a fee. Temporary licensure is effective for six months from issuance and applies to one appraisal assignment, which must be specified in the application. If the appraiser is unable to complete the assignment in six months, the appraiser may request an extension.

Nonresident appraisal reviewers who are performing an appraisal review on Connecticut real estate do not need to be licensed in Connecticut (permanent or temporary) as long as the reviewer is not conducting any fieldwork in Connecticut. Appraisal review is defined as "the act or process of developing and communicating an opinion about the quality of another appraiser's work."

QUESTIONS

1. All certified residential appraisers can appraise
   a. any property in Connecticut.
   b. a three-family house in Connecticut.
   c. a strip shopping center in Connecticut.
   d. a six-unit apartment complex in Connecticut.

2. Which type of license allows an appraiser to estimate the value of all properties utilizing federal funds?
   a. Certified general
   b. Certified residential
   c. Limited general
   d. Limited residential

3. A provisional license
   a. lasts for only four years.
   b. is renewable in four years.
   c. automatically renews for four years.
   d. can be reinstated every four years.

4. A licensed real estate salesperson is exempt from the appraisal licensing requirements when the salesperson
   a. has taken an appraisal course.
   b. does not charge a fee.
   c. performs what are referred to as "appraisal services" for real estate clients only.
   d. estimates the value of real estate as part of a market analysis conducted for a prospective seller.

5. To qualify as a limited appraiser, a person must have held a valid appraiser license originally issued on or before December 31,
   a. 1980.   c. 1992.
   b. 1990.   d. 1994.

6. An appraiser is required to follow USPAP, the
   a. United States Principles of Appraisal Practice.
   b. United States Appraisal Principles and Practices.
   c. Uniform Standards of Professional Appraisal Practice.
   d. Uniform Standards of Practical Appraisal Principals.

7. To qualify as a certified general appraiser, a person must meet _____ hours of education and _____ hours of experience.
   a. 180/3,000   c. 120/2,500
   b. 165/2,000   d. 90/2,000

8. What are the requirements to qualify as a provisional licensed appraiser?
   a. 75 hours of education, four years of experience, and an exam
   b. 75 hours of education, no experience, and an exam
   c. 75 hours of education, no experience, and no exam
   d. 30 hours of education, no experience, and no exam

9. A certified or licensed general or residential appraiser must take how many hours of continuing education every two years?
   a. 12   c. 20
   b. 15   d. 28

10. What type of transaction would not be considered a "federally related transaction"?
    a. The loan of money by a federally insured bank secured by a mortgage on property
    b. The sale of property by the Resolution Trust Corporation
    c. The purchase of property by a private party
    d. The refinancing of property by a federally insured institution

CHAPTER FOURTEEN

LAND USE CONTROLS AND PROPERTY DEVELOPMENT

■ OVERVIEW

The manner in which raw land is developed and subdivided or otherwise put to use is regulated by both state and municipal laws and ordinances. There are a number of state laws that directly affect the development and use of land and an equivalent number of state agencies authorized to oversee, administer, and enforce these laws. Additionally, local and regional planning authorities and economic development agencies have important, if not legislative, impact on the development and utilization of land. Consumer and private interest groups also affect decisions about how land is used.

WWWeb.Link

Connecticut municipality Web links, many of which contain detailed information on local land use control, can be found at *www.munic.state.ct.us/townlist.htm*.

In terms of residential construction, new home contractors and home improvement contractors are required to be registered with the state. There is both a New Home Construction Guaranty Fund and a Home Improvement Guaranty Fund from which a consumer can seek reimbursement for uncollectable damages. In terms of commercial construction, private contracts for building, renovating, or rehabilitating commercial or industrial buildings must contain payment schedule provisions.

■ PLANNING AND ZONING

Local Agencies

Some of the most important pieces of legislation concerning land use on the state level are the enabling statutes that authorize the formation and operation of local zoning and planning commissions and define their authority and manner of operation. State law permits local planning and zoning commissions to operate independently or as a single commission. No other agencies have a more critical impact on land resource development than these local authorities. It is by their actions and approval that the development of the area takes place, and it is their responsibility to adhere to whatever development plans they may have adopted.

Zoning commission.[1]   A zoning commission must have at least five and not more than nine members, with minority representation. Generally, the zoning commission is a legislative body, separate from and not controlled by the municipal legislative body. In towns of under 5,000 population and some of the larger cities, however, the town council members may be empowered by local ordinance to act as the zoning commission. Depending on local ordinance, the members of the zoning commission may be elected or appointed, but in all cases they must be *electors* (resident voters) of the municipality. The state enabling legislation also provides for the election or appointment of three alternate commission members and for the designation of one member of the commission as its chairperson.

Zoning commissions are authorized to control land use through such ordinances as they feel are necessary to safeguard the health and general welfare of the public and to oversee the prudent and productive development of the town's land resources. Chapter 124 of the Connecticut General Statutes outlines the more specific facets of land use and property development that are regulated by the local zoning commission. Included among those items regulated by the zoning commission are the

- height, size, and number of stories of various buildings and structures;
- percentage of a lot that a structure may cover;
- density of population;
- permitted uses within designated areas;
- height, size, and location of advertising signs; and
- location of specific areas for trade, industry, residences, and so on.

When any use or condition is found that violates zoning regulations, the local zoning officer (typically a building or housing code inspector) or other designated authority has the power to order the violation corrected and to impose fines until the situation is remedied.

If the zoning commission seeks to establish new regulations, designate new zones, or change the permitted uses in any area of an existing zone within 500 feet of a town boundary, it must hold a public hearing before formally adopting any of these changes or new regulations. All such proposals must be referred to the local planning commission and regional planning agency 35 days before the required public hearing.

Planning commission.[2]   Although it is common to see combined planning and zoning commissions in Connecticut, state law allows a municipality to maintain separate commissions. Planning commissions are composed of no fewer than five electors and three alternates (see Chapter 126 of the Connecticut General Statutes).

The principal duty of the planning commission is to prepare, adopt, and amend a plan of development for the town. This plan is essentially a statement of goals, policies, and standards relating to the town's physical and economic development. Any proposed zoning regulations or boundaries or any changes to existing zoning regulations or boundaries must be reviewed to determine whether such proposals are consistent with the plan of development.

The commission also has the authority to adopt *subdivision regulations* and to evaluate and approve new subdivision proposals submitted to it. It is important to recognize the amount of interplay between the state laws (such as inland wetlands legislation, discussed later in this chapter) and local ordinances in the overall process of subdividing and land development. Thus, the subdivider/developer must take all of these regulations into consideration before he or she makes a move on any particular project.

Variances and special permits.   There are two types of exceptions to the zoning regulations that may be obtained by a property owner. A *variance* is a permit to employ a particular use in an area that is not zoned for that use, and it runs with the land. A person seeking a variance must apply to the *zoning board of appeals*, a five-member to eight-member board that may be elected or appointed.[3] The zoning board of appeals must hold a public hearing and act on requests for variances within 65 days after proper applications have been submitted. The board will grant a variance if it determines that the characteristics of the site, unlike other similar sites, would cause the owner exceptional difficulty and unusual hardship in employing a permitted use. Economic hardship alone is not considered sufficient reason to grant a variance.

In contrast to the variance, there are certain uses that are permitted by the zoning regulations only if specific standards are met. An owner may obtain a *special permit* or *special exception* for such uses by applying to the zoning commission, the planning commission, or the zoning board of appeals. Before granting a special permit, the agency involved must first hold a hearing to determine if the required standards are fulfilled. Note that while all three agencies are empowered to grant special exceptions, only the zoning board of appeals may grant a variance.

Inland Wetlands Commission.   All municipalities must have an Inland Wetlands Commission that establishes the boundaries of inland wetlands and watercourses within a municipality and regulates the types of activities that can be conducted in these areas.[4] No regulated activity can be conducted in inland wetlands without a permit from the commission. The commission must consider a number of factors when deciding on an application, the most important of which is the environmental impact of the regulated activity. State statute requires that a permit shall not be issued by the commission unless it finds that a feasible and prudent alternative to the regulated activity does not exist.[5] *Feasible* means "able to be constructed or implemented consistent with sound engineering principles"; *prudent* means "economically and otherwise reasonable in light of the social benefits to be derived from the proposed regulated activity, provided cost may be considered in deciding what is prudent and further provided a mere showing of expense will not necessarily mean an alternative is imprudent."[6]

Connecticut also has a Tidal Wetlands Program that is run at the state level by the Department of Environmental Protection.

Village Districts.   Local zoning commissions are authorized to establish village districts as part of a municipality's zoning regulations. Such districts can have their own regulations protecting the district's historic, natural, and/or community character.[7]

Regional Planning Agencies

Chapter 127 of the Connecticut General Statutes authorizes the creation of regional planning agencies in any of the planning areas defined by the Office of Policy and Management (OPM). The OPM is responsible for guiding and coordinating the direction of land use in the state through its liaison work with the regional agencies and its own research efforts. The areas it defines as planning regions correspond roughly to the county jurisdictions that existed prior to the demise of county government in Connecticut. However, it is up to the director of the OPM to actually determine the area.

Regional planning agencies prepare comprehensive plans of development that encompass all the towns located within their jurisdictions. With these plans of development, planners make general recommendations for land use as well as recommendations concerning principal highways and freeways, airports, parks, playgrounds, recreational areas, schools, public facilities, and so on. After this comprehensive plan has been presented at a public hearing, it must be approved by a majority of the local representatives to the agency if it is to be adopted. Local representatives may be elected or appointed by the legislative authorities of the town they represent. Once adopted, the plan becomes a model to advise those implementing the planning process at the local level and, thus, may have some impact on any locally proposed land use that conflicts with its recommendations. But, more important, the regional plan is used in reviewing certain government grants to municipalities for land development, and it may have substantial impact in those cases.

Regional planning agencies are also authorized to assist local planning agencies in implementing the regional development plan and may provide technical assistance on a contract or voluntary basis to member municipalities.

WWWeb.Link   Information on Connecticut's Regional Planning Organization can be found at *http://www.opm.state.ct.us/igp/rpos/rpo.htm.*

■ DEVELOPING SPECIFIC TYPES OF PROPERTY

Subdivisions[8]

Connecticut statutes require that the *subdivision of a parcel of land into three or more parts must be approved by the local planning commission.* Approval requires that the developer of the parcel submit subdivision plans to the planning commission. Any plans submitted must conform to the subdivision regulations and other applicable development laws of the municipality in which the proposed subdivision will be located.

Although the specific requirements for subdivisions vary from locality to locality, virtually all commissions require the submission of an accurate development plan indicating the physical layout of the lots to be created, the roads to be constructed, the manner in which utilities will be provided to each of the proposed lots, and any other pertinent engineering or development data. The subdivision plans must be drawn up by a licensed surveyor and must meet the requirements of both local ordinances and state laws. Planning commissions are required to consider information on passive solar energy techniques (site techniques maximizing solar heat gain) when deciding a subdivision application. Once approved by the commission, all subdivision plans and maps must be filed in the town clerk's office within 90 days from the expiration of the appeal period (or in the case of an appeal, within 90 days of the resolution of that appeal).

The legal descriptions of each lot generally make specific reference to the original subdivision map and identify the lot in question by the number appearing on the original document. A typical plot map for a subdivision (Figure 14.1) appears along with a plot plan, which focuses on one property (Figure 14.2). The plan is one that a lender would typically require to make sure that the property is not in violation of any zoning, subdivision, or building line restrictions.

City and Town Development Act[9]

The comprehensive City and Town Development Act (CTDA) aids municipalities in their attempts to reverse their deteriorating employment, housing, and land resource conditions. The act deals with *development properties*, which are defined as any real or personal properties, including land, buildings, and other structures, acquired or to be acquired by the municipality and dedicated to the purposes of the CTDA. The CTDA empowers municipalities to do any of the following with respect to these development properties: (1) buy, (2) sell, (3) lease, (4) construct, (5) reconstruct, (6) rehabilitate, (7) improve, (8) finance, and (9) foreclose.

The CTDA, then, would allow a municipality to purchase structures in a deteriorated neighborhood, demolish them, erect new construction (for example, a new civic center) on the vacant parcels, sell the improved parcel, and finance the entire deal for the investors purchasing the property. CTDA allows Connecticut's municipalities to initiate programs on their own.

Planned Unit Developments (PUDs)

The PUD concept is described in the text. Chapter 124a of the Connecticut General Statutes allows municipalities to adopt the state's uniform regulations governing PUDs. The regulations, if adopted as a part of the local zoning ordinance, outline the standards, conditions, and application procedures for evaluating and approving PUDs. However, because of the flexibility given to local planning and zoning commissions in designing controlled projects, Connecticut municipalities are not required to adopt these regulations.

FIGURE 14.1

Subdivision Plan

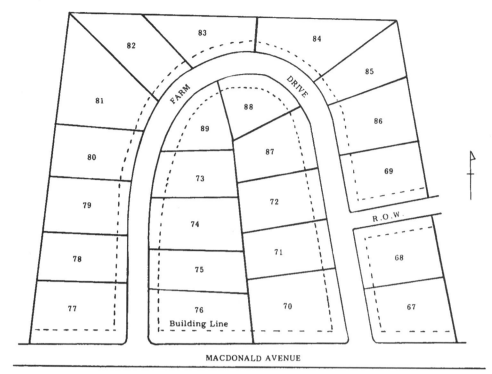

MACDONALD AVENUE

SCALE 1" = 100'

SUBDIVISION PLAN
OF
"COUNTRY FARM ESTATES"

John L. Sullivan Const. Co.
Willimantic, Conn.

Prepared by:

George Washington
Licensed Surveyor and
Professional Engineer

Accepted:

Tom K. Smith
Tom K. Smith, Chairman
Zoning Commission
7-4-76

Open-Space, Farm, or Forest Land

The state provides for local property tax relief for land held in any of these forms, provided that the owner meets the required qualifications for this relief and submits a proper application. The discussion of real estate taxes in Chapter 6 includes a more detailed discussion of the limitations on land use imposed by these designations.

Towns, at their discretion, may allow applicants for subdivision approval to pay a fee (or combination fee and land) in lieu of any requirement to provide open space. The fee is limited to 10 percent of the fair market value of the land to be subdivided prior to approval of the subdivision. The town must deposit such funds into a special account for open-space, recreational, or agricultural purposes. Exemption to this provision is granted for subdivisions of less than five parcels transferred for no consideration to certain members

FIGURE 14.2
Plot/Plan Mortgage Survey

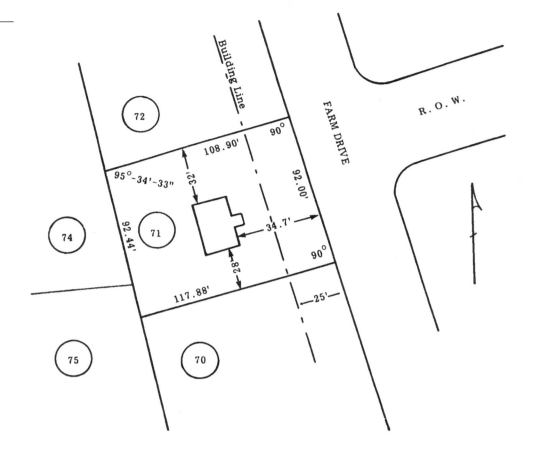

I HEREBY CERTIFY THAT THIS MAP IS SUBSTANTIALLY CORRECT. NO ZONING, SUBDIVISION, OR BUILDING LINE VIOLATIONS.

George Washington
Surveyor

PLOT PLAN/MORTGAGE SURVEY
JOHN L. SULLIVAN CONST. CO.
WILLIMANTIC, CONN.
SCALE 1" - 40' DEC. 20, 1976

of a family or for subdivisions providing 20 percent of their development for "affordable" housing purposes.

Town planning and zoning regulations may allow cluster developments, which are building patterns concentrating units on a parcel with at least one-third of the parcel left as open space for recreational, conservation, or agricultural purposes.

Affordable Housing Land Use Appeals Act[10]

This law was enacted to provide an affordable housing appeals procedure when a municipality denies an affordable housing development application. Its purpose is to encourage the development of affordable housing in the state. The act defines "affordable housing" as either "assisted housing" (through which one receives financial assistance under any government program for the construction or rehabilitation of low- and moderate-income housing and housing occupied by persons receiving rental assistance) or housing where not less than 30 percent of the units will be conveyed by deeds containing cov-enants and restrictions that require that such units be sold or rented at or below prices that will preserve the units as affordable (as defined in the law according to area median income) for at least 40 years.

The act shifts the burden of proof in an appeal of a development application denial from the developer to the municipality.[11] The municipality must prove that denial of an affordable housing development (1) is supported by sufficient evidence in the record; (2) is necessary to protect substantial public interests in health, safety, or other matters that it may legally consider; (3) is necessary because such public interests clearly outweigh the need for affordable housing; and (4) is necessary because such interests cannot be protected by reasonable changes to the proposed affordable housing development.

Municipalities are exempt from the act if at least 10 percent of the municipal housing is deemed affordable by the Commissioner of Economic and Com-munity Development. Towns are also allowed a moratorium from appeals of certain types of projects for four years after completion of other certain types of affordable housing projects in the town.

■ NEW HOME CONSTRUCTION

New home contractors must register with the Department of Consumer Pro-tection. A new home contractor is defined as someone who contracts with a consumer to build a new home or a portion of one before it is occupied. Additionally, new home contractors must include their registration number in all advertisements and must provide certain disclosures to consumers before entering into a contract.

Building officials must check registration certificates before issuing a contrac-tor a building or construction permit. If requested by a consumer, a contractor must return a deposit if 30 days have passed since work was to have begun and no substantial portion of the work has been completed.

New Home Construction Guaranty Fund

A consumer may seek reimbursement from this fund for damages caused by a new home contractor that the consumer is unable to collect. The reimburse-ment for a single claim is capped at $30,000.

Real Estate Licensees Exempted

Real estate licensees are specifically exempted from the new home construc-tion registration requirements as long as the licensee is working within the scope of his or her license.

■ HOME IMPROVEMENT

Home improvement contractors and salespeople must register with the Depart-ment of Consumer Protection. Home improvements are defined as repairs, replacement, remodeling, alteration, modernizing, and rehabilitation of any pri-vate or public dwelling in which the total cash price for all work agreed on between contractor and owner exceeds $200. It does *not* include (a) construction of new homes, (b) sale of goods by a seller who neither directly nor indirectly performs any labor in connection with installation or application of goods or materials, (c) sale of goods or services furnished for commercial or business use or resale, (d) sale of appliances, or (e) any work provided by an owner.

Municipalities are prohibited from issuing a building permit to a contractor who is not registered.

Home Improvement Contract[12]

To be valid and enforceable, a home improvement contract must (1) be in writing, (2) be signed by both owner and contractor, (3) contain the entire agreement, (4) contain the date of the transaction, (5) contain the name and address of the contractor, (6) contain a notice of the owner's cancellation rights, (7) contain a starting date and completion date, and (8) be entered into by a registered contractor. A contractor who has complied with (1), (2), (6), (7), and (8) but not (3), (4), and (5) is not precluded from recovering payment for work based on the reasonable services requested by the owner if the court determines that it would be inequitable to deny such a recovery.

Exemptions

Certain professionals and tradespeople are exempt from registering as home improvement contractors while working in their own profession or trade, for example, (1) government agencies and departments, (2) those who are involved with construction of a new home, (3) sellers of goods who neither arrange to perform nor perform any work in connection with an installation, (4) sellers of goods for commercial or business use, (5) sellers of appliances designed for easy installation, or (6) owners performing work on their own premises.

Home Improvement Guaranty Fund

A fund administered by the Commissioner of Consumer Protection has been established to reimburse homeowners who have suffered loss or damage by reason of the performance or nonperformance of registered home improvement contractors.[13] A $10,000 bond is required of each contractor for the use of the state or any person aggrieved by the contractor's action. The maximum that may be paid out of the Home Improvement Guaranty Fund on a single claim is $15,000. This fund also permits a homeowner to be reimbursed from the fund for attorney's fees.

■ COMMERCIAL/INDUSTRIAL CONSTRUCTION

Private contracts for building, renovating, or rehabilitating commercial or industrial buildings must contain a payment schedule. Unless agreed otherwise, owners must pay general contractors within 15 days after receiving a payment request, and general contractors must pay subcontractors within an additional 15 days. Also, retainage (amounts withheld from progress payments to a general contractor or subcontractor) under a construction contract is limited to 7.5 percent of the amount owed.

■ PRIVATE LAND-USE CONTROL

Private regulations affecting subdivision, land development, and land consist almost exclusively of deed restrictions and covenants. These are, essentially, voluntary restrictions that often fail to stand up in court under close scrutiny, primarily because many such private restrictions serve no legitimate public purpose. They are not usually considered as law and, when observed, are adhered to more on the basis of courtesy and mutual agreement than ironclad legality.

■ BUILDING ACCESSIBILITY

All units in R-2 buildings (multifamily dwellings) with elevators and ground floor units constructed or substantially renovated after July 1, 1991 (as well as R-2 buildings without elevators), must be adaptable for use by people with disabilities. In dormitories and boarding houses, 1 in 25 beds must be accessible to the disabled. The requirement for one-family and two-family attached dwellings constructed after July 1, 1991, is that one in ten units be accessible to people with disabilities.

WWWeb.Link

The Connecticut Building Code can be found at *http://www.state.ct.us /dps/DFEBS/OSFM.htm*. The Connecticut Fire Safety Code can be found at *http://www.state.ct.us/dps/DFEBS/OSFM.htm*. State officials are required to maintain a list of existing building exemptions and variations from these codes.

■ CONNECTICUT INTERSTATE LAND SALES

Occasions arise when real estate located in states other than Connecticut is advertised for sale and sold in Connecticut. Such activity can take place only under the provisions of either the Federal Interstate Land Sales Full Disclosure Act or the Connecticut Real Estate Licensing Laws Concerning the Advertising, Sale, Exchange or Other Disposition of Certain Real Estate Located in Another State (Sections 20-329a to 20-329m of the Connecticut General Statutes). The general purpose of the Connecticut law is to cover those instances that fall outside the jurisdiction of the federal laws. Appropriate filings with the Federal Office of Interstate Land Sales will generally exempt parties or individuals from the registration and compliance requirements of the Connecticut laws.

Whether the offering in Connecticut involves the sale of condominiums in Florida or raw land in Alaska, it must be registered with the Real Estate Commission and the secretary of state's office. The offer must comply with Sections 20-329a to 20-329m of the Connecticut General Statutes (as mentioned above), unless specifically exempted from the disclosure requirement by virtue of prior compliance with the federal law(s). Offerings must always be registered under Connecticut statutes.

Under the Connecticut statutes, registration and compliance involve the following general steps (although not necessarily in this order):

■ The offeror must submit documents, promotional plans, and advertising materials to the Real Estate Commission.
■ The offeror must appoint the secretary of state as the agent through whom actions and proceedings against the offeror may be served. Such appointment must be in writing.

■ The offeror must post a bond, as deemed appropriate by the Real Estate Commission, in favor of the state. The bond must be made with a surety company authorized to do business in Connecticut.

■ The applicant/offeror must apply for and receive a license from the Real Estate Commission that authorizes the offering and disposition in Connecticut of the property that is the object of the application and registration. Fees for such licenses are based on a sliding scale.

■ The offeror must appoint a resident Connecticut broker, who is responsible for compliance, as his or her representative in the state.

Once approved by the commission, the sale of properties outside Connecticut may proceed legally in accordance with the prescribed plan.

Only licensed real estate brokers in Connecticut are authorized to dispose of such property. Dispose is defined as sell, exchange, lease, and award. Under no circumstances may the brokers or parties to the disposition in any way advertise that the property in question has been inspected and/or approved by the Real Estate Commission or any other official, department, or employee of the state of Connecticut.

When an individual purchases property covered under Connecticut's Interstate Land Sales Act, he or she must be presented with a clearly identified copy of the prospectus, property report, or offering statement within 72 hours before signing a sales contract. The broker will retain a signed receipt.

Subdivisions of less than five parcels or lots; shares in real estate investment trusts; cemetery lots; and leases pertaining to apartments, stores, or offices generally are exempted from Connecticut interstate land sales regulations.

■ ENDNOTES

1. Chapter 124 of the Connecticut General Statutes.
2. Chapter 126 of the Connecticut General Statutes.
3. Section 8-5, et seq., of the Connecticut General Statutes.
4. Section 22a-42 of the Connecticut General Statutes.
5. Section 22a-41 of the Connecticut General Statutes.
6. Section 22a-38 (17), (18) of the Connecticut General Statutes.
7. Connecticut Public Act 98-116.
8. Section 8-25 of the Connecticut General Statutes.
9. Chapter 114 of the Connecticut General Statutes.
10. Section 8-30g of the Connecticut General Statutes.
11. See *West Hartford Interfaith Coalition, Inc. v. Town Council of West Hartford*, 228 Conn. 498 (1994).
12. Section 20-429 of the Connecticut General Statutes.
13. Section 20-432 of the Connecticut General Statutes.

QUESTIONS

1. The state law governing planned unit developments (PUDs) is incorporated into which of the following local ordinances if adopted by a municipality?
   a. Subdivision regulations
   b. Zoning regulations
   c. Plan of development
   d. Building code

2. A homeowner plans on hiring a contractor to build an addition. The following are all true about the home improvement business in Connecticut *except*
   a. home improvement contractors must be registered with the state.
   b. home improvement contracts must be in writing to be enforceable.
   c. a homeowner is prohibited from hiring a contractor that is not registered with the state.
   d. a homeowner may be able to collect losses caused by a registered home improvement contractor from a state fund.

3. Local planning and zoning commissions
   a. are always separate entities.
   b. may be a combined commission.
   c. must be separate entities.
   d. must be a combined commission.

4. Which of the following local authorities has jurisdiction over subdivision regulation?
   a. Planning commission
   b. Board of tax review
   c. Town clerk
   d. Assessor's office

5. A buyer is interested in building a deck off the back of his new house, but such structure would not be in keeping with the zoning regulations. The most likely procedure would be for the buyer to apply for a
   a. special permit.
   b. zone change.
   c. hardship exemption.
   d. variance.

6. Which of the following is excluded from Connecticut's law governing interstate land sales?
   a. Subdivisions under 50 lots
   b. Improved land up to 25 lots
   c. Real estate investment trusts
   d. Condominiums

7. How long before the signing of a sales contract for recreational lots outside Connecticut must the seller present a purchaser with a prospectus?
   a. 24 hours
   b. Within 72 hours
   c. Five business days
   d. One week

8. Applicants to sell real properties located outside Connecticut in this state must (if required to register)
   a. pay a 1 percent commission to the secretary of state's office.
   b. post a bond in favor of the state.
   c. observe a 1-month residency requirement.
   d. disclose the source of their principal income.

9. Subdivision plans in Connecticut must be drawn up by a
   a. local planning commission.
   b. building architect.
   c. licensed mechanical engineer.
   d. licensed surveyor.

10. Once approved by the planning commission, subdivision plans must be filed at the town clerk's office
    a. within 15 working days.
    b. within 90 days from the expiration of the appeal period.
    c. by the chairperson of the commission.
    d. by the tax assessor.

CHAPTER FIFTEEN

15

FAIR HOUSING AND ETHICAL PRACTICES

■ OVERVIEW

Connecticut fair housing law is substantially equivalent to Title VIII of the Federal Civil Rights Act. Although there is similar coverage in many areas of both state and federal laws, there still remains a certain amount of overlap and "underlap." In some instances, federal law provides greater coverage than state law, and in other instances state law provides greater coverage than federal law.

In Connecticut, it is illegal for a real estate licensee in the conduct of his or her business to discriminate against any person on the basis of race, creed, color, national origin, ancestry, sex, marital status, age, lawful source of income, familial status, physical disability, mental disability, learning disability, or sexual orientation. Although there are exceptions and exemptions for some property owners, there are no exceptions and exemptions for real estate licensees.

■ GENERAL CONSIDERATIONS

Antidiscrimination Laws and the Housing Market

Anyone who has traveled extensively throughout Connecticut can easily see that the majority of black and Hispanic households are located in the inner cities, while the suburbs and small towns of the state remain substantially all white. This pattern is obvious to anyone familiar with the Connecticut housing market.

While the causes of this dual housing pattern are open to question, it is clear that racial and ethnic discrimination continues to be a major problem in Connecticut. The existence of racial and ethnic discrimination has been documented by government studies and private investigations. Discrimination is not limited to racial and ethnic minorities, however, but includes practices that limit the housing choices of the elderly, families with minor children, persons with disabilities, and others.

Because of their critical role in the housing market, real estate agents are in a unique position to be a positive force for fair housing in Connecticut's housing market and to be instrumental in alleviating the existence and perpetuation of such discrimination.

Compliance with federal, state, and local fair housing laws is not just a lofty goal; it is a legal requirement. Real estate agents who violate these laws, whether by accident or design, risk serious civil and criminal penalties, including substantial fines and possible revocation of their real estate licenses. The first step in avoiding these consequences is to become thoroughly familiar with the requirements of the federal, state, and local fair housing laws and regulations. Because of the sheer number of such laws, and the complexity of their various prohibitions and exceptions, it is easy to become confused or unsure of exactly what is required. This chapter attempts to address such concerns. However, the safest way to avoid problems and ensure compliance with the law is simply not to discriminate or to participate in the discriminatory practices of others.

Understanding Fair Housing Laws

There is no single, all-inclusive, all-controlling fair housing law. Instead, there is a patchwork of various laws and regulations enacted or adopted by federal, state, and local governments. Each of these laws can apply to different protected classes (e.g., race, national origin, families with minor children), different kinds of real estate transactions (e.g., residential properties versus commercial properties), and different kinds of discriminatory practices (e.g., residential racial steering, discriminatory advertising, or blockbusting). Each level of government also has its own practices and procedures for enforcing its fair housing laws. To complicate things further, these laws can overlap. A given act of discrimination (e.g., denial of an apartment because of race) can violate a number of different laws and may be enforceable in federal court and in a state or local administrative agency, all at the same time.

To understand fully a fair housing law, one needs to know the classes of persons it protects, the types of real estate practices to which it applies, the acts of discrimination it prohibits, and how it is enforced. Because more than one law may apply to the same act of discrimination, it is important to be familiar with the provisions of every law that may apply to any given set of facts or real estate transactions.

Federal and state fair housing laws are intended to eliminate the effects of unintentional as well as intentional discrimination. The focus of fair housing laws is on the effect of a given act or omission, not on the state of mind of the principal. Therefore, practices and procedures that are perfectly innocent and benign in motive may violate the law if the effect is to discriminate because of membership in one of the classes protected by the law. To ensure compliance with fair housing laws, the professional conduct of real estate brokers and salespersons must be firmly based on their clients' legal and legitimate business needs as well as their own.

A popular misconception regarding fair housing laws is that they are designed to protect only minorities. While it is true that such laws arose out of discrimination against blacks and other ethnic minorities, their protection is available to all. Anyone may file a fair housing complaint if they have been discriminated against because of their race, sex, religion, or other protected class status. As will be discussed in greater detail below, it is also possible to bring a fair housing action if you are injured because of discrimination directed *toward someone else*. By providing a remedy for discrimination and, thus, helping to ensure a free and open housing market, fair housing laws serve the interests of the entire community. Fair housing laws exist for the protection and benefit of all.

Fair Housing Enforcement in Connecticut

The federal fair housing laws are discussed at length in the principles book. Those laws will be referred to in this chapter only as required for a full and complete understanding of fair housing enforcement in Connecticut.

The primary federal fair housing law, Title VIII of the federal Civil Rights Act of 1968, may be enforced by filing a private lawsuit in federal court or by filing an administrative complaint with the federal Department of Housing and Urban Development (HUD). Where a state or local government has enacted fair housing laws that are *substantially equivalent* to Title VIII, HUD is required to defer all fair housing complaints it receives from within that jurisdiction to the state or local fair housing enforcement agency created by that state or locality. A state or local fair housing law is considered to be substantially equivalent to Title VIII if its prohibitions and remedies are comparable to those of that federal law.

In Connecticut only the city of New Haven and the state, itself, have enacted laws substantially equivalent to Title VIII. Connecticut's fair housing laws are enforced by the Connecticut Commission on Human Rights and Opportunities. The New Haven Commission on Equal Opportunities is the enforcement agency for the city of New Haven.

 **WWWeb.Link**

The Connecticut Commission on Human Rights and Opportunities Web site is *www.state.ct.us/chro/*. The New Haven Commission's Web site is *www.newhavenparks. org/govt/gov31.htm*.

■ CONNECTICUT FAIR HOUSING LAWS

Connecticut's fair housing legislation was previously part of the public accommodations statute. Now, state law concerning fair housing[1] is separate from the law prohibiting discriminatory public accommodations practices.[2] These revisions made the Connecticut Fair Housing Law conform to the federal Fair Housing Act. Connecticut's fair housing law can now be found at Chapter 814c of the Connecticut General Statutes.

Definitions

Dwelling—Any building, structure, manufactured mobile home park, or portion thereof that is occupied as, or designed or intended for occupancy as, a residence by one or more families, and any vacant land that is offered for sale or lease for the construction or location thereon of any such building, structure, manufactured mobile home park, or portion thereof.

Housing For Older Persons

- Housing provided under any state or federal program that the Secretary of the U.S. Department of Housing and Urban Development determines is specifically designed and operated to assist elderly persons as defined in the state or federal program.
- Housing intended for, and solely occupied by, persons 62 years of age or older.
- Housing intended and operated for occupancy by at least one person 55 years of age or older per unit in accordance with the standards set forth in the federal Fair Housing Act and regulations developed pursuant thereto by the Secretary of the U.S. Department of Housing and Urban Development.

■ PROTECTED CLASSES IN CONNECTICUT

A protected class is a group of persons protected by statute from unlawful discrimination. Discrimination on the basis of any of the protected classes listed in Figure 15.1 is illegal.

■ DISCRIMINATORY HOUSING PRACTICES

Under Connecticut's fair housing legislation, the following discriminatory practices are prohibited:

1. To refuse to sell or rent a dwelling on the basis of a protected classification.
2. To discriminate against any person on the basis of a protected classification in the terms, conditions, privileges, or provision of services or facilities in connection with the sale or rental of a dwelling.
3. For purposes of items 1 and 2, discrimination against a person because of the physical, mental, or learning disability of any other person associated with such persons or any other person residing or intending to reside in the dwelling is also prohibited.
4. For purposes of items 1, 2, and 3, discrimination against a person with a physical, mental, or learning disability includes (a) refusing to permit the person to make reasonable modifications at the person's own expense to afford such person full enjoyment of the premises (permission may be conditioned upon a renter's agreeing to restore the interior of the premises to its original condition); (b) refusing to make reasonable accommodations in rules, policies, practices, or services if necessary to afford such person equal opportunity to use and enjoy a dwelling or premises; and (c) failure to design and construct certain multifamily dwellings that will be initially occupied after March 13, 1991, in accordance with the federal Fair Housing Act or after July 1, 1991, under state building codes (this includes buildings with four or more units and one or more elevators and ground floor units in other four-plus unit buildings).

FIGURE 15.1

Protected Classes in Connecticut

A.	Race	
B.	Creed	According to the Connecticut General Statutes (Sec. 46a-51(18)), "discrimination on the basis of religious creed" includes "discrimination related to all aspects of religious observances and practices as well as belief..."
C.	Color	
D.	National Origin	
E.	Ancestry	
F.	Sex	According to the Connecticut General Statutes (Sec. 46a-51(17)), "discrimination on the basis of sex" includes "discrimination related to pregnancy, child-bearing capacity, sterilization, fertility, or related medical conditions."
G.	Marital Status	
H.	Age	
I.	Lawful Source of Income	According to the Connecticut General Statutes (Sec. 46a-63(3)), "income derived from Social Security, supplemental security income, housing assistance, child support, alimony, or public or general assistance."
J.	Familial Status	According to the Connecticut General Statutes (Sec. 46a-64b(5)), "one or more individuals who have not attained the age of eighteen years being domiciled with a parent or another person having legal custody of such individual or individuals; or the designee of such parent or other person having such custody with the written permission of such parent or other person; or any person who is pregnant or in the process of securing legal custody or any individual who has not attained the age of eighteen years."
K.	Physical Disability	According to the Connecticut General Statutes (Sec. 46a-51(15)), "physically disabled refers to any individual who has any chronic physical handicap, infirmity, or impairment, whether congenital or resulting from bodily injury, organic processes, or changes from illness, including, but not limited to, epilepsy, deafness or hearing impairment, or reliance on a wheelchair or other remedial appliance or device."[3]
L.	Mental Disability	According to the Connecticut General Statutes, mental disability is defined as "an individual who has a record of, or is regarded as having one or more mental disorders, as defined by the American Psychiatric Association's Diagnostic and Statistical Manual of Mental Disorders." "Mental retardation means a significantly subaverage general intellectual functioning existing concurrently with deficits in adaptive behavior and manifested during the developmental period."
M.	Learning Disability	(This is a protected class only under the Connecticut fair housing law, currently not under the federal law.) According to the Connecticut General Statutes (Sec. 46a-51(19)), "learning disability refers to an individual who exhibits a severe discrepancy between educational performance and measured intellectual ability and who exhibits a disorder in one or more of the basic psychological processes involved in understanding or in using language, spoken or written, which may manifest itself in a diminished ability to listen, speak, read, write, spell, or do mathematical calculations."
N.	Sexual Orientation	(This is a protected class only under the Connecticut fair housing law, currently not under the federal law.) Having a preference for heterosexuality, homosexuality, or bisexuality or having a history of such preference or being identified with such preference. Excludes any behavior that constitutes a sex offense that is a violation of Part VI of Chapter 952 of the Connecticut General Statutes.

5. To advertise with respect to the sale or rental of a dwelling in a way that indicates any preference, limitation, or discrimination based on a protected classification.

6. To represent to any person because of a protected classification that any dwelling is not available for inspection, sale, or rental when such dwelling is so available.

7. To restrict or attempt to restrict the choices of any buyer or renter to purchase or rent a dwelling to an area that is substantially populated by persons of the same protected class as the buyer or renter (this is often termed *steering*).

8. To induce or attempt to induce any person to sell or rent any dwelling by representations regarding the entry or prospective entry into the neighborhood of a person or persons of a particular protected class (this is often termed *blockbusting*).

9. For any person engaging in residential real estate–related transactions, to discriminate against any person in making available such a transaction or in the terms or conditions of such a transaction because of a protected classification. (Note that a "residential real estate–related transaction is defined as either (a) the making or purchase of loans or providing other financial assistance for purchasing, constructing, improving, repairing, or maintaining a dwelling, or secured by residential real estate or (b) the selling, brokering, or appraising of residential real estate.")

10. To deny any person access to or membership or participation in any multiple-listing service, real estate brokers' organization, or facility relating to the business of selling or renting dwellings or to discriminate against him or her in the terms or conditions of such access, membership, or participation on account of a protected classification.

11. To coerce, intimidate, threaten, or interfere with any person in the exercise or enjoyment of, or on account of his or her having aided or encouraged any other person in the exercise or enjoyment of, any of the above granted rights.

Discrimination by Real Estate Associations or Boards

No association, board, or other organization that exists to further the professional or occupational interests of its members may refuse to accept a person as a member because of a protected classification.

This law applies only to associations, boards, and organizations of professions or occupations licensed by the state. Because Connecticut requires that all real estate brokers and salespersons be licensed, this law would apply to real estate associations. Violations of this law are punishable by a fine of $100 to $500.

Exceptions

Considerable caution must be exercised when relying on the exceptions contained in the state fair housing law. Many of the federal laws discussed in the main text apply to situations that come within one of the exceptions to the state law. None of the exceptions in Title VIII, for example, applies to single-family housing sales or rentals involving the services or facilities of a real estate broker, agent, or salesperson. Two other federal fair housing statutes (i.e., Sections 1981 and 1982 of the Civil Rights Act of 1866) contain no exceptions whatever. Because the Connecticut Commission on Human Rights and Opportunities has authority to prosecute violations of these federal laws (Deprivation of Rights Statute), the commission can still receive and act on complaints that fall outside the coverage of the state law. In questionable situations it is far easier and safer not to discriminate than to rely on statutory exceptions, which may lead to loss of a license or substantial financial penalties.

Because of the broad way in which the state fair housing law is written, its protections extend to persons who are injured, financially or otherwise, because of discrimination directed at someone else. For example, a white tenant who is evicted from an apartment because he or she has black friends can file a race complaint with the commission, even though the discrimination is not because of the tenant's own race but the race of his or her friends. Similarly, a real estate agent who loses a commission because a client refuses to sell to a Hispanic may file a national origin discrimination complaint based on the national origin of the Hispanic home seeker.

The following are exceptions under Connecticut fair housing law:

■ *In general.* Does not apply to the rental of a unit in a dwelling containing living quarters occupied or intended to be occupied by no more than two families if the owner actually lives in one of the two units (four units for sexual orientation category); does not apply to the rental of a room or rooms in a single-family dwelling unit if the owner actually maintains and occupies part of such living quarters as his or her residence

■ *Marital status.* Does not prohibit the denial of a dwelling to a man and a woman who are both unrelated by blood and not married to each other

■ *Age.* Does not apply to minors or to "housing for older persons"

■ *Familial status.* Does not apply to "housing for older persons" or to a unit in a dwelling containing units for no more than four families living independently of each other, if the owner of such dwelling resides in one of the units

■ *Lawful source of income.* Does not prohibit the denial of full and equal accommodations solely on the basis of insufficient income

■ *Sex.* Does not apply to the rental of sleeping accommodations provided by associations and organizations that rent all such sleeping accommodations on a temporary or permanent basis for the exclusive use of persons of the same sex to the extent that occupants utilize shared bathroom facilities (based on considerations of privacy and modesty)

■ *Sexual orientation.* Does not apply to an owner-occupied dwelling of single-family to four-family units, without the services of an agent and where no advertising has occurred

While there are certain exemptions for others, discrimination based on a protected classification is illegal for Connecticut real estate licensees. Licensees are not exempt from housing discrimination. In addition, racial discrimination has no exceptions under the Civil Rights Act of 1866.

■ ADMINISTRATIVE ENFORCEMENT

Connecticut Commission on Human Rights and Opportunities

The Connecticut Commission on Human Rights and Opportunities is the state administrative agency that has the authority to receive, initiate, and investigate complaints that are alleged to be violations of the fair housing statutes. It has offices throughout the state and employs its own legal counsel, staff, and investigators. It has the power to adopt, publish, amend, and rescind regulations consistent with and to effectuate the carrying out of its duties under the state law.

Complaint procedures. Any person claiming to be aggrieved by an alleged discriminatory practice may sign and file with the commission a complaint in writing under oath, which shall state the name and address of the person alleged to have committed the discriminatory practice and shall set forth the particulars thereof and contain such information as may be required by the commission. The complaint must be filed within 180 days after the alleged act of discrimination. The complaint is then served by the commission on the respondent within 10 days after filing, and the respondent then has up to 15 days to file a written response to the charges.

The complaint is then assigned to an investigator to determine if there is reasonable cause to believe a discriminatory practice has been or is being committed as alleged in the complaint. The commission may conduct conferences during the investigatory practice for the purpose of finding facts and promoting the voluntary resolution of complaints.

Findings and damages. If there is a determination made by the investigator of a "cause finding" to believe that a discriminatory act did take place, there will be an attempt to determine the damage suffered by the complainant as a result of this discriminatory act. This damage shall include but not be limited to the expense incurred by the complainant for obtaining alternate housing or space, storage of goods and effects, moving costs, and other costs actually incurred by him or her as a result of such discriminatory practice and shall allow reasonable attorney's fees and costs.

If the respondent does not agree to settle at this stage, a public hearing is scheduled. Such hearing is held before an impartial attorney, known as a *hearing officer*, appointed for that purpose. After a full public hearing, the hearing officer renders a decision and orders the relief appropriate to his or her determination. Decisions of the commission may be appealed in state court, all the way up to the Connecticut Supreme Court, if necessary. The commission may also seek the assistance of the state courts in enforcing any decision issued by a commission hearing officer. Such decisions may include an order requiring the sale or rental of the property at issue in the case, substantial money damages, and other forms of affirmative relief.

Connecticut Real Estate Commission Regulations

The Connecticut Real Estate Commission has direct authority over the licensing and regulation of the real estate industry in Connecticut. The commission is a subdivision of the Connecticut Department of Consumer Protection.

Administrative regulations adopted by the Real Estate Commission prohibit persons holding a real estate license in Connecticut from soliciting the sale, lease, or listing of a residential property on the grounds that such property will be declining in value because of the potential or actual movement into the neighborhood of persons of another race, religion, or ethnic origin. It is also a violation of this regulation for a real estate licensee to distribute, or cause to be distributed, materials or statements designed to induce residential property owners to sell or lease their properties because of such changes in a neighborhood. The real estate practice this regulation is designed to eliminate is called *blockbusting*. Such practices are also clear violations of Title VIII and the Connecticut fair housing laws.

Another regulation adopted by the Real Estate Commission requires that all real estate listing agreements contain words to the effect that "This agreement is subject to the Connecticut General Statutes prohibiting discrimination in commercial and residential real estate transactions (CGS Title 46a, Chapter 814c)."[4] This regulation ensures that all parties to a real estate listing agreement have clear notice that such agreements must comply with the requirements of the fair housing law.

Enforcement procedures.   The Connecticut Real Estate Commission has the authority to accept complaints alleging violations of the regulations issued by that commission. If, after investigation, the commission finds merit to such complaints, it will endeavor to eliminate the violation voluntarily. If those efforts fail, a formal public hearing will be held by the commission. Such hearings can lead to the suspension or revocation of any license issued by the commission and/or the issuance of a fine up to $2,000. Decisions of the Real Estate Commission can be appealed to a state court.

In addition, determination might also be made that punitive damages are warranted payable to the complainant in an amount not to exceed $50,000. The commission might also choose to seek a civil penalty against the respondent payable to the state to vindicate the public interest (1) in an amount not exceeding $10,000, if the respondent has not been adjudged to have committed any prior housing discriminatory practice; (2) in an amount not exceeding $25,000, if the respondent has been adjudged to have committed one other discriminatory housing practice during the five-year period to the date of the filing of the present complaint; and (3) in an amount not exceeding $50,000, if the respondent has been adjudged to have committed two or more discriminatory housing practices during the seven-year period prior to the date of the filing of the present complaint.

■ PSYCHOLOGICALLY STIGMATIZED PROPERTY

Brokers, salespeople, and owners are not liable to buyers or tenants for failure to disclose that a person who was HIV-positive or had AIDS occupied a property or that a suicide, murder, or other felony occurred on the property because by law these circumstances are not deemed material. Disclosure of knowledge about suicide, murder, or other felony is deemed material, however, if the purchaser/tenant advises the owner or licensee in writing that information that may have a psychological impact is important for his or her decision (note, however, that information about HIV-status still need not be disclosed).[5]

Effective October 1, 2004, this law changes. Sellers, landlords, and licensees will not be liable for failure to disclose a "nonmaterial fact," which is a fact related to whether a property occupant has or had a disease listed by the Public Health Commissioner, or the fact that there was a death or felony on the property.

■ ADAPTABLE AND ACCESSIBLE HOUSING REQUIREMENTS

Legislation was passed in 1992 requiring that the state building code be in substantial compliance with the Americans with Disabilities Act of 1990 (ADA) and the Fair Housing Amendments Act of 1988.[6] ADA provides accessibility guidelines that apply to newly constructed and renovated commercial buildings. The Fair Housing Amendments Act applies to all newly constructed multifamily residential dwellings.

■ PUBLIC ACCOMMODATIONS LAW

Section 46a-64 of the Connecticut General Statutes prohibits discrimination in any place of public accommodation. A place of public accommodation is defined as any establishment that caters or offers its services, facilities, or goods to the general public. The Connecticut law specifically states that this prohibition does not require that persons modify their property in any way. The federal ADA, however, does provide that structural changes to public accommodations must be made when they are "readily achievable."

■ IMPLICATIONS FOR CONNECTICUT REAL ESTATE BROKERS AND SALESPEOPLE

Because of their critical function in the housing market, real estate salespersons and brokers have a key role to play in the enforcement of fair housing laws. If real estate salespeople and brokers make an effort to comply with the letter and spirit of fair housing laws and cooperate with state and local fair housing enforcement agencies, they can make a substantial contribution to eliminating discrimination in Connecticut. They can also serve as an important source of information and education for the general public. If, on the other hand, real estate agents look for loopholes in the law and cooperate with persons who wish to discriminate, they risk serious legal consequences and perform a disservice to themselves, their profession, and their community.

Licensed brokers and salespeople are legally bound and ethically obligated to know and obey state and federal fair housing laws. Failure to do so will result in substantial financial penalties and possible license suspension or revocation. Equal housing opportunity is a legitimate and necessary component of everyone's civil rights. It is the duty and responsibility of the licensed broker or salesperson to ensure that this right is available to everyone.

■ ENDNOTES

1. Sections 46a-64b and 46a-64c of the Connecticut General Statutes.
2. Sections 46a-63 and 46a-64 of the Connecticut General Statutes.
3. The federal Fair Housing Act does not use the word *disability*, but rather prohibits discrimination on the basis of a person's *handicap*. The federal definition of handicap includes any physical or mental impairment that substantially limits one or more major life functions.
4. Section 20-328-4a(c) of the Connecticut Regulations Concerning the Conduct of Real Estate Brokers and Salespersons.
5. Sections 20-329cc through 20-329ff of the Connecticut General Statutes.
6. Public Act 92-71.

QUESTIONS

Are the following examples acts of housing discrimination under either the state or federal fair housing laws? Answer **yes** or **no** and explain.

1. In your capacity as a real estate agent, you receive a call from a landlord who owns a two-family house. Although the landlord does not live in the house, the landlord's mother lives on the first floor. The landlord wants you to rent out the second floor but says he does not want you to rent it out to any family with small kids. Is this discrimination? If so, what law or laws are being violated?

2. You are a real estate agent and you have a client with two small children who is interested in buying a condominium with two bedrooms. You find one for sale through the MLS but have learned that the condominium has a bylaw prohibiting minor children from living there. Could they refuse to sell to your client because she has small children if she is otherwise qualified to buy? What additional information may you need to know?

3. You have a client in a wheelchair who is looking for an apartment to rent. You find him a first-floor apartment in a three-family house where the owner lives on the second floor. Your client says the apartment is fine but he would like to install grab bars in the bathroom at his expense. The owner says he will rent your client the apartment but refuses to allow him to install grab bars regardless of who pays. Is your client being discriminated against? If so, what law or laws are being violated?

4. You own a single-family house and are renting out three rooms in the house to different tenants. You live in the house and you have decided you want to rent out the rooms only to women. A man applies for one of the rooms that you have advertised for rent in the newspaper. Is it discrimination if you refuse to rent to him because he is male? If so, what law or laws are being violated?

5. You are renting out a guest room in a house you own and live in. You do not advertise or use an agent but are renting it strictly by word of mouth. Is it discrimination if you refuse to rent to a black person because you would feel uncomfortable having that person live there?

6. You have just finished remodeling your three-family house on the east side of Bridgeport. You live on the first floor, and you decide you want to rent only to tenants who are gainfully employed. Is it discrimination if you refuse to rent to someone who is on welfare because they are on welfare? Is it discrimination if you refuse to rent to someone on Section 8 because they are on Section 8? If so, what law or laws are being violated?

7. You are a real estate agent and have a married couple in their mid-20s as clients who are interested in buying a co-op unit advertised in MLS. They have no children, but they are refused by the board of directors of the co-op because they are only selling to people 35 and over. This has always been the policy of the co-op since it was first built. Is this discrimination? If so, what law or laws are being violated?

8. You are a real estate agent and have a married couple in their late 20s with two minor children as your clients. They want to buy a two-bedroom co-op unit that has been advertised in MLS. They are refused for the same reason as the couple in item 7. The co-op is selling only to people 35 and over, which has always been its policy. Is this discrimination? If so, what law or laws are being violated?

9. You have a friend who is a single man in his late 40s who is confined to a wheelchair. He wants to buy a co-op unit that is being sold strictly by word of mouth without advertising and without the use of an agent. He has requested that he be allowed to build a ramp at his own expense. The board of directors of the co-op have decided they will sell him the unit but refuse to allow him to construct a ramp. Is this discrimination? If so, what law or laws are being violated?

10. You own a rooming house and live in a first-floor unit. There are seven rooms in all, which you rent out. You have decided you do not want to rent to any members of the Jehovah's Witnesses religion. You don't advertise or use an agent but rent out the rooms strictly by word of mouth. If you refuse to rent to someone because he or she is a member of this religion, would that be discrimination? If so, what law or laws are being violated?

11. You are an agent and receive a call from the owner of a single-family home who recently purchased a second home and wants you to rent out his first home. Although the home has three bedrooms, he does not want you to rent it to any family that has small children because he would eventually like to have his own daughter move into the house after she gets married and wants to make sure it remains in good shape. Can you legally take this listing and abide by the owner's wishes not to rent to any family with small children? Explain why it is or is not discrimination. If it is, what law or laws are being violated?

12. You own a seven-unit rooming house and someone who is handicapped and uses a wheelchair wants to rent one of the units. You live in the house and are willing to let him rent one of the rooms, but you have refused him permission to build a ramp at his expense. Are you guilty of discrimination? If so, what law or laws are being violated?

13. In the sale of a house you represent the seller, who has AIDS. You do not mention this fact to the buyer, and after the closing the buyer learns about it from a neighbor. The buyer threatens to sue you and the owner for not disclosing a material fact. Are either of you potentially liable?

16

CLOSING THE REAL ESTATE TRANSACTION

■ OVERVIEW

Most closings are conducted face to face in Connecticut, although it is not uncommon to have escrow closings in commercial transactions. The title procedures (with the exception that the buyer is typically responsible for title work) and closing statements are basically as described in the principles texts.

Although closings customarily are executed under the direction of legal counsel, a knowledgeable broker or salesperson can be invaluable to the buyer and/or seller. The broker or salesperson can assist by explaining the closing procedures and preparing net data for the buyer or seller to use as a guideline for expenses. The broker/salesperson can also assist by anticipating the many decision-making alternatives available to the buyer or seller in preparation for the settlement. Other benefits that can be offered by the agent are maintaining a time schedule for all parties involved in the transaction, keeping all parties informed of the current status of the settlement process, and conducting final inspection arrangements.

■ CLOSING PROCESS

Between the signing of the contract and the final settlement, both the buyer and the seller need direction, support, and encouragement. They must comply with time requirements to fulfill their obligations set forth in the contract. They must work diligently toward the final consummation of the contract completion. The buyer promises to obtain sufficient financing; the seller promises to obtain a clear, unencumbered title. Each promises to exchange one for the other at a designated date and hour at a specific location according to the contract. It is frequently the broker or salesperson who is instrumental in keeping the action flowing systematically toward settlement.

It is usual that the broker's client is the seller. To serve the client well, however, it may be necessary to assist the buyer with mortgage information. It may be appropriate to make arrangements for the buyer to meet with the mortgagee who can help obtain the *best* financing available. A knowledgeable agent knows the lending marketplace and can assist in directing the buyer toward successful, efficient finance sources.

Inspections usually are needed before the closing can be planned. These will vary from building inspections to termite inspections to inspections by appraisers, surveyors, and systems operations experts (i.e., heating/cooling, electrical). It is the agent who coordinates these various inspections and who frequently accompanies the inspector to open the building and assist in whatever way possible.

A walk-through inspection is a good practice that most agents require of both the buyer and the seller. This occurs immediately prior to the closing itself. Through this inspection, the buyer and the seller can be assured that all systems function properly and can be aware of the final condition of the property. Any adjustments necessary are resolved at the closing.

■ APPRAISALS

Lenders require that an appraisal be rendered by a qualified appraiser approved by the lending institution. It behooves the real estate broker and agent to cooperate with the appraiser's request for data. This not only creates professional teamwork but also develops the attitude of trust and confidence that better serves the client and customer and protects the public. Gathering data is only part of the appraiser's work. Those data must then be analyzed and substantiated to document the estimated value of the property.

The agent ensures that documents and escrow amounts are submitted to the closing attorney's office in sufficient time for adequate preparation for the closing. Confidential information is disclosed only to those who "need to know." The purchase price, terms of the contract, and financial data are considered private information—not to be shared with anyone until recorded for public record. The broker and salesperson are not permitted to reveal details of the transaction to those who are not parties to the transaction.

■ AT THE CLOSING

Because of the complexity of real property rights and the various forms used in the conveyance process, there is almost always at least one attorney involved in a conveyance, and in most cases two. The seller's attorney is responsible for preparing any documents necessary to convey title to the buyer, and the buyer's attorney conducts any title searches that might be required. Additionally, both offer legal counsel to their respective clients. A settlement typically takes place at either attorney's office.

When a real estate closing involves a mortgage loan or the assumption of one from a lending institution, another attorney is needed to conduct the closing for the bank. Thus, the legal representation for most closing situations can generally be divided into three areas: the seller's counsel, the buyer's counsel, and the lender's settlement (or closing) agent. Many banks allow the buyer to choose the attorney who will do the closing work for the bank, and as a result it is common for the buyer's and bank's attorneys to be the same person. However, some banks still require that their own attorney do their closing work and will not allow the buyer's counsel to fill the dual capacity. In either event, it is the responsibility of the closing attorney to calculate the prorations between buyer and seller, search the title, and prepare the mortgage note and deed. Real estate closings generally are held at the office of the closing attorney. There may be some instances, however, when a lender requires that the closing take place at the institution's offices.

Because the closing attorney does so much of the work involved with the loan settlement and conveyance, it is common to find the buyer without personal representation. However, the buyer may ask the closing attorney any reasonable questions he or she may have regarding the closing transaction. In general, the closing attorney is not required to offer legal counsel but should answer all other questions posed by any of the parties to the sale that are not in conflict with his or her client's interests.

Under no circumstances should a broker or salesperson advise a buyer against the use of legal counsel or attempt to offer legal advice. Both these actions are in violation of the license law and could cost brokers/salespeople their licenses. Although the real estate agent typically attends the closing to collect the commission, he or she does not actually participate in it.

Prorations or Adjustments

In Connecticut it is customary for the seller to pay the property expenses for the day of closing. Therefore, the seller's obligation for any accrued expenses ends on the day of closing, and the buyer reimburses the seller for any prepaid expenses beginning with the day after the closing.

When an item covering a period of time is prorated, or adjusted, between the buyer and the seller, it is the usual practice in Connecticut to use a 12-month (30 days each) or 360-day year to calculate the prorations. Of course, the buyer and seller may agree to waive or adjust the payment in accordance with their own agreement. An example would be the elimination of a property tax proration as an inducement to get the buyer to close earlier.

In Connecticut real property taxes are usually paid twice a year, on July 1 and January 1, for a tax year running from July to June. However, in several municipalities taxes are paid quarterly. The broker must understand the local tax payment schedule to provide accurate information to his or her clients regarding the tax proration.

■ MORTGAGE

In Connecticut the mortgage process is explained by the lender-interviewer. It may be helpful, however, to suggest questions the borrower may wish to ask to help him or her understand the mortgage obligations and alternatives more easily. Such questions might be: What points may *I* pay rather than having them taken from the loan? What is the capped rate for the life of the mortgage? What happens when I pay more principal than is required in the monthly payment? What are the alternatives to this particular mortgage? How often will the rate change? What is the rate based on?

Net data sheets may be used to the advantage of both the buyer and the seller. This information will give an estimate of what expenses to expect and what benefits can be anticipated. This information will include

- the contract sales price;
- earnest deposit money;
- the real property tax;
- insurance;
- prorated rents;
- security deposits;
- the private mortgage insurance premium;
- the assessments/special tax;
- the loan origination fee;
- points;
- fees for appraisals, credit checks, recordings, inspections, surveys, etc.;
- the broker's commission;
- the mortgage amounts (first, second, assumable, etc.);
- liens;
- title insurance;
- attorney fees;
- the conveyance tax;
- the transfer tax;
- warranties; and
- utilities (prorations).

QUESTIONS

1. In Connecticut who is responsible prior to closing for calculating the prorations between the buyer and seller, searching the title, and preparing the mortgage note and deed?
   a. Broker
   b. Salesperson
   c. Closing attorney
   d. Lender

2. Where do closings usually take place?
   a. Broker's office
   b. Lender's office
   c. Attorney's office
   d. Town clerk's office

3. Seller has paid the monthly condominium common charges of $180 for the month of June. If the closing occurs on June 20, what type of adjustment would usually be made?
   a. $120 in favor of Seller
   b. $120 in favor of Buyer
   c. $60 in favor of Seller
   d. $60 in favor of Buyer

4. The broker or salesperson may perform all of the following in preparation for the closing *except*
   a. maintaining a time schedule and providing net data.
   b. explaining closing procedures to both buyer and seller and anticipating decision-making alternatives.
   c. coordinating inspections and delivering documents and escrow monies to the appropriate attorney.
   d. conducting any title searches that might be required.

5. Salesperson represents BuyerOne in the purchase of First Avenue. Salesperson also represents BuyerTwo, who is interested in making an offer on a property on Second Avenue. To make an informed offer, BuyerTwo asks Salesperson what price BuyerOne contracted to purchase First Avenue for. Salesperson can disclose this information to BuyerTwo only after BuyerOne's
   a. offer is accepted.
   b. mortgage commitment has been signed.
   c. closing has occurred.
   d. deed has been recorded in the land records.

CHAPTER SEVENTEEN

ENVIRONMENTAL ISSUES AND THE REAL ESTATE TRANSACTION

■ OVERVIEW

Environmental issues and laws can have a significant impact on many real estate transactions. There is extensive federal legislation dealing with environmental problems. Connecticut has also promulgated extensive environmental legislation, which in some cases mirrors and in other cases is in addition to the federal law. The Connecticut Department of Environmental Protection is the primary state agency that has jurisdiction over the permitting and regulating of environmental activities, although many other state agencies also have their environmental niche.

The following provides a brief summary of Connecticut legislation on some of the more common environmental hazards that real estate brokers and agents should be aware of. This is by no means an exhaustive list and does not preclude or supersede any federal law in the area.

■ ASBESTOS

Asbestos is primarily regulated at the federal level. The Connecticut Department of Health Services has regulations requiring the abatement of asbestos in schools[1] and regulations outlining abatement procedures that mirror the federal law.[2] Asbestos contractors must be licensed.[3] The disposal of asbestos is regulated in Connecticut by the Bureau of Waste Management.[4]

WWWeb.Link

Information on Connecticut's Bureau of Waste Management is available online at *dep.state.ct.us/wst/index.htm.*

■ LEAD-BASED PAINT

Connecticut has enacted comprehensive legislation regulating lead-based paint in residential properties.[5] The law regulates when inspections and abatement are required, what type of inspections and abatement methods are allowed and how they are to be conducted, precautions to be taken when renovating or remodeling, training and certification of inspection and abatement professionals.

Under Connecticut law, inspections are not required on sale or lease of property. Inspections are only required in the following circumstances: (1) when a child (defined as a person under the age of six) has been diagnosed with an elevated blood lead level, that child's dwelling must be inspected; (2) if the child with an elevated blood lead level lives in a multifamily building, the other dwelling units in the building must be inspected; and (3) all day-care centers must be inspected prior to licensure and relicensure. While Connecticut law does not require inspections on transfer, many potential buyers and tenants may negotiate for an inspection as part of the transfer. (Note that federal law provides that all potential buyers be allowed a ten-day period after signing a purchase contract to conduct an inspection.) If a lead paint inspection reveals that there is lead paint present in a dwelling where a child resides, the lead inspector is legally required to report his or her finding to the local director of health and the state Department of Public Health (which then has the authority to order that abatement work be done).

Abatement is required in Connecticut if a child lives in the dwelling and there is defective lead-based paint. Additionally, if a child residing in the dwelling has an elevated blood lead level, certain intact surfaces must be abated (surfaces up to five feet from the floor that have a half-inch protrusion that children can chew, movable parts of windows, surfaces rubbing against movable parts of windows). Many municipalities have also passed ordinances regulating the presence of lead paint in housing.

There is a wave of recent litigation involving lead paint: tenants are suing landlords for lead paint poisoning,[6] and buyers are suing sellers and agents for nondisclosure of the presence of lead-based paint.[7]

WWWeb.Link   Connecticut's Lead Poisoning Prevention Program: *www.state.ct.us/dph/brs/lead/lead_program.htm.*

■ RADON

Contractors performing radon mitigation work must be registered with the Connecticut Commissioner of Consumer Protection under the home improvement contractor registration requirements.[8] A radon mitigation contractor will not receive a certificate of registration unless he or she attended a radon mitigation program approved by the U.S. Environmental Protection Agency and received a passing score on the national Radon Contractor Proficiency examination. The Department of Public Health and Addiction Services publishes a list of companies that perform radon mitigation and diagnoses.[9]

The Department of Public Health regulations establish safe levels of radon in potable water.[10]

WWWeb.Link Connecticut's Radon Program information: *www.state.ct.us/dph/brs/radon/ radon_program.htm.*

■ MOLD

Mold is a recent environmental concern. Some people are susceptible to mold toxins while others are not. There are no state laws dealing with mold disclosure or exposure. However, the presence of mold could potentially be considered a material property condition, and therefore any knowledge about mold should be disclosed by a property seller/landlord/agent to a potential buyer/tenant.

WWWeb.Link Connecticut's Department of Public Health offers a residential mold information pamphlet at *www.state.ct.us/publications/BCH/EEOH/mold.pdf.*

■ UREA-FORMALDEHYDE

Connecticut law has prohibited urea-formaldehyde foam insulation (UFFI) from being installed in any building or structure after June 1, 1981.[11]

■ WATER WELLS AND GROUNDWATER CONTAMINATION

The Connecticut Department of Environmental Protection (DEP) has identified and rated all of the groundwater and surface water in the state.[12] The water quality designations of all water resources are mapped. The master map is located at the DEP; copies of the map are available from the DEP Natural Resource Center.

The Connecticut Commissioner of Public Health has adopted regulations regarding the testing of water quality in private residential wells.[13] The regulations cannot require that a test be conducted as a consequence or condition of the sale of property containing a private residential well; however, water quality test results on a private residential well must be reported within 30 days of the test to the municipality's public health authority.

■ WATER DIVERSION

The Connecticut Water Diversion Policy Act prohibits a diversion of state waters unless a permit is obtained.[14] This permitting process is required for use of both surface waters and groundwaters. Waters are defined as *all tidal waters, harbors, estuaries, rivers, brooks, water courses, waterways, wells, springs, lakes, ponds, marshes, drainage systems and all other surface or underground streams, bodies or accumulations of water, natural or artificial, public or private, which are contained within, flow through or border upon this state.*

Application to divert waters must be made to the DEP. There are activities that are exempt from requiring a permit, such as certain wells, storm drainage systems, and roadway crossings or culverts.

The DEP also regulates discharges into the waters of the state.[15] A permit must be obtained to discharge pollutants. The issuance of such a permit does not convey any property rights; therefore, discharges may still be in violation of the common law under riparian rights theories.

 Information on Connecticut's coastal and watershed systems can be found at *www.yale.edu/ccws* and *www.ctriver.org*.

■ UNDERGROUND STORAGE TANKS

Property owners in Connecticut can be held liable for cleanup costs and damage associated with leaking underground storage tanks, and sellers who do not disclose the presence of an underground tank to buyers may have to take back the property.[16] Many municipalities in Connecticut have enacted ordinances requiring the removal of older residential underground storage tanks. The Commissioner of Environmental Protection regulates nonresidential underground storage tanks.[17]

Connecticut has established an Underground Storage Tank Petroleum Fund for expenses related to releases of petroleum from underground storage tanks and third-party damages.[18] The party responsible for the release must still bear all costs of the release that are less than $10,000 or more than $1 million.

 Connecticut's Underground Storage Tank Program information: *www.dep.state.ct.us/wst/ust/indexust.htm*.

■ HAZARDOUS WASTE

Property owners in Connecticut can be held liable for cleanup costs associated with hazardous waste on their property, even if they were not responsible for the spill or discharge.[19] Connecticut does have an innocent landowner defense for those acquiring polluted property after a spill or discharge, but it only limits liability to the imposition of a lien against the property.[20] The state's lien on a polluted parcel is limited to the appraised value as if uncontaminated plus administrative costs. Liability for pollution cleanup costs for lenders acquiring title to property through foreclosure or a deed in lieu of foreclosure is limited to the value of the property.[21]

 Information on Connecticut's Bureau of Waste Management programs can be found at *www.dep.state.ct.us/wst/index.htm.*

Property Transfer

Connecticut requires an assessment of any discharge, spillage, uncontrolled loss, seepage, or filtration of hazardous waste at an "establishment" prior to the *transfer of ownership* of the property.[22] An establishment is defined as any (1) real estate or business operation that generated a defined amount of hazardous waste; or (2) place where hazardous waste was handled, stored, or disposed of; or (3) dry cleaning, furniture stripping, and vehicle body repair facilities. Certain forms are to be filed, an inspection must be executed, and an analysis of the findings and cleaning of land as deemed appropriate by the DEP must be performed.

 Information on Connecticut's Property Transfer program can be found at *www.dep.state.ct.us/pao/download.htm#PTP.*

■ WASTE DISPOSAL SITES

The DEP maintains an inventory of sites in Connecticut where hazardous or toxic wastes have been disposed (these sites do not necessarily pose a threat to public health or the environment).[23] The DEP is required to furnish the inventory list, updated quarterly, to the town clerk of each municipality, to be maintained in the land records. The list includes each site's name, the name of the town it is located in, the type of material and disposal activity involved, the present groundwater classification of the site, and general information about the site's current status.

The construction of hazardous waste facilities requires a Certificate of Public Safety and Necessity from the Connecticut Siting Council.[24]

WWWeb.Link Information on the Connecticut Siting Council can be found at *www.state.ct.us/csc.*

Disclosure of Off-Site Conditions

A seller that provides written notice to a potential purchaser about the availability of the DEP inventory lists has legally met his or her duty to disclose the presence of off-site hazardous waste facilities; if such disclosure is given, the agent is also excused from liability for failure to disclose off-site hazardous waste conditions.[25] The notice needs to be given either before or at the time of the signing of the purchase contract. The Purchase Contract in Chapter 7 contains a provision giving such notice. Figure 17.1 provides an example of the notice in a separate document.

F I G U R E 17.1

Hazardous Waste Notice

REALTOR®

NOTICE OF AVAILABILITY OF HAZARDOUS WASTE FACILITY INFORMATION

Property Address: _____

Town: _____

Buyer is notified that the Connecticut Department of Environmental Protection is required pursuant to Section 22a-134f of the Connecticut General Statutes to furnish lists of hazardous waste facilities located within the town to the Town Clerk's office. Buyer should refer to these lists and the Department of Environmental Protection for information on environmental questions concerning the Property and the lands surrounding the Property.

_____
Firm's name

_____
Signature of Licensee

I/We acknowledge that I/we have been notified of the availability of lists of hazardous waste facilities on _____.
          Date

_____
Buyer's (or Tenant's) signature

_____
Buyer's (or Tenant's) signature

©2002 Connecticut Association of REALTORS®, Inc.

EQUAL HOUSING OPPORTUNITY

■ ENDNOTES

1. Section 19a-333 of the Connecticut General Statutes.
2. Section 19a-332, et seq.
3. Section 20-435 of the Connecticut General Statutes.
4. Section 22a-252 of the Connecticut General Statutes.
5. Sections 19a-111, et al., of the Connecticut General Statutes and Sections 19a-111-1 through 19a-111-11 of the Department of Health Services Regulations.
6. *Hardy v. Griffin*, 41 Conn. Supp. 283 (1989); *Copeland v. Peoples Savings Bank*, 1993 Conn. Super. Lexis 445 (1993).
7. *Tackling v. Gorman*, filed in New London Superior Court (1992).
8. Section 20-420 of the Connecticut General Statutes.
9. Section 19a-14b(d) of the Connecticut General Statutes.
10. Section 19a-14b of the Connecticut General Statutes.
11. Section 29-277 of the Connecticut General Statutes.
12. Section 22a-351 to 352 of the Connecticut General Statutes.
13. Section 19a-37 of the Connecticut General Statutes.
14. Sections 22a-365 through 22a-378 of the Connecticut General Statutes.
15. Section 22a-427 of the Connecticut General Statutes.
16. *Diamond v. Varcinek*, 2326 Conn. 737 (1993).
17. Section 22a-449(d) of the Connecticut General Statutes.
18. Section 22a-449c of the Connecticut General Statutes.
19. *Starr v. Commissioner of Environmental Protection*, 226 Conn. 358 (1993).
20. Section 22a-452a of the Connecticut General Statutes. (Revised by PA 95-190.)
21. Id.
22. Section 22a-134a of the Connecticut General Statutes.
23. Section 22a-8a of the Connecticut General Statutes.
24. Section 22a-114 to 133 of the Connecticut General Statutes.
25. Section 20-327f of the Connecticut General Statutes.

QUESTIONS

1. The primary Connecticut state agency having jurisdiction over environmental matters is the
   a. Real Estate Commission.
   b. Department of Consumer Protection.
   c. Department of Environmental Protection.
   d. Environmental Management Commission.

2. What are the ramifications of a residential seller (who has children) allowing a potential purchaser to conduct a lead paint inspection?
   a. The seller may be ordered to abate defective lead paint.
   b. The seller will have to pay for the inspection.
   c. The potential purchaser will be prohibited from purchasing.
   d. There are none.

3. Robert and Cheryl own their own home where they live with their five-year-old son Bobby. Knowing their house contains some surfaces with lead paint, Bobby was tested for elevated blood levels—the tests showed he had no lead in his system. Does Connecticut law require that Robert and Cheryl take any action with regard to the lead paint in their home?
   a. Yes, they must abate all lead paint.
   b. Yes, they must abate defective lead paint.
   c. No, as long as Bobby does not have an elevated blood lead level, they need not conduct any abatement.
   d. No, abatement of lead paint is required only in rental housing.

4. Calvin has ordered a home inspection, including testing of the well water, for a home he is purchasing. The results of the water quality test must be
   a. kept confidential by the firm conducting the test.
   b. reported to Calvin only.
   c. reported to Calvin and the seller of the property.
   d. reported to the municipal public health authority.

5. A purchase and sale agreement has been signed for the sale of a facility that was previously operated as a dry cleaners. Connecticut law requires
   a. an assessment of the presence of any hazardous waste prior to the transfer of ownership.
   b. a payment made to the Connecticut DEP of up to $100,000 for potential cleanup costs.
   c. that the contract be reviewed by the EPA.
   d. that the seller must pay the cost to clean up any hazardous waste.

6. Kerry discovers that there is an underground oil storage tank in her backyard. Which of the following would *not* apply to her situation?
   a. Kerry may be required to remove the tank.
   b. Kerry may be held liable for cleanup costs if the tank has leaked.
   c. Kerry should not disclose the presence of the tank to a potential purchaser.
   d. If she recently purchased the property and the seller did not disclose that the tank was there, Kerry may be able to rescind the transaction.

INTRODUCTION TO REAL ESTATE INVESTMENT

■ OVERVIEW

Under Connecticut law *real property securities dealers* must hold real estate licenses. The license law contains specific provisions covering their operations and licensing.

The terms *real property security* and *real estate security* have been applied almost universally to any security that has real estate as an underlying asset. A security is generally a share of any interest-bearing investment. Real estate itself, however, is never a security. A security is created by the manner in which the real estate asset is packaged, managed, and marketed. For example, a partnership or trust might be formed to purchase a property. To raise sufficient funds for the purchase, the partnership or trust would issue and sell shares. In effect, the investors are financing the project, and the shares represent claims of ownership of the partnership or trust (whose only asset is the real property).

■ THE SECURITIES MARKET

Packaging real property investments for multiple or group ownership is not a recent phenomenon on the real estate scene. It has been a widely used technique to pool the financial resources of small investors to allow investment in properties outside the reach of all but the wealthiest of investors. Small-scale investors have neither the financial nor managerial resources to purchase and operate large investment properties. By splitting a large real estate investment into small shares and by retaining the management responsibilities, the real property securities dealer or real estate syndicator can offer an attractive investment medium to the average investor. These securities allow the investor to reap the benefits of real property ownership without the attendant management responsibilities. The benefits would include income, tax shelter, and capital appreciation. Specific types of securities may be structured to maximize a particular benefit, such as a tax shelter, while others may provide all three benefits in equal proportion.

The market for both real property securities and real estate syndicate securities achieved spectacular growth in the 1980s when an unprecedented number of syndications and real estate investment trusts were formed. Because of a combination of mismanagement, lack of adequate regulation, and a severe economic downturn in the late 1980s and early 1990s, many newly formed syndicates and trusts experienced failure. Only the best managed and capitalized remained solvent. However, these real estate investments will probably make a comeback, and these securities may again be common means by which the small investor can buy into a large-scale real estate investment. Properly packaged, marketed, and managed, both types of real estate securities can be a profitable experience for dealer, syndicator, and investor alike.

■ CONNECTICUT REGULATIONS ON THE SALE OF SECURITIES

While many types of investment offerings involving real estate may be classified as real estate securities, the Connecticut General Statutes delineate all such investments as either *real property securities* or *real estate syndicate securities*. The laws outline specific regulations for the sale of each type of security. Real property securities are composed principally of real estate investment trusts (REITs). Real estate syndicate securities, on the other hand, generally take the form of shares in a general or limited partnership, although syndicates may be organized into other forms of ownership. Real estate syndicates tend to have fewer investors than REITs and involve only one or two properties.

In Connecticut each type of real estate security is regulated under a separate law. Real property securities are regulated under Chapter 392 (Sections 20-329o to 20-329bb), an extension of the real estate license law. Real estate syndicate securities fall under the jurisdiction of Chapter 826—Real Estate Syndicates (Sections 47-91 to 47-115). *Both laws are administered by the Connecticut Real Estate Commission.*

Under Connecticut law the seller of real property securities is called a *real property securities dealer*. Any person who acts as a real property securities dealer *must be licensed as a real estate broker and have his or her license specifically endorsed by the Real Estate Commission.* The seller or *syndicator* of real estate syndicate securities, however, is not required to have any special licensing and *is not required to have a real estate license to sell syndicate shares.* In addition, there are subtle but significant variations in the conditions under which each type of security can be marketed.

Commission's Authority

The Commissioner of Consumer Protection, with the advice and assistance of the Real Estate Commission, may make and enforce whatever regulations are considered necessary to regulate the marketing and sale of both real property securities and real estate syndicate securities. In addition, the commission may prescribe the qualifications of dealers and syndicators and oversee their actions. The following paragraphs outline the commission's general authority regarding each type of security and provide a basic overview of the procedures required to market them in Connecticut. The chart emphasizes the different requirements for the two types of securities (see Figure Appendix A.1).

Connecticut Securities Transactions

	Real Property Securities	**Real Estate Syndicate Securities**
Securities covered	Shares in an REIT—may involve many properties	Shares in a syndicate—generally involve only one property
Regulated by	Real Estate License Law	Real Estate Syndicate Law
Administered by	Connecticut Real Estate Commission	Connecticut Real Estate Commission
Seller	Real property securities dealer—licensed broker + special endorsement	Syndicator—no licensing required
Permit to sell	Required information submitted with application	Prospectus submitted with application
Fee	No fee	$300 to $1,500 based on total value of interests issued in Connecticut
Purchaser receives	Written statement containing required information	Prospectus containing required information
Records and reports	1. Copies of written statements to purchasers executed by purchasers retained for at least four years 2. Financial report to commission within 60 days from close of usual business period	Books, records, sales accounts maintained—may be subject to commission's examination
Advertising materials must be to commission	Ten days before use	Three business days before use
Penalties for violation	$5,000 and/or one to five years' imprisonment	$1,000 to $10,000 and/or up to ten years' imprisonment
Civil suits must be initiated within	Three years from date of transaction	Two years from date of transaction or one year from detection of violation—whichever expires first

■ REAL PROPERTY SECURITIES

Permit To Sell

Dealers in real property securities must obtain permits from the commission to sell any real property security in Connecticut. Applications for these permits must be in writing and accompanied by whatever information regarding the security issue and/or the applicant the commission requests.

Fees

Although the Connecticut license law reserves the right for the Commissioner of Consumer Protection, with the advice and assistance of the Real Estate Commission, to levy a "reasonable" fee for the submission of an application or the issuance of a permit, no specific fee is prescribed at present, and the commission does not charge any application fee.

Required Statement to Purchaser

Any dealer who sells or attempts to sell a real property security must present a written statement on the property to the purchaser. The dealer must personally sign and deliver this statement to the purchaser, who must, in turn, sign and return an executed copy to the dealer. *The dealer must retain all signed statements for at least four years.* The statement must contain the following information:

- The legal description or address of the property subject to the lien that secures the note or contract being made or sold
- The name and address of the fee owner of the property
- Available information regarding the ability of the person liable for the obligation to meet his or her contractual payments
- A description of any improvement on the property
- A description of any streets, sewers, water mains, curbs, and gutters on or adjacent to the property
- The terms and conditions of the contract or note being made or sold, including information about the principal balance owed and whether the payments are current
- A statement of the approximate balloon payment on the note or contract being made or sold, which must appear prominently in words and figures
- The terms, conditions, and balance of all prior and existing liens on the property and the status of these accounts
- The amounts and terms of tax liens and assessments
- An appraisal of the property made by either the dealer or an independent fee appraiser (the purchaser may waive this requirement by obtaining his or her own appraisal and indicating this to the dealer)
- A statement as to whether the real property securities dealer is acting as a principal or as an agent
- A statement that the transaction is in compliance with the provisions of Chapter 329 (real estate license law) that pertain to real property securities
- Any other information the Commissioner of the Department of Consumer Protection, with the advice and assistance of the Real Estate Commission, may require from time to time by regulation

Advertising

In marketing real property securities, a dealer is required to submit to the commission for approval *at least ten days before use* any materials he or she wishes to use in advertising the securities. If the commission disapproves of the materials because they include false or misleading statements or material omissions, it will prohibit the dealer from using them. If the commission does not reply to the dealer within ten days after receipt of the materials, the dealer may consider them approved.

Financial Report

The Connecticut license law also requires that real property securities dealers furnish the commission with financial data. Within 60 days from the close of the dealer's usual business period, he or she must file with the commission a financial report prepared by a certified public accountant. The report must include the total number and dollar value of sales for the period (whether as principal or agent), information concerning the handling and disposition of all funds related to these sales, and any other information required by the Commissioner of the Department of Consumer Protection with the advice and assistance of the Real Estate Commission. If the dealer fails to provide an annual financial report, the commissioner may order an audit, the cost of which will be borne by the dealer.

Exemptions

The license law requirements regarding the sale of real estate securities do not extend to the sale of notes or contracts under investment participation pools or to the sale of certificates based on notes or contracts used as collateral. This exemption refers primarily to sales in the secondary mortgage market through such agencies as Fannie Mae (the Federal National Mortgage Association) and Freddie Mac (the Federal Home Loan Mortgage Corporation).

Also exempted are dealers who sell other types of securities and deal with transactions involving the sale of promissory notes secured by mortgage deeds as opposed to shares of a syndication in which a trust deed is the principal asset.

Because the real property securities dealer is permitted to deal only in real estate securities, he or she is exempted from the laws that regulate sales of other types of securities and fiduciary arrangements.

Enforcement and Penalties

Prohibited acts. Under the license law provisions relating to real property securities, any person found guilty of any of the following acts may be fined up to $5,000 by the court and/or imprisoned for one to five years:

- Knowingly making any false statement or representation, or filing or causing to be filed with the commission any false statement or representation in a required report
- Issuing or causing to be issued any advertisement or other material concerning any real property security that contains any statement that is deliberately false or misleading
- In any respect willfully violating or failing to comply with any provision of the laws pertaining to real property securities dealers or with any order, decision, demand, requirement, or permit of the commission
- With one or more other persons, conspiring to violate any permit or order issued by the commission or any provision of said sections

Suspension and Revocation of License

If the commission feels that a dealer is violating provisions of the license law as it relates to real property securities or conducting his or her business in an unsafe or fraudulent way, the commission may follow the procedure outlined under suspension or revocation of a license (Section 20-320). In addition, the dealer may appeal the decision in accordance with Section 20-322.

Civil Action for Injury from a Transaction

Any person who sustains an injury resulting from a real property security transaction that was in violation of the license law may recover damages plus 7 percent interest through a civil action. The action must be initiated within three years from the date of the transaction.

Appeals

Appeals entered by any person aggrieved by a commission regulation, order, or decision must be initiated in the same manner as described in the license law under the suspension and revocation of licenses (Section 20-322).

■ REAL ESTATE SYNDICATE SECURITIES

Permit To Sell and Prospectus

Syndicators wishing to sell any real estate syndicate securities in Connecticut must also apply in writing to the Real Estate Commission for a permit. A syndicator's application must be accompanied by a copy of the *prospectus,* or printed statement of information about the proposed issue, that will be distributed to purchasers. The commission requires that the prospectus include the following information:

- The name, residence, and principal business address of the issuer
- The names and residences and business addresses of all officers or members of the corporation, partnership, or joint venture if the issuer is a corporation, partnership, or joint venture
- A detailed statement of the plan of syndication including, but not limited to, the form of entity and the number and aggregate amount of the real estate syndicate securities proposed to be sold
- A copy of partnership or other agreements governing the rights, duties, and liabilities of members or participants
- A legal description of the real property, including a detailed description of any existing or proposed improvements
- A true statement of the condition of the record title to the real property, including all encumbrances
- A statement disclosing any covenants, conditions, or restrictions
- The detailed terms of the property acquisition, including, but not limited to, the down payment and the amount, periodic payment, and terms of any encumbrances
- A description of the type or types of real properties intended to be acquired if the plan of syndication provides for the acquisition of unspecified property or properties
- A statement disclosing any management agreement, including the amount of any fee, compensation, or promotional interest to be received by the issuer or any other persons in connection with the formation and management of the syndicate
- The name of any escrow depository
- A statement disclosing the amount, terms, and conditions of fire, liability, and hazard insurance
- Any other information required by the commission's regulations

Note that the information required for the prospectus is essentially equivalent to the data included in the written statement that a dealer must submit to a purchaser of a real property security.

The prospectus may contain considerably more data than the minimal amount required by the commission. However, all information that is included in the prospectus must be submitted to the commission along with the application for a permit to sell.

Fees

Under the real estate syndicate law, a syndicator must pay a fee when filing a permit application. The amount of the fee is based on a sliding scale from $300 to $1,500, depending on the aggregate, or maximum, value of the interests to be issued in Connecticut. For the purpose of this law, value is equivalent to the proposed sales price. A similar fee formula is used for applications involving increases and/or changes in existing security issues.

Prospectus to Purchaser

As indicated above, a syndicator must give a copy of the syndicate's prospectus to every purchaser of a real estate syndicate security. The prospectus essentially provides a collection of all the pertinent information about both the syndicate and the real property underlying the syndicate.

Advertising

In marketing real estate syndicate securities, a syndicator must submit to the commission for approval any advertising materials he or she wishes to use *at least three business days* before use (or whatever shorter period the commission agrees to allow). As with real property securities, the syndicator may not use any advertising materials of which the commission disapproves. In addition, the syndication law exempts the media from any liability for advertising placed by a seller of real estate syndicate securities.

Required Records

The real estate syndicate law requires that the issuer of syndicate securities maintain a complete set of books, records, and accounts on sales. On the commission's request, the issuer must report to the commission any interests sold by the syndicate (including the amount and disposition of proceeds). The commission has the right to examine the issuer's accounts at any time and will be reimbursed by the issuer for the costs of any out-of-state travel required to make such examinations.

Exemptions

The real estate syndicate law exempts the following types of securities from its jurisdiction:

- Syndicate securities in oil, gas, or mining titles or leases
- Interests in mutual water companies
- Real estate investment trusts falling under provisions of the license law
- Syndicate securities registered under the Federal Securities Act of 1933
- Condominium interests covered under the Common Interest Ownership Act
- Syndications not construed as public offerings and involving sales or offers to fewer than 18 persons
- Any other transactions not intended by the commission to be covered by this law

Enforcement and Penalties

Prohibited acts. The real estate syndicate law calls for punitive measures similar to those prescribed under the license law provisions regarding real property securities. The syndicate law does not, however, identify specific violations, but rather generalizes on violations and associated penalties. Any person found guilty of violating the law or any of the commission's regulations may be fined from $1,000 to $10,000 and/or imprisoned for up to ten years.

Cease and desist orders. If the commission feels that a syndicator is violating the syndicate law or conducting his or her business in an unsafe or fraudulent way, the commission may order the syndicator to desist and refrain from such conduct or to stop all security sales. The seller/syndicator may submit a written request for a hearing within ten days after receiving the order. The hearing will be held within the time limits and provisions set in the real estate license law.

Civil action.   As with real property securities, any person who sustains an injury as a result of a syndicate security transaction may recover damages under a civil suit. However, the law limits the conditions under which an aggrieved party may file a suit as well as the types of violations that can be considered under the real estate syndicate law. If a syndicator/seller has made false statements or if the security was unqualified for sale, the syndicator/seller may make a written offer to repurchase the security (plus interest and/or actual damages) from the buyer. In such cases, if the buyer either accepts the offer or fails to accept it *within 30 days* after it was received, he or she loses the right to sue. When the syndicator/seller does not make such an offer, the buyer may sue for the consideration originally paid for the security plus interest at the prevailing legal rate. If the original purchaser no longer owns the security, the judgment will be apportioned according to the length of time each individual owned the security.

Any actions brought under the real estate syndicate law must be initiated *within two years* of the date of the transaction or within one year from the date the violation was actually detected by the plaintiff—whichever period expires first.

Appeals.   Appeals and/or hearings under the real estate syndicate law are handled similarly to those brought under the license law provisions regarding real property securities.

QUESTIONS

1. Under Connecticut law any person who acts as a real property securities dealer must
   a. be licensed as a real estate broker.
   b. have his or her license endorsed by the Real Estate Commission.
   c. Both a and b
   d. No special licensing is required.

2. Which of the following does *not* have to be included in the statement a real property securities dealer must present to a purchaser of such securities?
   a. The name of the fee owner of the property
   b. A list of improvements on the property
   c. The terms and conditions of the contract or note being sold
   d. The uses to which adjacent properties are being put

3. A real property securities dealer submits promotional material to be used in selling securities to the commission for its approval. If the dealer does not hear anything within seven days, he or she
   a. must wait three more days before doing anything.
   b. may assume the commission has approved the materials.
   c. must resubmit the materials.
   d. may make a written request for a hearing.

4. Which of the following would be considered a real property security?
   a. Shares in a limited partnership
   b. Shares in a real estate investment trust
   c. Shares in a real estate syndication
   d. Shares in a construction company

5. A civil action to recover damages from a real property security transaction must be initiated within what period?
   a. One month
   b. Six months
   c. One year
   d. Three years

6. Which of the following is *not* required to sell real estate syndicate securities?
   a. A permit to sell
   b. A prospectus
   c. A real estate broker's license
   d. All of the above are required.

7. Which of the following investments is *not* regulated by the real estate syndicate law?
   a. Syndications of fewer than 18 persons and not involving public offerings
   b. Limited partnership
   c. Joint venture
   d. Syndicates in real estate titles

8. How many days prior to use must materials used in advertising a real estate syndicate security be submitted to the commission for examination?
   a. Three business days
   b. Three calendar days
   c. One week
   d. Ten business days

9. When submitting an application for a permit to sell a real estate syndicate security, the syndicator must also include a
   a. photograph of the property.
   b. copy of the prospectus.
   c. sworn affidavit identifying the syndicator.
   d. certified partnership tax return for the most recent year.

10. Under the license law, a real property securities dealer must file with the commission within 60 days of the close of the business period
    a. a copy of the revised statement on the offerings.
    b. a financial report showing the total number and dollar volume of sales for the period.
    c. the complete books of the firm.
    d. the names and addresses of the property owners.

STATE SOURCES OF INFORMATION

State of Connecticut

State of Connecticut Web site
www.state.ct.us

Real Estate License Laws/Education

Connecticut Licensing Information Center
www.ct-clic.com

Connecticut Real Estate Commission*

Connecticut Real Estate Appraisal Commission*

Department of Consumer Protection*
*165 Capitol Avenue
State Office Building
Hartford, CT 06106
www.state.ct.us/dcp

Center for Real Estate and Urban Economic Studies
University of Connecticut
2100 Hillside Road, Unit 1041RE
Storrs, CT 06269-1041
(860) 486-3227
www.business.uconn.edu/realestate

PSI Real Estate Licensing Examination Services
100 West Broadway, Suite 1100
Glendale, CA 91210-1202
(800) 733-9267
candidate.psiexams.com/index.jsp

Test Centers:
45 S Main Street, Ste. 209   488 Main Avenue
West Hartford, CT   Norwalk, CT

Real Estate Brokerage

Connecticut Association of REALTORS®, Inc.
111 Founders Plaza, 11th Floor
East Hartford, CT 06108
(860) 290-6601 / (800) 335-4862
www.ctrealtor.com

Connecticut CCIM Chapter
www.ctccim.com

New England Regional REALTOR®
newengland.realtorplace.com

Board of REALTORS®
Referenced on CAR's Web site,
www.ctrealtor.com/resources/localboards.htm

Connecticut MLS Services
www.ctrealtor.com/resources/mls-list.htm

Legal

General Statutes of Connecticut (updated January 2003)
www.cga.state.ct.us/2003/pub/titles.htm

Connecticut State Library
www.oslib.org

Connecticut Bar Association
www.ctbar.org

Connecticut On-line Commercial Recording Database
www.sots.state.ct.us

Megan's Law Sex Offender Registry
www.state.ct.us/dps.Sex_Offender_Registry.htm

Municipal Information and Records

Municipality Web sites
www.munic.state.ct.us/townlist.htm

Leasing

Connecticut Property Owners Association
www.ctlandlord.com

Fair Housing

Connecticut Fair Housing Center
221 Main Street, Suite 204
Hartford, CT 06106
(860) 247-4400
E-mail: CTFairHsng@aol.com

Fair Housing Association of Connecticut
45 Lyons Terrace
Bridgeport, CT 06614
(203) 576-8323

Commission on Human Rights and Opportunities
90 Washington Street
Hartford, CT 06106
(860) 566-7710
www.state.ct.us/chro

Office of Protection & Advocacy for Persons with Disabilities
60B Weston Street
Hartford, CT 06120
(860) 247-4300
www.state.ct.us/opapd

Office of Fair Housing & Equal Opportunity, HUD
www.hud.gov/local/index.cfm?state=ct

Municipal Fair Housing Offices or Commissions
Check local telephone book

Housing

Department of Economic & Community Development,
Housing Department
www.state.ct.us/ecd

Listing of Local Housing Authorities
www.state.ct.us/ecd/cwp/view.asp?a=1098&Q=249720&ecdNav=1

**Economic
Information**

Department of Economic Development
865 Brook Street
Rocky Hill, CT 06067
(860) 270-8000
www.state.ct.us/ecd

Connecticut Center for Economic Analysis
www.lib.uconn.edu/ccea

Connecticut Policy and Economic Council
www.cpec.org

Connecticut Market Data
www.hickoryhill.com

Connecticut Economic Resource Center
www.cerc.com

Mortgages

Department of Banking
44 Capitol Avenue
Hartford, CT 06106
(860) 240-8299
www.state.ct.us/dob

Connecticut Mortgage Bankers Association
www.cmba.org

Connecticut Bankers Association
www.ctbank.com

Connecticut Housing Finance Authority
99 West Street
Rocky Hill, CT 06067-4005
(860) 721-9501
www.chfa.org

Environmental Issues

Department of Environmental Protection
165 Capitol Avenue, Room 117
State Office Building
Hartford, CT 06106
(860) 424-3000
www.dep.state.ct.us

Office of Lead Paint
Department of Public Health
150 Washington Street
Hartford, CT 06106
(860) 509-7229
www.state.ct.us/dph/brs/lead/lead_program.htm

Underground Storage Tank Information
www.sp.uconn.edu/~hydrogeo/deprept.htm
www.dep.state.ct.us/wst/ust/indexust.htm

Architecture/ Engineering

Architectural Licensing Board
www.state.ct.us/dcp

Connecticut State Board of Landscape Architects
www.state.ct.us.dcp

State Board of Examiners for Professional Engineers & Land Surveyors
www.state.ct.us.dcp

Department of Transportation
www.dot.state.ct.us

CONNECTICUT TRANSACTION DOCUMENTATION

Outline of Required Documentation in Connecticut Residential Purchase and Sale Transaction

Initially	**Written Agency Agreement** (or Consent to Subagency)
Marketing/Locating Property	**Real Estate Agency Disclosure Notice given to Unrepresented Persons** (given to unrepresented parties the agent works with) **Lead Hazard Information Pamphlet** (given to potential Purchasers if housing built before 1978)
Open House	**Post sign or display pamphlet disclosing Agent's agency relationship**
If Firm Represents Both Buyer and Seller in Transaction	**Dual Agency Consent Agreement** - *or* - **Dual Agency/Designated Agency Notice and Consent Agreement**
Prior to Offer	**Connecticut Property Condition Disclosure Form** (completed by Seller, given to Buyer, attached to offer, binder, contract) **Lead-Based Paint Disclosure Statement** (if housing built before 1978; completed by Seller, given to Buyer, attached to contract) **CIOA Public Offering Statement** (if initial sale of condo, co-op, or PUD; given to Buyer before contract signed)
At Time of Contract	**Purchase and Sale Agreement** **Hazardous Waste Notice** (can be included as part of Purchase Agreement) **Resale Certificate** (if resale of condo, co-op, or PUD; given to Buyer before conveyance)

CONNECTICUT SPECIFIC REAL ESTATE MATH APPLICATIONS

Real estate professionals must have a working knowledge of mathematics, as much of real estate involves working with numbers in a variety of contexts. The principles textbooks detail the basics of real estate math; this appendix will focus only on real estate math applications where Connecticut specific law or customs dictate computations.

■ PERCENTAGES

Brokerage Commissions (Chapter 2)

A brokerage firm's compensation (under both listing agreements and buyer agency agreements) is usually set as a percentage of the sales. Further, a salesperson's share of the commission is usually set as a percentage of the broker's commission. If a co-brokerage firm is involved, the co-brokerage firm's share of the commission is usually set as a percentage of the listing broker's commission.

■ **EXAMPLE** A seller listed a home for $220,000 and agreed to pay the listing brokerage firm a commission of 6 percent of the sales price. Through the multiple-listing service, the listing brokerage firm agreed to pay any brokerage firm that introduced the buyer to the property 50 percent of the commission collected. The brokerage firm that introduced the buyer to the property has agreed to pay 50 percent of its share of the commission to its salesperson working with the buyer. If the house sold for $205,000, how much commission did the salesperson receive?

Listing brokerage firm's commission = 6% of $205,000 = .06 × 205,000 = $12,300
Share to buyer brokerage firm = 50% of $12,300 = .50 × $12,300 = $6,150
Share to buyer brokerage firm's salesperson = 50% of $6,150 = .50 × $6,150 = $3,075

Property Taxes (Chapter 6)

Real estate is taxed at the municipal level in Connecticut. Annual property tax is calculated by dividing a property's assessed value by $1,000 and then multiplying by the town's tax rate. The assessed value of a parcel of real estate is 70 percent of its market value. Tax rates vary by municipality, but all are expressed in mills (and are equivalent to dollars of tax per thousand dollars of assessed value).

■ **EXAMPLE**   An office building in Wallingford has a market value of $550,000. Wallingford's mill rate is 37 mills. What should the annual property tax be?

Assessed value = 70% of $550,000 = .70 × 550,000 = $385,000

Indicated annual property tax = $\dfrac{\$385,000}{1,000} \times \$37 = 385 \times 37 = \$14,245$

Note that actual property taxes may vary from indicated property taxes, depending on the municipality's opinion of market value.

Conveyance Taxes (Chapter 8)

Connecticut levies two taxes upon the conveyance of residential real estate: (1) a municipal conveyance tax of .11 percent of the sales price; and (2) a state conveyance tax of .5 percent of the first $800,000 of the sales price, and 1 percent for any amount over $800,000. For nonresidential property, the municipal conveyance tax rate is still .11 percent, but the state conveyance tax rate is a straight 1 percent.

Note: For the time period of March 15, 2003, to June 30, 2005, the municipal conveyance tax rate is .25 percent. On and after July 1, 2005, the municipal conveyance tax will revert back to .11 percent (unless the legislature chooses to extend the increase).

In addition to the above state conveyance taxes, 18 "targeted investment communities" have the option of imposing an added .25 percent to the municipal conveyance tax, which would increase the total municipal conveyance tax in these communities to .50 percent.

For purposes of all examples and questions in this book, the .11 percent municipal tax rate is used. Adjustments would have to be made in real life accordingly if the town/time frame required one of the different rates.

■ **EXAMPLE**   A house in Stamford sells for $1,300,000. What is the total conveyance tax to be paid?

Municipal conveyance tax = $1,300,000 × .0011 = $1,430
State conveyance tax = $800,000 × .005 = $4,000
    + ($1,300,000 – 800,000) × .01 = $500,000 × .01 = $5,000
    = $4,000 + $5,000 = $9,000
Total conveyance tax = $1,430 + $9,000 = $10,430

Calculation of Purchase Price Based on Conveyance Tax (Chapter 8)

Connecticut does not require that a deed state actual consideration paid for property, but the amount of town conveyance tax paid in relation to the sale is always stamped on a recorded deed. The sales price can be calculated by looking at the conveyance tax paid. This is done by dividing the town conveyance tax paid by the town conveyance tax rate in effect at the time of conveyance.

■ **EXAMPLE**   The conveyance tax stamp on a recently recorded deed states that $328.90 was paid for town conveyance tax. What was the sales price of the property?

Sales price = $\dfrac{\$328.90}{.0011} = \$299,000$

■ PRORATIONS (CHAPTER 16)

Statutory Year

When an item covering a period of time is prorated, or adjusted, it is the usual practice in Connecticut to use a 12-month (30 days each) or 360-day year.

■ **EXAMPLE**   Seller's property is rented for $600 a month, paid on the first of the month. The closing on the property to the buyer is scheduled for April 20. At closing, how much will seller reimburse buyer for this item?

Number of days owed = 30 days – 20 days = 10 days
Per day rent = $600 per month / 30 days = $20
Proration = $20/day × 10 days = $200

Through Day of Closing

In Connecticut, it is customary for the seller to pay the property expenses for the day of closing. Therefore, the seller's obligation for any accrued expenses ends on the day of closing, and the buyer reimburses the seller for any prepaid expenses beginning with the day after closing.

■ **EXAMPLE**   Seller paid $125 in condominium common charges for the month of July. The closing is set for July 17. At closing, how much will buyer reimburse seller for this expense?

Number of days owed = 30 days – 17 days = 13 days
Per day common charge rate = $125 per month / 30 days = $4.17
Proration = $4.17/day × 13 days = $54.21

Property Taxes

In most municipalities in Connecticut, real property taxes run from July 1 to June 30 and are paid twice a year in arrears on July 1 and January 1. Given that taxes are paid in arrears, the seller will owe the buyer from the most recent payment date (July 1 or January 1) through the day of closing.

■ **EXAMPLE**   The annual property tax on a house is $3,600. The property is scheduled to close on March 15. What is the proration?

Number of days owed = 30 (Jan) + 30 (Feb) + 15 (Mar) = 75 days
Per day tax = $3,600 per year / 360 days = $10 per day
Proration = 75 days × $10 per day = $750
Credit to buyer, debit to seller (because in arrears)

ELECTRONIC SIGNATURES AND CONTRACTS

This appendix consists of a legal alert written by Eugene Marconi, General Counsel of the Connecticut Association of REALTORS®, Inc., for the Connecticut Association of REALTORS®, Inc. It is reprinted with permission of the Connecticut Association of REALTORS®, Inc.; all rights are reserved.

ELECTRONIC SIGNATURES

Attorney Eugene A. Marconi, General Counsel

October 8, 2001
Revised July 30, 2002
Revised May 20, 2003

■ INTRODUCTION

For several years now, REALTORS® have been bombarded by pundits urging REALTORS® to enter the new age of electronic communications. Web sites, e-mails, and instant messaging have become as much a part of the REALTORS®' tool kit as MLS books and the telephone were several years ago.

Many REALTORS® have adapted their practices to the electronic age by using fax machines. Most REALTORS®, however, did not realize that the law, to a large extent, had not caught up to the electronic age and was not far advanced from the days of the quill pen and ink well.

This Legal Alert will discuss Connecticut law concerning signatures and legislative attempts to bring the law (albeit kicking and screaming) into the electronic age including the Electronic Records and Signature in Commerce Act and the Connecticut Uniform Electronic Transactions Act ("CUETA").

■ CONNECTICUT LAW AND "WET" SIGNATURES

Connecticut courts have attempted to define a "signature" for many years. The last Connecticut Supreme Court case defining a signature occurred in 1975. In that case, the Court stated that "a signature is the name of a person written with his own hand to signify that the writing which precedes accords with his wishes or intentions." As you can see, the Connecticut courts traditionally favored a so-called "wet" signature, where the signer took pen in hand and signed his or her own name, made a mark or other distinguishing writing. Using such a definition, neither a faxed signature nor an electronic signature was valid.

Connecticut courts have not been entirely oblivious to technological change, however. Connecticut had several cases in the late 19th and early 20th centuries dealing with that technological revelation, the rubber stamp. In the rubber stamp cases, the courts dealt with the question as to the validity of signing a document by means of a rubber stamp. These cases are useful for two reasons. First, this is an instance where the Connecticut courts authorized use of something other than a true "wet" signature. Second, the courts engaged in a useful discussion as to the reasons for requiring a signature. Essentially, there are two reasons for requiring a signature. The first is that a signature shows that the person intended to be bound by what is written in the document. The second reason is that the signature shows that the document is the authentic document. It is useful to keep these concepts in mind as these concepts also carry over into the world of electronic signatures.

■ ENTER CONGRESS

Several states adopted legislation authorizing electronic signatures. This legislation varied; some were simply authorizing the electronic signature of documents and others specifying that certain technologies be used to produce an encrypted or secure signature. Congress began to get nervous over the various approaches that these states adopted. Believing that there should be one approach in use throughout the country and that this approach should not involve the adoption of any particular technology, Congress passed the Electronic Records and Signature in Commerce Act, also known as "E-sign." This Act preempts all state legislation to the contrary for contracts involving interstate commerce. Generally, real estate is so intertwined in interstate commerce that virtually all real estate transactions, especially those involving financing, are interstate commerce. Let us take a closer look at the Electronic Records and Signature in Commerce Act.

■ ELECTRONIC RECORDS AND SIGNATURE IN COMMERCE ACT

The Act applies to every sort of electronically transmitted signature. Therefore, it includes e-mails and facsimile transmissions commonly known as faxes. REALTORS®, therefore, have guidance from Congress as to how to obtain a signature on a document transmitted through a fax machine. The Act goes on to state that an electronically signed document is the equivalent of a written document with a so-called "wet" signature. This is so despite any requirement in state law that a document be in writing or be signed. As all REALTORS® will recall from their Principles and Practices course, a contract for the sale of real estate is not enforceable unless it is in writing. This is called the Statute of Frauds. As a result of this Act, the Statute of

Frauds can be met electronically as well as with paper and ink. Similarly, Connecticut's statute requires that listing and buyer representation agreements be in writing and signed. The requirements for these agreements can also now be met electronically.

The Act is technology-neutral. An "electronic signature" is defined very broadly. It is an "electronic sound, symbol, or process, attached to or logically associated by a person with the intent to sign the record." In other words, it does not matter whether an encrypted signature is used or whether any encryption is used. So long as the parties are agreeable to contracting electronically and can agree on what constitutes a "signature," the use of that agreed upon signature will be adequate to properly execute the electronic document.

■ PROTECTION FOR CONSUMERS

Congress was also worried about consumers being forced to contract electronically or being put in a position where they were not able to send and receive electronic documents but were bound by the electronic documents. Therefore, Congress required that a notice be given to a consumer. A "consumer transaction" was defined as one for family or household purposes. The typical real estate transaction would, therefore, be a "consumer transaction" for purposes of the Act.

Consumers who are asked to contract electronically must be provided with a notice. As you might imagine, the notice must meet certain requirements. These are:

1. consumers affirmatively consent to the use of electronic records;
2. consumers receive a "clear and conspicuous" statement informing them of the right to receive records in paper or in non-electronic form, the right to withdraw consent regarding electronic transactions, and the process for requesting paper records;
3. consumers receive a statement of the "hardware and software requirements" for access to and retention of electronic records; and
4. consumers consent electronically in a manner that "reasonably demonstrates" that they can access the information.

As can be seen from this list, the statement that "the parties agree to be bound by their faxed signatures" contained in many Board and company listing agreements, buyer representation agreements, and purchase contract forms does not meet the Act's requirements for consumer transactions. REALTORS® *should therefore not rely on these statements for the fax execution of listing agreements, buyer representation agreements, and purchase contracts in residential transactions.* A form of notice that meets the Act's requirements is attached to this Legal Alert and can be found on CAR's Fax-On-Demand service at (800) 335-4862 or at *www.ctrealtor.com*. This addendum can be used in listing agreements and buyer representation agreements. It should also be noted that the CAR Purchase and Sale Agreement form incorporates the required notice and can be executed electronically.

■ ENTER THE CONNECTICUT LEGISLATURE

Congress granted permission for a state to adopt its own electronic signature legislation. Any state that adopted the Uniform Electronic Transactions Act ("UETA") "substantially in its reported form" could do so without preemption by E-sign. Connecticut enacted Public Act 02-68 "An Act Concerning the Connecticut Uniform Electronic Transactions Act" in the 2002 session. The Connecticut version of the Uniform Electronic Transactions Act is known as "CUETA" and took effect October 1, 2002. The Act applies to every transaction and contract except for wills and those documents that are recorded in the land records. The Act provides that an electronic record or electronic signature is attributable to a person if it was the act of the person. Whether an electronic record or electronic signature was the act of the person may be shown in any manner. In other words, evidence that a faxed signature bears a very great resemblance to the pen and ink signature of the person executing the document can be used to show that the faxed signature was the act of that person. This does not mean that the simple statement contained in board and company forms is sufficient to have a document executed by fax.

CUETA does answer certain questions that E-sign left unanswered. CUETA provides that an electronic record is "sent" when (a) it is addressed properly or otherwise directed properly to an information processing system that the recipient has designated or uses for the purpose of receiving electronic records or information of the type sent; (b) from which the recipient is able to retrieve the electronic record; (c) is in a form capable of being processed by that information processing system; and (d) enters the information processing system outside the control of the sender. In other words, a fax is "sent" when you run it through the fax machine and it enters the telephone line with the proper phone number. An e-mail is sent once the "send" button is hit and the e-mail enters the telephone line. An electronic record is "received" when it enters the information processing system of the recipient or someone the recipient has designated or uses for the purpose of receiving electronic records. So a recipient who asked that the contract be faxed to an office supply center "receives" the document when the document reaches the office supply center's fax machine. However, if the sender is aware that the electronic record was not actually sent or received, the legal effect of the sending or receipt is determined by Connecticut law governing contracts in general or by the terms of the contract itself.

In addition, CUETA states that unless otherwise expressly provided for in the electronic record or agreed upon between the sender and recipient, the electronic record is deemed to be sent from the sender's "place of business" and to be received at the recipient's "place of business." If the sender or the recipient do not have a "place of business," then the sender or recipient's residence is considered to be the "place of business." Since the parties can establish the "place of business," it is possible to use a third party, like the parties' REALTOR®, as the "place of business." However, this means that the REALTOR®'s e-mail or fax will continue to be used as the "place of business" unless the parties subsequently agree otherwise.

There are several items in CUETA that REALTORS® should note. *First, the notices required by federal law for consumer transactions apply to residential real estate transactions.* Therefore, an electronic record, which includes a fax, should not be used in the purchase and sale of a residence unless the federal law's notice requirements are met. **Please note that under both CUETA and E-sign, a simple statement in a listing, buyer representation agreement, or purchase and sale contract that the parties agree to be bound by their faxed signatures is insufficient to create a legally binding electronic signature.** Further, in order to avoid arguments over the location of the recipient's "place of business" the electronic document should indicate where the electronic record is to be faxed or e-mailed and that is the only address or telephone number that should be used. Therefore, REALTORS® electronically contracting should obtain the e-mail address or fax number where the consumer wishes to send and receive electronic documents to avoid questions over whether the consumer's residence or employer is the consumer's place of business. The CAR addendum for listings and buyer representation agreements meets the requirements of both E-sign and CUETA. The CAR form "Purchase and Sale Contract" also meets the requirements of both E-sign and CUETA.

■ ADVICE FOR REALTORS®

1. Remember that E-sign and CUETA apply to all forms of electronic contracting and electronic execution of documents including faxes, e-mails, instant messaging, and other forms of electronic communications.
2. Do not rely on statements in Board form and company form agreements stating "that the parties agree to be bound by their faxed signatures" for residential transactions. As a result of E-sign and CUETA, these statements do not meet the requirements to validate an electronic signature for a consumer transaction. Only those documents electronically executed using the proper notice mandated by E-sign and CUETA will be effective.
3. REALTORS® seeking to have documents electronically executed in foreign countries should be aware of the Acts in those countries and of the statutes in those countries concerning electronic execution of documents. They may or may not be the same as U.S. law.

■ SUMMARY

Congress and the Connecticut legislature have spoken on the electronic execution of documents and have established rules for the electronic execution of these documents. REALTORS® varying from these rules risk having consumers argue that their listing agreement, purchase and sale contract, or buyer representation agreement has not been properly executed and is therefore invalid. Since the rules are not particularly extensive or troublesome in order to execute documents electronically, REALTORS® should begin using the notice to ensure that there can be no claims that the required documents were not validly executed.

THIS LEGAL ALERT FOR REALTORS® IS INTENDED FOR GENERAL INFORMATION PURPOSES AND IS NOT INTENDED TO PROVIDE LEGAL ADVICE ON ANY SPECIFIC FACTS. IF YOU HAVE SPECIFIC QUESTIONS CONCERNING YOUR OWN SITUATION, PLEASE CONSULT YOUR ATTORNEY.

F I G U R E **E.1**

Addendum for Use of Electronic Signature and Record

ADDENDUM FOR USE OF ELECTRONIC SIGNATURE AND RECORD

This Addendum is used with one or more of the following documents (check all that apply):

☐ Listing Agreement dated:

☐ Buyer Representation Agreement dated:

You agree that we may use an electronic record, including fax or e-mail, to make and keep this Agreement.

You need not agree to use an electronic record. By a written notice to us, you have the right to withdraw your consent to have a record of this Agreement provided or made available to you in electronic form, but that does not permit you to withdraw your consent to the Agreement itself once it has been signed. We will provide you with a paper copy of this Agreement should you request one in writing to us at the address, e-mail, or fax number listed below. Your agreement to use an electronic record applies only to this particular real estate transaction and not to all real estate transactions in which you are a party.

For access to and retention of faxed records, there are no special hardware or software requirements beyond access to a fax machine or fax modem and accompanying software connected to a personal or laptop computer. For access to and retention of e-mail records, you will need a personal or laptop computer, Internet account, and e-mail software or Web browser.

I wish to use (check one)   ☐ Fax machine.   My fax number is:_____

                               ☐ E-mail.   My e-mail address is:_____

All electronic records will be sent to the fax number or e-mail address noted above unless you inform us of any change in your e-mail address or fax number in writing to the Brokerage Firm address, e-mail or fax number set forth.

_____	_____
Signature	Brokerage Firm
_____	_____
Print Name	Brokerage Firm address
_____	_____
Signature	Brokerage Firm e-mail
_____	_____
Print Name	Brokerage Firm fax number

©2000-2002 Connecticut Association of REALTORS®, Inc.
Revised July 30, 2002
Revised May 7, 2003

REALTOR®

ANSWER KEY

Following the answers in the Answer Key are references to pages of the text where points are discussed or explained. These references are made to help you make maximum use of the tests. If you did not answer a question correctly, *restudy the course material until you understand the correct answer.*

CHAPTER 1
Real Estate Brokerage
and Agency

1. b (2)
2. a (18)
3. b (2)
4. b (5)
5. d (11)
6. d (12)
7. a (14)
8. b (18)
9. b (14)
10. a (20)
11. d (19)

CHAPTER 2
Listing Agreements and
Buyer Agency Contracts

1. c (27)
2. c (27)
3. a (27)
4. c (46)
5. c (46)
6. c (46)
7. a (49)
8. b (48)
9. d (45)
10. a (45)
11. d (48)
12. a (48)

CHAPTER 3
Interests in Real Estate

1. d (52)
2. c (52)
3. d (53)
4. a (54)
5. c (53)
6. c (54)
7. b (54)

8. a (54)
9. c (55)
10. a (55)

CHAPTER 4
Forms of Real Estate
Ownership

1. d (57)
2. a (63)
3. b (63)
4. c (58)
5. b (58)
6. a (58)
7. d (59)
8. c (61)
9. c (61)
10. a (62)

CHAPTER 5
Legal Descriptions

1. c (65)
2. a (65)
3. b (67)
4. b (67)
5. d (67)
6. c (65)

CHAPTER 6
Real Estate Taxes and
Other Liens

1. b (69)
2. d (69)
3. a (70)
4. d (70)
5. b (71)
6. b (71)
7. c (72)
8. a (73)
9. a (73)
10. c (71)

CHAPTER 7
Real Estate Contracts

1. c (78)
2. c (96)
3. b (76)
4. a (77)
5. a (77)
6. c (97)
7. a (98)
8. b (98)
9. c (96)
10. d (97)

CHAPTER 8
Transfer of Title

1. a (103)
2. b (106)
3. b (105)
4. b (105)
5. c (104)
6. c (101)
7. a (102)
8. b (103)
9. b (104)
10. d (105)

CHAPTER 9
Title Records

1. b (108–9)
2. b (108)
3. c (108)
4. a (109)
5. d (109)
6. a (110)
7. c (112)
8. c (110)
9. b (110)
10. d (109)

CHAPTER 10
Real Estate License Laws

1. b (115)
2. c (116)
3. a (116)
4. a (116–17)
5. d (117)
6. a (118)
7. c (116–17)
8. d (119)
9. a (120)
10. a (119)
11. a (120)
12. a (121)
13. b (123)
14. d (123)
15. d (126)
16. c (124)
17. b (129)
18. c (129)
19. d (120)
20. d (123)
21. b (130)
22. c (130)
23. c (119)

CHAPTER 11
Real Estate Financing:
Principles/Practice

1. a (136)
2. a (137)
3. b (138)
4. a (137)
5. d (142)
6. a (140)
7. b (139)
8. b (140)
9. d (141)
10. a (142)

CHAPTER 12
Leases

1. d (147)
2. b (148)
3. b (148)
4. d (148)
5. b (159)
6. b (157)
7. c (158)

8. d (154)
9. a (154)
10. b (158)
11. c (161)
12. c (161)
13. a (154)
14. a (157)

CHAPTER 13
Real Estate Appraisal

1. b (168)
2. a (168)
3. a (169)
4. d (166)
5. b (168)
6. c (170)
7. a (170)
8. c (170)
9. d (171)
10. c (167)

CHAPTER 14
Land Use Controls and
Property Development

1. b (178)
2. c (181–82)
3. b (175)
4. a (177)
5. d (176)
6. c (184)
7. b (184)
8. b (183)
9. d (178)
10. b (178)

CHAPTER 15
Fair Housing and Ethical
Practices

1. **Yes,** this would be discrimination under both the state and federal laws that cover two- to four-family houses that are not owner-occupied. The owner's mother living in the house does not make it owner-occupied when the owner lives elsewhere.

2. **No,** they cannot refuse to sell to your client with minor children unless they are claiming the complex qualifies as "housing for older persons," which means 80 percent occupied by those 55 and over or 100 percent occupied by those 62 and over. The fact that they have such a bylaw prohibiting minor children would not be relevant because there is no such exception recognized under either state or federal law. Unless they can prove they are "housing for older persons," their refusal to sell to your client would be a violation of both state and federal law.

3. **Yes,** this is discrimination under the state law. It stipulates that the owner has to allow the tenant to modify the apartment to make it accessible if the tenant is willing to pay to have it done. Federal law does not apply because it exempts up to four-family, owner-occupied dwellings.

4. **No,** since it is four rooms or less and the owner lives in one of the four units, the federal law does not cover it. The state law does not apply because it is an owner-occupied rooming house.

5. **Yes,** under the Civil Rights Act of 1866, there are no exceptions when race, color, or national origin is involved.

6. **Yes,** the state law includes "source of income" as a protective class. Therefore, you cannot refuse to rent to someone simply because they

receive public assistance. Needless to say, if the income that person receives is not sufficient to be able to afford the rental, the person can be denied for that reason. The federal law does not cover "source of income" and does not apply.

7. **Yes,** this is discrimination under the state law because it indicates with regard to "age" that the only exceptions are minors and "housing for older persons." Unless the co-op can demonstrate it falls in this category, it can't discriminate because of age. The federal law does not apply here because it does not cover age and the couple doesn't have minor children to make it a "familial status" complaint.

8. **Yes,** now if a couple is denied because of age, they can complain under the federal law covering "familial status" because the policy of selling to only those 35 and over has a discriminatory impact on families with minor children. Unless the co-op complex qualifies as "housing for older persons," it will be discrimination under both the state and federal laws covering "familial status" and under the state law covering "age."

9. **Yes,** this would be discrimination under the state law, which does cover single-family homes without exception. Federal law does not apply because the property is being sold

without advertising or the use of an agent.

10. **Yes,** it would be discrimination under the federal law, which covers more than four rooms or units that are owner-occupied. The state law does not apply because it is a rooming house and the owner lives in the building.

11. **No,** if you abide by the owner's wishes, you will be guilty of discrimination under both the state and federal laws. The state law covers all single-family homes, and the federal law covers single-family homes that are either advertised or leased using an agent.

12. **Yes,** it would be discrimination under the federal law, which only exempts up to four owner-occupied units. A seven-unit rooming house would be covered whether the owner lives there or not. The state law does not apply because it is an owner-occupied rooming house.

13. **No,** brokers, salespeople, and sellers are not liable for failing to disclose to a buyer that the property was previously occupied by a person with AIDS.

CHAPTER 16

Closing the Real Estate Transaction

1. c (201)
2. c (200)
3. c (201)
4. d (199)
5. d (200)

CHAPTER 17

Environmental Issues and the Real Estate Transaction

1. c (204)
2. a (205)
3. b (205)
4. d (206)
5. a (208)
6. c (207)

APPENDIX A

Introduction to Real Estate Investment

1. c (214)
2. d (216)
3. a (216)
4. b (214)
5. d (217)
6. c (218)
7. a (219)
8. a (219)
9. b (219)
10. b (216)

INDEX